MW00561708

Subjectivity and
the Signs of Love

American University Studies

Series II
Romance Languages and Literature

Vol. 214

PETER LANG
New York • Washington, D.C./Baltimore
Bern • Frankfurt am Main • Berlin • Vienna • Paris

James M. Hembree

Subjectivity and the Signs of Love

Discourse, Desire, and the Emergence of Modernity in Honoré d'Urfé's *L'Astrée*

PETER LANG
New York • Washington, D.C./Baltimore
Bern • Frankfurt am Main • Berlin • Vienna • Paris

Library of Congress Cataloging-in-Publication Data

Hembree, James M.
Subjectivity and the signs of love: discourse, desire, and the emergence
of modernity in Honoré d'Urfé's L'Astrée / James M. Hembree.
p. cm. — (American university studies. Series II, Romance
languages and literature; vol. 214)
Includes bibliographical references and index.
1. Urfé, Honoré d', 1567–1625. Astrée. 2. Subjectivity in literature. 3. Self in
literature. 4. Identity (Psychology) in literature. 5. Semiotics and literature.
I. Title. II. Series. III. Series: American university studies.
Series II, Romance languages and literature; vol. 214.
PQ1707.U7A2   843'.4—dc20   95-40412
ISBN 0-8204-2817-5
ISSN 0740-9257

Die Deutsche Bibliothek-CIP-Einheitsaufnahme

Hembree, James M.:
Subjectivity and the signs of love: discourse, desire and the emergence
of modernity in Honoré d'Urfé's L'Astrée / James M. Hembree.
–New York; Washington, D.C./Baltimore; Bern; Frankfurt am Main;
Berlin; Vienna; Paris: Lang.
(American university studies: Ser. 2, Romance
languages and literature; Vol. 214)
ISBN 0-8204-2817-5
NE: American university studies / 02

The paper in this book meets the guidelines for permanence and durability
of the Committee on Production Guidelines for Book Longevity
of the Council of Library Resources.

© 1997 Peter Lang Publishing, Inc., New York

All rights reserved.
Reprint or reproduction, even partially, in all forms such as microfilm,
xerography, microfiche, microcard, and offset strictly prohibited.

Printed in the United States of America.

Table of Contents

Et considerez combien Amour est mauvais maistre, et combien il paye mal la peine de ceux qui le servent: il donne à ces amants tout ce qu'ils sçauroient desirer, car il faict qu'ils meurent d'amour l'un pour l'autre, et il n'y a point de desir en leur ame plus ardent que celuy de cette reciproque volonté; mais comme s'il estoit jaloux que les humains jouyssent de ces contentemens, qui sont les plus grands que les immortels puissent avoir, il veut qu'ils ignorent le bien qu'il leur faict, et que dans cette ignorance, ils n'en jouyssent point!

L'Astrée III, 12

Part One: The Anatomy of a Paradigm Shift

1

Subjective Interiority and the Problem of Symbolic Reference: Montaigne, Descartes, and d'Urfé

After a brief historico-geographical exposition, *L'Astrée*'s plot-line begins *in medias res* with a lovers' quarrel that culminates in the heroine's fateful command of banishment and Celadon's suicidal leap into the river Lignon. With the principal lovers thus estranged, the narrative proceeds through several thousand pages in which reconciliation, though clearly implied as the wished-for consummation, takes place only in sequels composed by authors other than d'Urfé himself. Since d'Urfé evidently felt no urgency to bring his plot to conclusion, and in fact deferred its resolution indefinitely, we are left with the question of its inherent resolvability, and hence, of the work's coherence as an ideological and aesthetic structure. Does the narrative's internal logic project a resolution which an untimely death prevented d'Urfé from elaborating for his readers? Does it contain a logical paradox or conflict of values that precludes the possibility of "closure?" Or, finally (and this will be the thrust of my argument), does *L'Astrée* possess a kind of unity to which logical closure is incidental—a dynamic unity of process, for example, as opposed to the static unity of a finished product? Any response in turn inevitably implies a judgment about the period mentality of which *L'Astrée* is widely acknowledged to be the most perfectly realized literary expression.[1] The larger project I would like to undertake, then, is to discover whether "baroque" culture may be reduced to the vertiginous sense of metamorphosis and theatricality engendered by a breakdown of traditional metaphysical conceptions of order, or whether it possessed within itself the epistemological resources upon which an alternative unifying vision might have been, and perhaps ever so briefly was, established.

In answer to the question of formal coherence, I will argue that both the estrangement of the lovers and the prolonged irresolution of the plot reflect a crisis of interpersonal knowledge that occurred in the late sixteenth and early seventeenth centuries. During that period, an epochal shift from a cosmological to a psychological conceptualization of personal identity engendered a corresponding shift in the epistemology of signs. But because the second transformation lagged behind the first, there ensued a period of cultural adjustment during which the dominant representational paradigm was radically incommensurate with the emerging reality of the self. To state the matter in slightly different terms: an intensification of subjective self-awareness in the early modern period invalidated the traditional means of self-representation, predicated on the epistemological priority of an objective ontological and symbolic order,[2] before a new means of self-representation, predicated on the epistemological priority of subjective consciousness, had taken its place. Baroque self-representation is characterized by the irreconcilable opposition of an interior psychological space which had begun to establish itself as the central *locus* of personal identity, and an objective order of signs which had no relevance to the self defined as a function of interiority. As a result, the central problem of d'Urfé's narrative is the difficulty of achieving authentic self-representation in the absence of a coherent semiotic model. His fictional lovers face an intolerable dilemma: on the one hand, a self-affirming quest for erotic fulfillment destroys intersubjective guarantees of meaning and renders interpersonal knowledge impossible, while on the other, participation in an objective symbolic order entails the sacrifice of subjective autonomy and the repression of erotic desire.

Although the narrative exhibits an ambivalence characteristic of discourse suspended between conflicting semiotic models, it is not without an internal logic of resolution and closure. I will approach *L'Astrée* as the chronicle of a quest which is at once psychological and epistemological because its consummation requires the accommodation of interior privacy with an intersubjective symbolic order which ultimately transforms the ontological status of both. D'Urfé recognizes that the psychological subject receives his desires from the discourses and institutions of the society into which he is born, and is therefore less than autonomous and self-creating, while those institutions and discourses are historically relative and culturally produced, rather than providentially established reflections of a transcendent, metaphysical reality. The narrative projects a resolution predicated on neither the sacrifice of self in order to accede to meaning, nor the subordination of intersubjective meaning to the whims of private fancy, but a process of socialization by which the subject and the symbolic order become reciprocal reflections of each other.

My analysis will conclude that the solution d'Urfé provides to the problem of intersubjective reference is neither medieval nor modern, neither object-centered nor subject-centered, but historicist, and in that sense, characteristically Baroque.

Previous critics who have commented on the thematic and formal coherence of *L'Astrée* may be divided into two principal groups. There are those for whom a unity of signification reinforced by a dominant aesthetic norm is the *sine qua non* of a successful literary work, and who consequently seek to establish the narrative's inner logic at the expense of its ethical, epistemological and generic diversity. The virtual impossibility of reconciling *L'Astrée* with an ideal of this sort in all likelihood accounts for the lack of critical attention it has received in spite its enormous popularity in the seventeenth century. Other critics insist upon the co-existence in the text of incompatible aesthetic ideals, theories of knowledge or ethical systems, only to find in that fact a mechanism of indeterminacy precluding the possibility of logical closure. As a transitional work, they argue, *L'Astrée* is hopelessly divided against itself, caught in an unresolvable paradox, and incapable of resolution. My own analysis will therefore fill a gap in the corpus of *L'Astrée* criticism by taking into account d'Urfé's juxtaposition of medieval and modern modes of conceptualization, while offering an interpretation that confirms our intuitive sense—shared by readers from d'Urfé's day to our own—of the coherence of the whole.[3] I will show that the narrative derives its inner logic not from epistemological norms indigenous to one or the other side of the cultural divide, but rather from the interrogative process through which d'Urfé and his readers, vicariously in the persons of fictional characters, experiment with epistemological alternatives in their quest for a criterion of truth in the interpretation of signs. It is precisely the possibility of intersubjective meaning that is at issue in *L'Astrée* with the result that to impose a normative meaning on the text in advance is to pre-empt the discussion in which d'Urfé is primarily engaged.

In response to the larger question of the epistemological resources inherent in the baroque mentality, I will suggest that the transition from an object-centered to a subject-centered paradigm of self-presentation takes place in three phases, according to an internal logic suggested by T.S. Kuhn's theory of paradigm shifts. The first phase produces a skeptical critique of the traditional foundations of meaning which reaches an impasse precisely because it remains dependent upon the metaphysical presuppositions whose validity it calls into question. At this stage, which is characteristic of Montaigne's *Essais*, the opposition between the subject and the symbolic order remains absolute and unresolved. The second phase, reflected in *L'Astrée*, anticipates the emergence of a new subject-centered epistemological model, but ultimately rejects it. Here, we find a dual critique of both the declining and the emergent paradigms, superseded by a third "historicist" perspective. It is only in the final phase of cultural adjustment, exemplified by the writings of Descartes, that subjective interiority acquires legitimacy not only as the *locus* of authentic selfhood, but as the founding principle of a new theory of intersubjective knowledge.

The analysis of early modern intellectual culture in terms of the internal logic of a paradigm shift will enable me to position d'Urfé's work in relation not only to those of the other towering figures of the period in France— Montaigne and Descartes—but to those of the great literary mediators of modernity in England and Spain—Shakespeare and Cervantes. *L'Astrée*, I will argue, deserves to be considered as a cultural monument of the first rank, possessing an historical significance, if not an aesthetic quality, equal to that of *Othello* and *Hamlet* on the one hand, and *Don Quixote* on the other. It will also lead to the conclusion that certain characteristics of the paradigm shift that takes place in "premodernity"—the relativization of discourse, and the historicist response to the problem of meaning—have been replicated in the "postmodern" transition through which we are currently living. The profound affinities between premodern and postmodern epistemological crises underscore the trans-historical relevance of *L'Astrée*, and suggest its importance as a text that enhances our understanding not only of a former era, but of aspects of cultural experience which are perennially, if only at distant intervals, renewed. We, more than any generation perhaps since 1660, are in a position to understand a narrative whose principal characters embark on a quest for meaning.

The intrinsic justification for attributing the defining formal and ideological features of *L'Astrée* to its status as a transitional work is to be found in d'Urfé's own historical self-awareness. In the "Lettre au Berger Celadon" that prefaces the second volume (1610) d'Urfé establishes, as one of the central organizing principles of his work, the tension between two irreconcilable patterns of life and thought associated with two historical periods, and exemplified by different kinds of lovers. One lover adheres to the values and customs of "un autre siècle" based on the principle of fidelity, while the other adheres to those of "celui ou nous sommes" based on the principle of change. Celadon, who exemplifies the former, finds himself completely at odds with his contemporaries. "Que l'âge ou nous sommes est bien contraire à ton opinion!" d'Urfé tells him. "On dit maintenant qu'aimer comme toi, c'est aimer à la vieille Gauloise, et comme faisaient les chevaliers de la Table Ronde, ou le Beau Tenebreux." Actions that in another era would have elicited admiration now earn contempt: "On se rira plutôt de ta peine qu'on ne voudra imiter ta fidelité." Instead of being regarded as a hero Celadon seems a victim of "une étrange humeur." The incommensurateness of two historical ages, two ethical systems and two ways of conceptualizing the real, cannot be more clearly apparent than when the exemplary behavior of one is regarded as madness by the other.

The principle difference between the two kinds of lovers in the letter takes us to the heart of the reconceptualization of the psychological subject that initiates the estrangement with which the narrative begins, and which reflects the general direction taken by the evolution of subjectivity in the early modern period. The lover who emulates the ancients sacrifices any vestige of an individuated ego that would prevent him from proclaiming his mistress' beauty and goodness to the world. He achieves his destiny as a lover, and the highest expression of his true self, by submitting to the authority of an ideal reality that transcends him, and demands his absolute surrender. The lover who exemplifies the values of the current age, by contrast, engages in a campaign of erotic conquest designed to affirm the priority of the individual ego. Positing himself as the autonomous center of his own identity, he achieves his destiny as a lover, and the highest expression of selfhood, by appropriating the objects he desires.

These two modes of affectional life are, moreover, inseparable from alternative means of self-representation. The first lover discloses his inner truth by becoming wholly identified with, and transparent to, the "other" of whom he is both "témoin" and "témoignage." The complete surrender of his will enables him to become a living hieroglyph or mark of what he has seen, eliminating the polarities of self and other, sign and signified. The second reveals himself by means of words and deeds over which he exercises complete "authorial" control precisely because they are, as d'Urfé tells us, "différents du coeur." The transparency of the lover who *is* a sign, gives place to the hiddenness of the lover who uses signs to reveal or conceal at will the thoughts and intentions of a self-enclosed interiority.

These two modes of affectional life and the means of representation they imply stand at the two extremes in the paradigm shift that occurred at the dawn of the modern era. Throughout the period spanning the sixteenth century and the first two thirds of the seventeenth, an object-centered paradigm of self-representation gradually gives way to a subject-centered paradigm, transforming the conceptualization of the individual in both socio-psychological and epistemological aspects. Personal identity ceases to be regarded as the function of an individual's location in an objective ontological order, and comes instead to be regarded as the function of private capabilities and desires actualized by an autonomous, self-determining will. The fulfillment of a teleological purpose yields to the rational pursuit of self-interest as the means of achieving happiness and the highest good.[4] At the same time, the epistemological subject ceases to be regarded as a *locus* of innate ideas which constitute within the rational soul an imprint of the world writ small, and comes instead to be regarded as a transcendental consciousness that exists independently of the external order, and which "knows" both self and world as objects to be analyzed according to the principles of its internal logic. Reason as an inscription in the rational soul of the over-arching *logos*, gives place to the self-enclosed mathematical rationality of the Cartesian *cogito*.[5]

This gradual turning from cosmology toward psychology as the source of personal identity, and from universal *logos* toward self-enclosed rationality as the foundation of knowledge, is paralleled by a transition from signification to representation as the dominant structure of symbolic reference.[6] In the traditional model, a word or action, or any sign whatever, "refers" in so far as it serves as an indication of an object's location within an over-arching pattern. The epistemological guarantee of "signification" is to be found in the mutual participation, or embeddedness, of the sign and what it signifies in a providential order which establishes their relation as an objective fact, and whose discovery depends upon the mind's *a priori* possession of an ideational correlative of that relation. Stated in slightly different terms, the objective order which at once determines personal identity and imparts knowledge by imprinting itself in the rational soul, appears in a third locality, in visible signs displayed throughout the phenomenal world—in the book of nature, social institutions and language, all of which are regarded as parallel reflections of a single transcendent reality. In the emergent paradigm by contrast, a sign "refers" in so far as it serves as an arbitrary marker or substitute for the object in the processes of thought. The epistemological guarantee of reference as "representation" is to be found not in an ontologically real relation (i.e. a relation of inherency) between sign and signified, but rather in the ability of an autonomous conceptualizing faculty to verify the correspondence between signs and objects available to direct perception, and which refer to nothing beyond themselves. In Richard Rorty's words, "the Inner Eye surveys these representations hoping to find some mark which will testify to their fidelity."[7]

The transition from signification to representation as the dominant model of symbolic reference was, moreover, a necessary rather than a merely coincidental feature of the modern, subject-centered paradigm. The triumph of self-interest as an ethical value, and of the transcendental *cogito* as the seat of knowledge, both require as a logical precondition, the recognition of the conventional origin of the symbolic order in both its institutional and linguistic manifestations. Because, within the traditional paradigm, signs are providentially given, rather than created by man, they impose themselves as the very material embodiment of the order in which he is inscribed as both desiring and knowing subject, and in which he recognizes the image of an innate identity from which he can never be free. Only when the knowing subject becomes the originator and author of meaning, rather than a passive recipient of meanings providentially given, will signs cease to be revelations of an objective order within which he finds an indication of his metaphysical destiny, and become instead a means by which he represents his own affective and perceptual experience to himself and others. At the conclusion of the historical trajectory we have been describing, the institutions of a "market society" will exist in a similar relation to the autonomous psychological subject as a discourse of objective reference will exist in relation to the autonomous epistemological subject. Created by man, for the fulfillment of human aspirations and for the purposes of human thought, institutions on one hand, and language on the other, become expressions of his affective and cognitive freedom, embodying not an objective *a priori*, but the structure of his own heart and mind.

In spite of their differences, the object-centered and the subject-centered paradigms of symbolic reference both offer the possibility of achieving, if only as an ideal, a perfect correspondence between subjective self-awareness and the representation of personal identity within a supra-personal order of signs. Each, in other words, possesses an internal mechanism that assures in advance that individuals will recognize and acknowledge the accuracy of representations which have been verified with reference to an intersubjective criterion. The subjective authentication of discourse in the traditional structure of signifying relations is predicated upon the immanence of being in the world of space and time. The personal identity imprinted within the soul of the individual and the symbolic order which renders identity visible to others are parallel manifestations of a single metaphysical truth. In the representational paradigm it is predicated on the transparency of social institutions and language to the inner world of the individuals by and for whom they were created. While the traditional model resolves the problem of authentication by granting epistemological priority to a supra-personal metaphysical order in which all minds participate, the subject-centered paradigm resolves it by granting epistemological priority to a self-enclosed rational structure which all individual minds possess. In the first instance, signs are deemed to be "true" to the extent that they correspond to a universally intuited location of the subject in an objective hierarchy. In the second, they are deemed to be "true" to the extent that they correspond to the undisguised intentions and desires of the subject empirically apprehended by ancillary means such as eavesdropping, spying, secret reports, etc.

It is precisely the reciprocal fit between sign and self, subject and symbolic order, as established on either objective or subjective foundations that *L'Astrée*, and other representative works of early modernity, call into question. It is as though a gap occurs in the history of thought during which no single semiotic model predominates. The objective-metaphysical foundations of meaning have been invalidated by the valorization of subjective consciousness as an autonomous center of personal identity, while a subjective-empirical foundation of meaning has not yet been formulated to take its place.[8] As a result, the subject, construed as the very antithesis of intersubjective meaning, and the symbolic order, reduced to the status of a cultural fiction, constitute irreconcilable polarities separated by a seemingly irreparable logical void.

Before proceeding further, it will be useful to reflect for a moment upon the theoretical possibility and the intrinsic structure of paradigm shifts, since only a working model of the process by which structural change occurs will permit us to evaluate *L'Astrée*'s largely ignored but entirely crucial role in mediating the emergence of the modern paradigm alongside the more familiar texts of Montaigne and Descartes. Ideally, such a model will permit us to recognize not only the *uniqueness* of each contribution but, in some limited sense, its *necessity* according to the inner logic change itself.

Critics and theorists committed to the extreme textualism[9] most notoriously proclaimed by Derrida in the often cited phrase, "il n'y a pas de horstexte," have encountered difficulties in explaining, or even discussing, the transition between one historically limited mode of conceptualization and the next. Textualist theory, of course, derives from the Saussurian premise that meaning is produced within a relational structure in which each signifier derives its value from the other signifiers in a closed system. Since language possesses only relations and no positive terms, Saussure tells us, no direct correspondence is possible between the signifiers and reality as such. The initial foreclosure of the real, moreover, is rendered completely invisible to the thinking subject by his or her seamless integration into the signifying system within which thought inescapably occurs. An extra-discursive reality—whether the affective reality of the subject, or the empirical reality of the external world—to which signs may be held accountable no longer presents itself to the mind since the real as perceived by a discursively constructed subject is always-already a product of the discourse in question. Thus, it is frequently pointed out that any statement must not only *be* true, but "*in* the true," in order to be received as "knowledge." When every aspect of human thought and feeling is considered to be determined by the very structure whose permutations one is attempting to explain, it becomes impossible to identify an agent capable of initiating change. Historians of culture who subscribe to the textualist thesis have therefore tended to conceptualize cultural transitions as ruptures in the symbolic order available to be described empirically but not to be reduced to extra-discursive causes.[10]

The particular relevance of the foreclosure of reality by structure to our study of epistemological paradigm shifts hinges on the claim that a symbolic system not only establishes fixed relations among signs, but imposes a fixed configuration of relations among the subject, the symbolic order, and the objects of thought at a level of discourse to which I have referred as "the structure of symbolic reference," to which Timothy Reiss refers variously as "the signifying relation" or a "discursive logic," and which lies at the root of Foucault's conception of the "episteme." We have already implicitly illustrated this point by describing two systems of signifying relations distinguished by the relative positions assigned to the knowing subject. The medieval or object-centered paradigm posits both personal identity and the structure of reason as intra-mental inscriptions of an overarching *logos*, while the modern or subject-centered paradigm posits the subject as the ontologically autonomous and self-determining center—indeed the "proprietor"—of his own identity and mental faculties or powers. It should be stressed that the status assigned to the subject is not a reflection of consciously formulated theories of subjectivity or concepts of human nature—or at least not exclusively so—but rather of the very structure of symbolic reference itself. To the extent that the subject thinks at all, he must, of necessity, take upon himself his role as passive recipient *vis à vis* a providentially established order of significations in the one instance, or, in the other, as the author and determining origin of signification, verifying the referential transparency of arbitrary signs.

While the complete interdependence of thought and the symbolic order poses difficulties for textualist theories of change, some of these difficulties seem to me to reflect an unnecessary theoretical extremism. Because structuralist assumptions of even the purest sort question only the *accessibility* to thought, and not the *existence*, of an extra-discursive reality, the presumption that that which has been foreclosed—either within the subject, or in the external world—thenceforth lacks any capacity to influence the development and future course of the symbolic order seems inadequate to the assumptions of textualist theory itself. The initial foreclosure of reality would, on the contrary, seem to suggest the existence of a *locus* of perennial resistance external to the symbolic order—a great, unrepresentable plenitude welling up from within the subject, and a limitless empirical manifold welling up from the external universe—which exerts a continuous, destabilizing pressure against it, and forces, from time to time, the emergence of new and (at least potentially) more inclusive paradigms.

The existence of an exterior to discourse which continually impinges upon the intrinsic coherence of representational models is a fundamental assumption of T.S. Kuhn's theory of scientific paradigm shifts. His work seems particularly suggestive for a study of baroque self-representation because, while avoiding the difficulties to which an extreme, poststructuralist position leads, it provides a theoretical framework in which it is possible to discuss the complex interaction between the self, as the object of representation, and various semiotic models competing for dominance.

For Kuhn, a paradigm is not so much a conceptual structure that forecloses the real absolutely, as a dominant expanatory model which can, at any time, be challenged by the appearance of empirical facts which fail to fit the expectations it imposes. His central purpose, and his 'structuralist' deviation from conventional philosophy of science, is to insist upon the epistemological priority and self-perpetuating nature of paradigms—complex systems of authorized investigative procedures, laboratory instruments, standard illustrations, and professional relationships—which engender powerful inertial resistances to innovation, and even render certain facts of nature invisible. Kuhn departs from an extreme 'textualist' position, however, by asserting that such systems are accountable in the final analysis to facts which exist beyond their borders. The decision to reject one conceptual model in favor of another "involves the comparison of both paradigms with nature and with each other."[11]

Both the constitutive role of the paradigm, and its ultimate accountability to external reality come into play in Kuhn's theory of scientific discovery. At variance with the traditional positivist view that discoveries occur in an instant, at a particular time and place, and result from the pioneering work of single individuals, Kuhn argues convincingly that they are processes which involve the cumulative contributions of numerous people, unfold over relatively long periods of time, and possess a characteristic internal structure. The path to discovery begins when the scientist first observes empirical data which exceed the predictive capabilities of his explanatory model. Because the paradigm has not prepared him for what he observes, he cannot assimilate it into his store of significant facts. Instead, he regards it as an "anomaly" to be ignored, or falsifies it by inventing specious explanations that save the paradigm at the expense of the data. The inadequacy of these responses, however, results in an extended period of "crisis" during which the anomaly poses an increasingly unanswerable challenge to the reigning paradigm. The "discovery" proper does not occur until a wholesale transformation of the paradigm establishes a new set of primary assumptions and investigative procedures within which the formerly aberrant fact becomes a confirmation of anticipated truth. Kuhn summarizes as follows:[12]

Discovery commences with the awareness of anomaly, i.e., with the recognition that nature has somehow violated the paradigm-induced expectations that govern normal science. It then continues with a more or less extended exploration of the area of anomaly. And it closes only when the paradigm theory has been adjusted so that the anomalous has become the expected. Assimilating a new sort of fact demands a more than additive adjustment of theory, and until that adjustment is complete—until the scientist has learned to see nature in a different way—the new fact is not quite a scientific fact at all.

To the extent that subjective interiority emerges as a fact of psychological and practical experience before it can be assimilated as a meaningful (i.e. representable) aspect of human self-understanding, Kuhn's theory provides a useful tool for analyzing the semiotic paradigm shift that takes place in the early modern period.[13] Subjective self-awareness initially subsists as an "anomaly" within an object-centered paradigm of symbolic reference, before being "discovered" when a subject-centered paradigm takes its place, at the end of an extended period of "crisis" during which the two paradigms are inconclusively juxtaposed, and third alternatives explored. In what follows, I will argue that Montaigne represents the period of "anomaly," Descartes the moment of "discovery," and that the intervening period of "crisis" takes its most characteristic form in d'Urfé's *L'Astrée*. Although Montaigne launches a subjectivist critique of a system of signifying relations predicated on the epistemological priority of the objective order, he can only conceptualize subjective consciousness as a subversive force, and not as the foundational principle in an alternative theory of meaning. Descartes overcomes the epistemological crisis engendered by the Montaignian critique when he establishes the marginalized element of the old paradigm as the determining center of the new. When subjective consciousness replaces Being as the horizon of symbolic reference—that is to say, as the theoretical source of a reality that refers to nothing beyond itself and therefore grounds the meaning of signs—"signification" gives way to "representation" as the dominant semiotic model. Between these two extremes, d'Urfé occupies an intermediate position characterized by a double-edged skepticism leveled on the one hand against Being, and on the other against subjective consciousness. Sharing Montaigne's rejection of the traditional model, but refusing in advance the Cartesian alternative, he offers a third response according to which the sign itself is epistemologically prior to both metaphysical and subjective absolutes. The baroque paradox by which self and sign stand in irreconcilable opposition will, for d'Urfé, be resolved by the possibility of interpellating the psychological subject into historically relative communities of discourse.

Perhaps more than any other figure, Montaigne demonstrates the intensification of subjective self-awareness, and the concomitant de-realization of transcendent Being, with which modernity begins. He opens the *Essais* by establishing his own thought processes as his principal object of study.[14] Retreating from public life, he allows his mind to "s'arrester et rasseoir en soy," and sets out to record his ideas in whatever order they appear ("De l'oisiveté"). The valorization of subjective privacy is coupled with an insistent devaluation of the objective ontological order. At variance with the medieval notion that the soul bears within itself the marks of divinity, Montaigne frequently reiterates the incommensurateness of becoming and Being. In the "Apologie" he tells us that God is wholly 'other': "C'est à Dieu seule de se cognaistre et d'interpreter ses ouvrages" ("Apologie," II, 165); and again, when mocking Plato for assuming the surname "divine," he says: "S'il y a quelque chose du mien, il n'y a rien de divin." If we are to conceptualize the truths of God with any justice at all, "il faut les imaginer inimaginables, indicibles et incomprehensibles, et parfaictement autres que celles de nostre miserable experience" ("Apologie," II, 184). The ontological gap makes its appearance as well in terms of humanity's "ignorance des causes premières et des principes" ("Apologie," II, 226).

Although subjective consciousness affords Montaigne a vantage point from which to launch a skeptical critique of the entire ontological tradition originating in Classical and Christian sources, it does not yet provide an alternative foundation of intersubjective reference precisely because his skepticism itself remains dependent upon the theory of meaning whose validity he calls into question. Montaigne, no less than Plato, identifies reality with the transcendence and permanence of absolute Being, and conceptualizes the foreclosure of being as the foreclosure of the real itself, and hence, of an intersubjective horizon of symbolic reference. Far from inaugurating a subject-centered paradigm of self-representation in which a determinate authorial identity discloses itself in a discourse of objective reference, the failure of immanence deprives the mind of its intrinsic stabilizing principle (i.e. the intra-mental inscription of the *logos* of being), and the collective symbolic order of its intersubjective meaning (i.e. its inherent relation to metaphysical reality). From this double consequence arise the two most consistently reiterated themes of the *Essais*, and indeed, of baroque literature as a whole: the infinite mobility of the self, and the theatricalization of public appearance.[15] Everything pertaining to the subject, uniquely and originally *subjective*, regardless of its intrinsic interest, can only be represented as grotesque illusion and laughable chimera, while everything pertaining to the collectively established symbolic order, deriving its authority from public acceptance, can only be regarded as a cultural fiction.

Throughout the *Essais*, subjective consciousness subsists as a violently destructive presence in the midst of an ossified and increasingly irrelevant structure of conventional discourses and institutions. While chastising the intellectual establishment for its neglect of self-reflection, and insisting that he understands himself better than any external thing ("Du repentir," III, 21), it never occurs to Montaigne (as it would to Descartes) to construe subjective consciousness as a self-sufficient rational structure transcending the limitations of corporeal existence, and capable of serving as a *locus* of permanent, unmoving truths. Instead, the separation of becoming from Being engenders the infinite mobility, not only of the world of sense phenomena, but of thought itself: "Il n'y a aucune constante existence, ny de notre estre, ny de celuy des objects. Et nous, et nostre jugement, et toutes choses mortelles, vont coulant et roulant sans cesse" because, he explains, "nous n'avons aucune communication à l'estre" ("Apologie," II, 266). Separated from Being by an unbridgeable gulf and cast back, as it were, on its inward and private resources, the mind is not a transcendental consciousness, *locus* of clear and distinct ideas, but a center of protean activity producing an endless chain of "chimères et monstres fantasques." Human minds in their pure, unencumbered essence, resemble "des terres oisives," rich and fertile but teeming with useless weeds, or wombs bringing forth "des amas et pièces de chair informes," or finally, runaway horses casting about "desreiglez, par-cy par-là, dans le vague champ des imaginations" ("De l'oisiveté," I, 69–70).

At the same time, traditional linguistic codes, philosophical systems, and institutional structures within and through which subjective consciousness assumes a determinate social and moral identity become, in his eyes, a network of empty cultural artifacts standing in diametric opposition to the fluidity of thought. His insistence upon writing as a man and not as an author (made the more famous by Pascal's reiteration), assigns a greater truth-value to the spontaneous emanations of private consciousness than to the objective realities traditionally assumed to be embodied in the external order of signs. Authors, Montaigne complains, "se communiquent au peuple par quelque marque particulière et estrangère; moy, le premier, par mon estre universel, comme Michel de Montaigne, non comme grammarien, ou poète, ou jurisconsulte" ("Du repentir," III, 21). The remark is not merely a statement of stylistic preference, but an implicit rejection of the metaphysically guaranteed fit between the discursive mode—the "marque" which he here denounces as "estrangère"—and the intellectual discipline and social estate of the speaker.

He extends his critique of the conventional symbolic order to comprehensive systems of thought and institutions. Concluding his disquisition on classical opinions about the nature of man and the soul, he traces the origins of orthodox belief to the playful inventiveness of ancient philosophers—"la liberté [...] et gaillardise de ces esprits anciens"—and the partisan motives of their followers—"chacun entreprenant de juger et de choisir pour prendre parti." Future generations forgot or suppressed the knowledge of origins, and circumscribed the protean vagaries of mind within static structures of belief enforced by "civile authorité et ordonnance" and legitimized by "l'approbation commune" ("Apologie," II, 225; 420). His famous pronouncement on the relativity of laws reflects an equally uncompromising insistence on the priority of human thought in all of its diversity to a metaphysical *a priori.* Taking aim at those who predicate the universal validity of laws on the assumption that "il y en a aucunes fermes, perpetuelles et immuables, qu'ils nomment naturelles, qui sont empreintes en l'humain genre par la condition de leur propre essence," he declares that ethical principles in fact originate in "cette mer flotante des opinions d'un peuple ou d'un Prince, qui me peindront la justice d'autant de couleurs et la reformeront en autant de visages qu'il y aura en eux de change-mens de passion" ("Apologie," II, 245; 437). Custom alone lends them an air of legitimacy: "Les loix prennent leur authorité de la possession et de l'usage" ("Apologie," II, 248; 440).

The opposition of an autonomous subject conceptualized as a *locus* of ceaseless and indeterminate change on the one hand, and conventional symbolic order conceptualized as a collection of arbitrary customs and historically relative prejudices on the other, renders determinate self-knowledge and self-representation impossible. To the extent that the author affirms himself by

recording the contents of his own mind, he is incommensurate with any determinate representational structure or symbolic model. To the extent that he
appears to himself and to others as an object of determinate knowledge, he has
had to alienate or repress the central motivations, and arrest the natural movement, of his inner being. Montaigne accepts the incommensurateness of the
two as a given. Authentic self-representation occurs only in the solitude to
which he retreats when writing the *Essais*. There he gives free reign to the
"chimeras and fantastic monsters" of his unbridled mind ("De l'oisiveté"),
and, seeking knowledge only of the moment, represents himself in passage
("Du repentir," III, 20). The possibility of social intercourse by contrast
requires his participation in conventional modes of discourse, beliefs and institutions which lack any inherent relation to subjective experience. Hence his
well-known fideism. Deploring eccentricity in the public sphere, he pays lip-
service to orthodox opinion because without it "je ne me sçauroy garder de
rouler sans cesse" ("Apologie," II, 235; 428).

Because a structure of signifying relations in which meaning is predicated on the priority of an objective ontological order cannot, by its very nature, accommodate subjectivity as anything other than anomaly or illusion, it
must undergo one of those radical transformations which, as Kuhn remarks,
seem to transplant us to an entirely different universe. It will be the accomplishment of Descartes in the *Discours de la méthode*, but even more defini-
tively in the *Méditations*,[16] to consummate the "discovery" of subjective
consciousness as the horizon of symbolic reference replacing transcendent
being in an entirely new epistemological paradigm.

He accomplishes this by means of a dramatic inversion of Montaigne's
skeptical critique of immanence in which the chimera and fantastic monsters
of subjective privacy, and the distorting lens of cultural prejudice, are made to
figure not as proofs of the 'otherness' of being, but as threats to subjective
self-presence. The thinking self who recognizes the perils to the objective
grasp of external reality posed by the radical subjectivism of a mind impris-
oned in a hallucinatory world of its own creation (i.e. our senses may be
deceiving us, we may be dreaming) and by the naturalization of arbitrary
prejudices (i.e. our minds are colonized against their will by "ancient and
commonly held opinions") transcends them both. The formulation of the
transcendental ego, in turn, permits the reciprocal correspondence between the
two elements of the baroque paradox—subjective privacy and the symbolic

order—to be reestablished. It provides at once a principle of stability for the unbridled mind, and an extra-discursive ground of experience with reference to which representational accuracy may be verified. Because it exists independently of the desiring self the *cogito* organizes and directs the passions toward rational ends, and because it exists logically prior to the means of representation, it can assure the transparency of confessional speech. Self-representation under the new paradigm will be predicated on the capacity of a transcendental knowing self to represent the private experiences of the psychological, desiring self objectively to others in a discourse subjectively verified with reference to its object.

The consequences for self-representation are apparent in Descartes' *The Passions of the Soul* (1645–1646), which exemplifies the characteristics of self-analysis practiced by later seventeenth-century moralists such as Pascal, La Rochefoucauld and La Bruyère. No longer do moralists interpret the passions as symptoms of ontological states, nor do they regard them, in Montaignian fashion, as yet one more manifestation of the infinite mobility of thought, but rather, as an expression of the self-enclosed desiring self, available for rational analysis and representation like any other object. No doubt, objections to such a claim will immediately occur to readers familiar with texts such as the *Maximes* of La Rochefoucauld which call attention to an irreducible irrationality at the core of human nature which cannot be transcended and "objectified." My point is not, however, that the later seventeenth-century moralists share Descartes' complacent faith in the ascendancy of reason, but that the possibility of conceptualizing a subject divided between a transcendental rational faculty and an inward tendency toward irrationality is itself eminently Cartesian. Prior to the inception of the modern "split subject," the purpose of the analysis of the passions was to reorient the will toward ontologically appropriate objects—the good and the beautiful—and away from ontologically inferior ones—material forms—to the end that the soul might assume its true place in the hierarchy of being, and fulfill its teleological purpose. The entire project of the moralists after Descartes, and the purpose of the neo-classical "analyse des sentiments," is to inoculate the self-enclosed rational faculty against the biases imposed by equally self-enclosed forces of irrationality, for only by remaining free and detached in its transcendence can the *cogito* assure the transparency of the mental—and hence of the linguistic—representations. When Pascal warns that imagination rules the world, he takes issue with Cartesian optimism regarding the powers of reason, but not with the self-enclosed privacy and binary structure of the Cartesian subject. The same holds true when La Rochefoucauld exposes the subversive potential of "amour-propre" by demonstrating its modes of operation, its capacity to infiltrate every aspect of thought and feeling, and to appear in the guise of reason itself.

Within the historical process through which a new paradigm of self-representation emerged, the works of Montaigne and Descartes would appear, at least superficially, to represent a continuous development, the latter proceeding logically from the former. While Montaigne refutes the objective, ontological correspondence of sign and self by analyizing it from the vantage point of subjectivity, Descartes establishes the representational correspondence of sign and self by methodologically reducing knowledge to the subject's primary and unshakable awareness of his or her own existence: "I think, therefore I am." It would seem that the *Méditations* carry the skeptical project of the *Essais* to its logical conclusion by establishing the subject not merely as the *locus* of skeptical resistance, but as the guarantor of truth, and the horizon of symbolic reference.

The apparent continuity, however, is illusory. The skeptical critique of traditional ontology which inaugurates the paradigm shift, and the skeptical critique of objective reference which completes it, apprehend the effects of subjectivity on the determination of meaning from different sides of a cultural divide.[17] Just as Montaigne cannot escape the object-centered structure of signifying relations whose validity he calls into question, Descartes presupposes the subject-centered structure with which the *Méditations* ostensibly conclude. It is only because the contents of subjective consciousness have *already* replaced the spontaneous disclosure of being as the horizon of symbolic reference, that the principal threat to intersubjective meaning arises from the "epistemological" difficulty of proving the correspondence between intra-mental and extra-mental registers, rather than from the "ontological" difficulty of apprehending the footprints of being in the shifting sands of temporal life.

These differences may be briefly illustrated by the inflection each philosopher imparts to an identical arsenal of skeptical *topoi*. Of the four major causes of doubt enumerated in the *Méditations*—the senses are unreliable (145), we could be dreaming (145–46), an evil genius may be deceiving us (148), and "ancient and commonly held opinions" dominate our minds (148)

—all but the third are already familiar to us from Montaigne, and for that matter, from classical Greek precedents. In each instance, however, Montaigne employs them to demonstrate the inaccessibility to human thought of the unmoving truths of being, while Descartes employs them to illustrate the impossibility of verifying the correspondence of mental representations to the empirical world outside our heads. Instead of arguing that the senses deceive (Montaigne, 447), he argues that we are capable of producing sensory hallucinations without any link to a real exterior whatever (145), and finally that we are deceived not *by* the senses, but in believing that we *have* senses (149). Instead of presenting dreaming as a metaphor of the uncertainty of waking perception (Montaigne, 451), he argues that neither one nor the other can be proven to correspond to anything that exists outside the mind (146). Even the traditional skeptical motif of custom, which seems by definition to imply that the thinking subject is not alone in the universe, becomes an illustration of radical solipsism, rather than of the individual's co-participation in a collective symbolic order. For Montaigne, custom refers to the shared beliefs of an historically situated community, and is itself an external phenomenon impinging, along with sensory objects, on the mind, whereas for Descartes custom refers only to the private prejudice that leads us to infer the existence of an external reality from our awareness of mental images. Custom, in other words, does not shape our perceptions, but is, like the senses and mental perceptions, a figment of our imaginative faculty. These differences are epitomized in the contrast between the Montaignian thematics of movement—"le grand branloir" (the condition of becoming cut off from Being), and the Cartesian thematics of deceit—the "evil genius" (the misrepresentation within the mind of external objects).

The only skeptical argument for which we are unable to find any Montaignian precedent—i.e. an evil genius may be deceiving us (148)—is original precisely because it presupposes the transcendental subjectivity with which the *Méditations* conclude, and is therefore not only the crowning cause of doubt, encompassing and superseding all others, but the beginning of a reconstructive movement:

> I shall then suppose, not that God who is supremely good and the fountain of truth, but some evil genius not less powerful than deceitful, has employed his whole energies in deceiving me; I shall consider that

> the heavens, the earth, colours, figures, sound, and all other external
> things are nought but the illusions and dreams of which this genius has
> availed himself in order to lay traps for my credulity. (148)

In this anthropomorphic deity, envisioned not as the determining origin and immanent sustaining presence of an objective order, but as a self-enclosed subject, existing apart from creation and imposing his arbitrary will upon it, we see already an anticipation of the Cartesian *cogito*, capable of deceiving others by design, but perfectly lucid and detached in itself. All of the tributaries of Cartesian doubt flow into the single danger of misrepresentation, which is to say the interposition of an erroneous image of reality between an autonomous knowing subject and a world which, in the absence of deceit, would present itself directly to thought as an object referring to nothing beyond itself. Having already, in the initial stage of his argument, implicitly established the existence of a transcendental epistemological subject in the person of the evil genius, Descartes need only provide a rationale for believing in the voluntary restraint that prevents a good and loving God from deceiving his creatures in order to posit the mind of the individual as an intersubjective epistemological ground.

Given the incommensurate frames of reference implied by Montaigne's "que sais-je," and Descartes' methodological doubt, we are forced to conclude that the paradigm shift does not occur as a continuous intertextual development within their works, but rather as a consequence of events that take place in the conceptual space between them. Indeed, although Descartes' skeptical method is incommensurate with classical and even Montaignian antecedents, which remain, as we have seen, within the "ontological" tradition, he does not invent "epistemological" doubt, but rather takes it over from the imaginative literature—both drama and prose—of the late sixteenth and early seventeenth centuries which, because it contains the arguments of both "ontological" and "epistemological" varieties of skeptical thought, provides a kind of bridge between them. In the decades immediately preceding the Cartesian "discovery" of consciousness, Shakespeare and the Jacobean playwrights in England, Cervantes in Spain, and d'Urfé in France, simultaneously produce a literature of deceit in which multitudes of charlatans and dupes, "evil geniuses" and their victims, pursue self-interested designs against the still visible backdrop of a cosmic moral order.[18] This fact suggests that the logical movement that permits the emergence of a subject-centered theory of knowledge includes, as a necessary mediating step, a reprioritization of the sources of error in which the *misrepresentation* of the objects of knowledge comes to be regarded as a greater peril than their ontological "otherness." The origins of Cartesian subjectivity, in other words, may be traced to a gradual shift in the complexion of early modern skepticism which renders the formulation of the transcendental ego a necessary and inevitable reconstructive response.

L'Astrée, which enjoyed immense popularity in the decade immediately preceding the appearance of the *Discours de la Méthode* (1637), contains a double critique of the object-centered and the subject-centered epistemologies of signs. An experience of subjective interiority associated with the birth of love, which strikes with visceral force and militates against the possibility of intersubjective meaning, lies at the very heart, at the point of origin, of everything that happens in *L'Astrée*. The consequences for providential guarantees of meaning are immediately apparent. For d'Urfé as for Montaigne, the authentic inward self separated from transcendent sources of being stands in irreconcilable opposition to an external symbolic order conceived as a conventional fiction. D'Urfé's characters are continually beset by (and the obstacles to consummation are almost invariably related to) the difficulty of mediating the seemingly unbridgeable gulf between self and sign, subject and symbolic order, so that the self represented to others and which thereby acquires an intersubjective status, is also the self of subjective experience. To the extent that they act on their erotic impulses, they disappear from the domain of the representable, and they reappear as knowable selves only to the extent that their private impulses have been repressed or canalized or molded by conventions that are inauthentic. While Descartes resolves this paradox on the side of subjective consciousness, however, predicating the transparency of the arbitrary sign on the capacity for objective self-reflection of the transcendental *cogito*, d'Urfé exposes transparency as a pretense which merely conceals the fact that discourse, liberated from objective controls of meaning, inevitably becomes a vehicle for the self-generated illusions, and conventional prejudices of the speaker. D'Urfé's modernity lies not in his affirmation of subjective consciousness as a new horizon of symbolic reference, but rather in his simultaneous critique of two representational paradigms in a manner that leaves the signs of love ambiguously suspended between them. The symbolic universe of *L'Astrée* is a liminal one. The critic must always avoid anchoring it on one or the other side of the theoretical divide between the medieval and the modern, for *L'Astrée* is representative of both and neither.

The mediating role of *L'Astrée* is evident not only in a juxtaposition of modern "epistemological" with traditional "ontological" varieties of skepticism, but in a relative gain for the autonomy and continuity of subjective consciousness that differs markedly from Montaigne and anticipates a more modern view. For the author of the *Essais*, the mind lacks an intrinsic principle of stability that would permit it either to engage in systematic deceit and self-deception, or to be reduced to a determinate shape and identity by external social authority: "On le bride et garrote de religions, de loix, de coustumes, de science, de preceptes, de peines et recompenses mortelles et immortelles," Montaigne tells us, "encores voit-on que, par sa volubilité et dissolution, il eschappe à toutes ces liaisons." Lacking a determinate psychological or affective identity, the subject possesses no "handle" by which it might be grasped: "C'est un corps vain, qui n'a par où estre saisi et assené; un corps divers et difforme, auquel on ne peut assoir neud ni prise" ("Apologie," II, 224; 419). It is precisely the elusive changeability of thought that renders the subjective authentication of any fixed representation of self impossible for Montaigne, and which compels him to accept an insuperable awareness of interior distance—of being at once inside and outside the collective symbolic order. In *L'Astrée*, by contrast, the proliferation of self-directed villains, such as Semire, Laonice, Polemas and Climante, implies a gain for the intrinsic continuity and self-enclosure of consciousness that not only foreshadows the Cartesian *cogito* in its negative form as the "evil genius," but also, and more importantly, lays the foundation for an "historicist" response to the problem of authenticating discourse. An intrinsically coherent nexus of recurrent desires provides a kind of affective handle, or lever by which the subject may be systematically re-integrated into the community, and the discrepancy between subjective experience and collectively ratified representations of identity effaced. Neither an *a priori* order of being nor a transcendental consciousness guarantees the relation between the self and its representation in speech and gesture, but rather the subjective ratification of an arbitrary symbolic system.

The experience of interiority that destabilizes the symbolic universe of d'Urfé's narrative may best be understood in the context of a long pre-history in which sexual desire functions as one of the most important "anomalies" contributing to the emergence of a new structure of signifying relations. It has long been customary for historians of ideas to find a prototype of the Cartesian *cogito* in the religious interiority of Augustine.[19] More recent views of the period have emphasized the interdependence of the self-enclosed knower who seeks to possess the world as an object of thought with the acquisitive psychology of the merchant who regards the world as an object to be appropriated for self-interested use.[20] It seems no less reasonable, in view of our analysis of *L'Astrée*, to suggest that the Cartesian epistemological subject may have become a theoretical necessity partly due to the appearance of a new form of romantic love. The philosopher who knows the contents of his own mind more readily than any external thing has at least as much in common with the brooding, self-reflective lover as with the introspective saint and the possessive, self-seeking merchant, all of whom exemplify, in their respective domains of human endeavor, a similar experience of subjective interiority.

The pre-history in question begins with the eleventh-century troubadours whose poetry celebrates love as a personal, sentimental experience poised in opposition to officially sanctioned alliances.[21] Ultimately, however, although "courtly love" begins as one of the breaking points through which subjectivity makes its appearance in the midst of the objective order, it fails to realize its full subversive potential. Rather than foster the emergence of an autonomous, knowing and feeling consciousness, the courtly tradition imposes an ethic of self-emptying which reinforces the metaphysical assumptions of the *status quo*, and reproduces an identical structure of signifying relations. Social authority merely gives place to the will of the mistress as the absolute law to which the individual must submit in order to be known. And just as the officially sanctioned social structure derives its legitimacy from a presumed relation to a higher order of being (and not merely to political or class interests), the will of the mistress derives its binding power from her status as the embodiment of a metaphysical ideal of goodness and beauty (and not merely as an individuated ego governed by self-interest). The lover succeeds through self-transcendence, rather than through self-affirmation. Subjective interiority can no more be imagined as the determining center of meaning within the symbolic universe of courtly love than in the dominant order.

The authority of the chivalric code, however, was not destined to last even as a widely accepted ideal. Johan Huizinga has argued that the *Roman de la Rose*, composed in the middle to late thirteenth century, retains the chivalric ethic only as an empty formalism, and that the pastoral literature of the fourteenth and fifteenth centuries increasingly displaces philosophical idealism with an overtly erotic vision.[22] It is as though the egoistic energies that gave birth to courtly love were destined to reassert themselves, and to shake off the yoke of sublimation by which they had been impressed into the service of an objective symbolic order.

It is against the background of the chivalric tradition and its decline that we are able to recognize in d'Urfé's conceptualization of love a movement toward a paradigm shift which will permit the previously marginalized sentiments of the individual to be granted legitimacy and meaning, and to become, as it were, "a new fact of nature." In *L'Astrée*, love reasserts itself as a *locus* of resistance on the part of the individual to the objective order of being reflected not only in officially sanctioned social relationships (including, but not limited to marriages), *but also* in the chivalric code. The first evidence that the change has taken place appears in the opposition between the individual and coercive social institutions. Newly awakened to the imperative of erotic desire, the d'Urféan lover rejects parental authority, the company of friends, and even, eventually, the economic responsibility of tending sheep. A simultaneous gap opens between the inner truth of the individual and the conventional codes of courtly speech. Intensely preoccupied with the discrepancy between expression and feeling, d'Urfé's lovers regard the highly wrought discourse of knights and ladies as a mask that conceals rather than reveals the inner truth of the self, and continually raise the question as to whether an amorous compliment or vow has been motivated by love or merely by "courtoisie."

As phenomenological reflections of a providentially established pattern of life, however, these institutions and linguistic codes not only impose constraints upon the psychological subject, but provide the only means of representation by which personal identity may be known. One knows the inner merits or "prix" of an individual by the institutional function the heavens have given him to perform (Silvandre explains this in an early discourse with Diane), while courtly speech serves primarily to illuminate, in the manner of an interpretive gloss, the lover's place in an objective order of being. As a consequence, the autonomy of the desiring self can be achieved only at the expense of the aspirations of the knowing self, and *vice versa*. On the one hand, the affirmation of self-interest blocks the traditional path to interpersonal knowledge, and brings with it the threat of an impenetrable atomism. On the other, participation in the inter-subjective symbolic order entails the sacrifice of all that is authentic to the private self.

It will be useful here to describe in general terms the epistemological architecture of the main narrative in the light of the internal structure of the paradigm shift initiated by the birth of love, in preparation for a more detailed treatment of each phase of development in subsequent chapters.

D'Urfé's exploration of the problem of symbolic reference as it relates specifically to self-representation in the frame narrative produces two inter-locking triadic structures centered on the characters of Astrée and Celadon respectively. Each structure begins with the baroque dilemma in which the subject finds himself caught between the poles of subjective interiority and arbitrary custom, and each concludes by seeking to transcend the choice between intolerable alternatives in a different way. In the first, Astrée initiates an abortive attempt to establish subjective guarantees of transparency in self-representation, but finds herself constrained to accept the authority of collective perception as the criterion of personal truth instead. In the second, Celadon attempts, regressively, to adhere to objective, metaphysical guarantees of symbolic reference, but finds himself engaged in a process of transformation that tends toward his submission to collective norms, and re-integration into the community with which Astrée has become identified at the conclusion of the first. Throughout the two phases of narrative development, the relation between Celadon and Astrée parallels that between the subject and the objective order under the traditional paradigm which grants priority to the latter. Astrée represents the reality, the pole star of the true self, to which Celadon must become transparent in order to become fully realized and fully visible. It is only in his reconceptualization of the supra-personal order as a function of social rather than metaphysical reality that d'Urfé departs from the traditional object-centered paradigm.

As though to call attention to the rupture that love engenders between the inner self and the collective symbolic order, d'Urfé situates the lovers' first encounter in the symbol-laden context of a public ceremony—the Festival of Venus (I, 111–117). In the aftermath of their newly awakened self-awareness, every attempt at self-expression deepens the chasm that separates them from the ritual life of the community. In flagrant transgression against the laws of the temple, Celadon disguises himself as a woman in order to gain access to Astrée in the course of a ritual enactment of the myth of Paris. As a result, the disclosure of private thoughts and feelings takes place, from the outset, at the expense of the intersubjective symbolic order. They experience the identical dilemma once again when their love comes into conflict with the wishes of their parents who, later, replace the temple authorities as the principal representatives of the objective order within which personal identity and interpersonal relationships are pre-ordained and represented.

Under Astrée's influence the lovers at first attempt to transcend the alternatives of solipsism and fideism (affirmation of self at the expense of representation, and representation at the expense of self) in the direction of modernity. They reject the ontological-symbolic order as irrelevant to the inner truth of the self and seek to establish interpersonal knowledge on the basis of transparent, confessional speech. As autonomous knowing subjects, representing themselves to each other in a discourse of objective self-reference, however, the lovers find it impossible to escape the destructive effects of self-interest which motivates deceit and self-deception alike. Instead of entering a state of untroubled transparency, they find themselves in the world of the "evil genius" where each self-enclosed epistemological subject, though apprehending the empirical world directly as an object, strives to advance his private interests by misrepresenting the truth he clearly and distinctly perceives. The result is an intolerable Hobbesian war of all against all enacted in the domain of discourse, and presided over by such characters as Semire, Mandrague, Laonice, Climante, and Polemas, and in which the lovers themselves, as a measure of self-protection against "les plus mesdisants," become inextricably engaged.

Deceit in itself, however, is not an insurmountable obstacle. In the same way that the transcendental ego is already implicit in the personality of the deceiver (i.e. the Cartesian evil genius) the vindication of truth is implicit in the very structure of the representational sign. Just as the former presupposes the existence of an autonomous, knowing subject at the origin of discourse, the latter presupposes the existence of an objective referent available to direct, unmediated apprehension. The restoration of transparent, interpersonal knowledge requires merely that the lovers verify the claims of those who would impose upon them.

The decisive obstacle to self-representation in confessional speech is rather to be sought in the fact that objects, detached from their context in a supra-personal order, are never perceived as they are in themselves, but always mediated by the desires and inward fancies of the beholder. The subject, confronting the world as an object that refers to nothing beyond itself, inevitably reconstitutes what he sees according to the bias of his gaze, with the result that a discourse purporting to be transparent merely blinds us to our capacity for self-deception. The first response to the logical void that opens between subject and symbolic order, solipsistic self and arbitrary custom, ends by sliding back into one of the two sides of the original dilemma. The heroine's journey from the initial paradox of self and sign, through an abortive attempt to establish a subjective foundation for intersubjective reference, leads circularly to a relapse into solipsism. The command of bannishment by which Astrée forbids Celadon to appear in her presence marks this failure diagetically. Thenceforth, the lovers' physical separation serves as a reminder of the impenetrable self-enclosure that prevents them from representing themselves to each other.

At the same time, an endlessly renewed polemic on behalf of objective, metaphysical foundations of meaning pervades the narrative and provides a potential corrective to Astrée's error. But because the epistemological priority of the ontological-symbolic order has been irreversibly invalidated by the experience of romantic love with which Astrée's journey began, a reversion to the traditional model is no longer possible. Instead, the promise of authentic self-representation lies in a third direction. Astrée will be persuaded to accept the authority of collective opinion which, though external, exists in a kind of reciprocal exchange with the inner self.

In the frame narrative, the critique of subjective consciousness as an epistemological ground concludes with Astrée's autobiographical discourse in the fourth book of volume one. Here, by sharing her story with Phillis and Diane, Astrée relinquishes proprietary rights to her own identity, and establishes an intersubjective criterion of truth in the collective perceptions of her peers. These three friends, in fact, through a mutual sharing of their personal narratives, become the nucleus of an ideal community that forms around Astrée after Celadon's disappearance and which, by arrogating to itself the power to arbitrate disputes and to determine matters of fact, imposes standards of justice and truth which counter-balance the rapacious violence of self-interest and the vertiginous play of solipsistic fancy. Numerous lovers and pilgrims join the group as the narrative progresses, in each case positing themselves as knowable subjects by exteriorizing their inner truth in public discourses which subsequently, and after having been duly discussed and examined, acquire the status of objective representations of fact even though the facts as such can seldom be verified. Each member of this "discursive community" is who she is because the others believe her to be so, while the coercive effect of the collective gaze is mitigated by the participation of each individual in the creation of his or her personal myth.

The second triadic structure begins with the estrangement that results from the failure of the subject-centered paradigm, and encompasses Celadon's development throughout. If Astrée leans toward a proto-modern response to the problem of meaning, however, Celadon seeks to return to the symbolic universe of a former era. Henceforth, for him, the objective order will be represented neither by the ceremonial structure of religious observance, nor by officially sanctioned social relationships, but by the symbolic and metaphysical system of courtly love, the entire force of which comes to be concentrated in Astrée's command of banishment: "Va t'en desloyal, et garde toy bien de te faire jamais voir à moy que je ne te le commande" (I, 13).

The command, which precipitates Celadon's suicide attempt, and initiates the separation of the lovers, continues, at the surface level of the plot, to be the principal obstacle to reconciliation throughout the narrative. Astrée has forbidden Celadon to appear in her presence until she explicitly summons him. Since she doesn't know where he is, however, she cannot reverse her order even after recognizing her error, while Celadon, for his part, refuses to reveal his location for fear of violating a command he continues to regard as absolute. This situation would merely be absurd were it not for the fact that the command is also the functional link between Celadon and an entire system of self-representation. It appears to him as the supreme ethical imperative—the mythical Astraea is, of course, the goddess of justice (see note 21, below) — imposed by the objective order within which he aspires to be recognized as the living realization of the Perfect Lover, who is, as we have already pointed out, a being without interiority because wholly absorbed in the metaphysical reality from which he receives the final cause of his existence. In the broadest possible sense, the command is the originary prohibition through obedience to which the subject sacrifices the real (that undifferentiated, unstructured reality that cannot even be imagined or thought because it exists outside the field of representation), and assumes a place in a self-enclosed, supra-personal symbolic system. It functions in a manner precisely equivalent to the process of interpellation which Althusser has so vividly illustrated as "hailing"—the act of naming or designating an individual who, by the reciprocal act of recognizing the name as his own, implicitly assumes the identity (the mode of subjectivity) prepared for him by the discursive order of which the name is but a part, and from which it derives meaning as a name.[23]

Because the symbolic and metaphysical order of courtly love had already lost its relevance for d'Urfé's contemporaries who had ceased to conceptualize identity as the function of an objective, ontological order, the command and Celadon's obedience to it are the subject of much highly self-conscious reflection within the narrative. In the prefatory letter "Au Berger Celadon," d'Urfé anticipates the incredulity of his readers, and attempts to justify Celadon's behavior in terms of his adherence to the culture of "ancient Gaul." Within the narrative, Celadon encounters many—most notably Leonide and Adamas—who point out the absurdity of his obedience, which alienates him from the object of his desire, and logically precludes the possibility of discovering the reason for Astrée's displeasure and of enacting practical measures toward reconciliation. He consistently dismisses their counsel, however, as he must do, because his bizarre and self-sacrificial posture stems not from an exaggerated respect for the egoistic wishes of a headstrong mistress, but from his attempt to identify with the higher order of being that he imagines her to represent. In his mind, any transgression would, by asserting his subjective autonomy, invalidate the ontological subordination that establishes him as Astrée's true lover, and undermine the objective determination of meaning which permits that bond to be represented and known.

But Celadon's identity is not exhaustively defined by his obedience to an external command. An irreducible interiority remains which neither he, nor any of d'Urfé's lovers, can escape, and which, because it cannot be represented within the symbolic and metaphysical order of courtly love, produces a discrepancy between subjective experience and the objective system of signification through which his publicly recognized identity appears. Although Astrée's law for him is absolute, he exists in unresolvable conflict with it, unable to reconcile the twin objectives of the lover's quest—to be known as a true lover, and to satisfy an egocentric longing to enjoy her sexual favors. By rigorously adhering to her command, he may prove his identity as a perfect courtly lover at the price of the caresses which alone would satisfy subjective desire. Or, by appearing before her without her permission, he may secure the enjoyment of her physical presence at the price not only of his status as perfect lover, but of the very possibility of interpersonal knowledge.

Each of the two aspects of the baroque dilemma—self-representation at the expense of personal authenticity, and personal authenticity at the expense of self-representation—becomes the focus of one of the two major phases in Celadon's sentimental and spiritual apprenticeship under the direction of the high priest, Adamas. The first phase takes place during the period of retreat at the Temple de l'Amitié, which extends throughout the first two-thirds of the narrative; the second, in the course of the famous cross-dressing episodes which begin at the end of the third volume when Celadon returns to Astrée's hamlet disguised as a priestess. The two phases are distinguished primarily by Celadon's evolving relation to Astrée's command.

Celadon achieves the extreme limit of obedience and self-emptying during his sojourn at the Temple d'Amitié where, sacrificing the fulfillment of the erotic desire with which subjective autonomy has become identified, he surrounds himself with an elaborate symbolic structure representing the collective historical and spiritual memory of the inhabitants of the Forez, of which Astrée herself becomes the focal point, and reigning deity. As the site of two pilgrimages undertaken by Astrée and her circle of friends (in Books II and III), the temple becomes the central manifestation of an intersubjective symbolic order within which Celadon assumes his place not only as a knowable subject, but as a subject whose identity is metaphysically defined in terms of his transparency to a transcendent ideal. As "l'amant parfait," he is a living mark or sign commemorating the goodness and beauty of the beloved. The fact that he achieves his status as knowable subject only at the expense of subjective fulfillment is most poignantly illustrated by the episode of the "vain tombeau" in which the shepherds erect an empty tomb in Celadon's memory, a cultural symbol from which all vestiges of subjective presence have been removed.

Near the end of volume three, upon the insistence of Adamas, Celadon returns to the hamlet where, living with Astrée and her friends under the assumed identity of the druidess Alexis, he enjoys intimacies which would be denied him were he to appear undisguised. It is here that the paradox between subjective authenticity and the symbolic order of courtly love produces the highest peak of emotional conflict. By interpreting Astrée's command literally to mean only that he must not allow himself to be seen, he attempts to fulfill at one and the same time his obligations as a perfect lover, and the imperatives of desire—to preserve his identity within the objective symbolic order concretely displayed in the Temple de l'Amitié, while at the same time getting around the prohibition that constitutes his identity within that order. Rather than escape the choice between the intolerable alternatives of self-representation without authenticity, and authenticity without self-representation, however, he merely finds himself on the latter side of the dilemma. The disguise which facilitates his access to Astrée, and permits the fulfillment of his desires, also renders him invisible to her even as he lives with her on intimate terms. When the undisclosed interiority which had been the latent center of identity during his sojourn in the Temple becomes the functional center during his sojourn in the hamlet, he immediately disappears from the field of representation. He is either known, and denied erotic pleasure at the temple of love, or erotically gratified and unknown in Astrée's bed chamber. He laments this paradox at the culminating moment in his personal development when all alternatives for reconciling representation and subjectivity have been exhausted:

> O Dieu! dit-elle, qu'Alexis serait heureuse sans Celadon et que Celadon serait heureux sans Alexis! Que si j'estois veritablement Alexis, et non pas Celadon, que je serais heureuse de recevoir ces faveurs d'Astrée, mais combien le serais-je encore plus si, estant Celadon, elles ne m'estoient pas faites comme estant Alexis! Fut-il jamais amant plus heureux et plus mal-heureux que moi? heureux pour estre chery et caressé de la plus belle et de la plus aimée bergère du monde, et malheureux pour sçavoir asseurément que ces faveurs qui me sont faites seroient changées en chastimens et en supplices, si je n'estais courvert du personnage d'Alexis. (III, 605)

Since confessional self-disclosure, along with the entire subject-centered system of signifying relations upon which it depends, has already been discredited as an avenue to interpersonal knowledge, Celadon's dilemma would seem to be unresolvable. But throughout his adventures, unbeknownst to himself, he is gradually being prepared for reconciliation under conditions that bring both the meaning of Astrée's command and the definition of personal identity within the sphere of social authority represented by a community of like minded peers. Astrée's status as the embodiment of a collective social ideal radically alters the orientation of Celadon's mental journey. She continues to represent his highest good, the possession of which coincides with the hero's complete self-realization. But she does so neither as a metaphysical ideal to which he must become wholly transparent, nor as an autonomous, self-determining ego to whom he must submit, but as the affective link by which he will be reintegrated into the community, and accede to the collective symbolic order. Through his experiences under the guidance of Adamas, his identity, like the identities of all who participate in the discursive community of which Astrée is the center, will be re-established as a function of the collective gaze.

While Astrée's command continues, in Celadon's view, to represent the ethical imperative of an objective ontological order to which he must submit if he wishes to demonstrate his status as perfect lover, it has long since been recognized by everyone else in their circle of friends as the expression of a finite, self-enclosed subjectivity whose tendency toward irreducible, anarchistic egotism can be moderated only by collective standards of justice. Early on, Astrée perceives the injustice of a command which functions not as a means to test the truth, in an objective, metaphysical sense, of Celadon's love, but as an act of vengeance for an imaginary affront to possessive desire. As we have seen, her autobiographical narrative marks the moment when she publicly refers her subjective impulses to the collective judgment of her friends. Insofar as Astrée symbolizes the idea of justice, the laws of love which provide the intersubjective criterion by which true lovers are recognized, have been brought down out of the heavens and established on social rather than metaphysical foundations. Thenceforward, no law, including the command of banishment, is binding until it has been ratified by the community.[24]

In itself, however, the triumph of the collective gaze as the criterion of truth in self-representation does not assure the subjective authentication of discourse. Rather, it would appear to be little more than a capitulation, in a manner reminiscent of Montaignian fideism, to the tyranny of custom as a means of escaping the vagaries of solipsistic fantasy. We would be forced to conclude that d'Urfé, unable to resolve the paradox of baroque self-representation, merely affirms the rights of society over those of the individual, and the arbitrary objective order, over the polymorphous and unstable energy of the autonomous subject.

D'Urfé, however, calls attention to the limitations of a fideistic response. The destructive potential of social authority would seem to be the central import of the narrative's innumerable "procès d'amour"—lovers' quarrels arbitrated in the presence of the assembled community by a judge who embodies the collective voice. Lovers who submit to judicial decrees ratified by their peers invariably do so at the expense of personal authenticity, and to the detriment of health and happiness. This clearly appears in the aftermath of each of the trials when plaintiffs faint dead away, fall desperately ill, or resort to violent, self-destructive measures in an effort to comply with a law that fails to reflect authentic personal desires. We need only remember Calidon's illness, Celidée's self-disfiguration, and Adraste's madness.

Closing the gap between the self and the symbolic order therefore requires an additional step. It is not toward an act of heroic self-repression that Celadon's journey progresses, but toward the complete reconciliation, valid at the deepest levels of affective life, between subjective self-awareness and a socially constructed, historically relative, vision of the real. D'Urfé envisions a *dénouement* in which subjective desire and the intersubjective symbolic order determine and reflect each other reciprocally—in which the representation of identity provided by the one becomes subjectively true for the other, and in which the inner truth of the one leaves an indelible mark in the other.

D'Urfé's preoccupation with the processes by which such accommodations occur accounts for the proliferation of ritual performances throughout the narrative where they serve to effect a transference of affective energy which renders the collective symbolic order subjectively authentic.[25] Adamas relies on Astrée's dual role as the object of subjective desire and the embodiment of the collective consciousness as a means of drawing Celadon imperceptibly back within the compass of the institutional and discursive order of Forezian society. Instructing his pupil in the history of Gaul and in the doctrines of druidism, Adamas "lui assaisonnait tous ses conseils par quelque dessein d'amour" (II, 320), and encouraging him to build a temple in honor of the druidic trinity, he exploits Celadon's repressed eroticism as a means of motivating his adoration of the gods:

> Mais d'autant que le druide avait opinion que, s'il ne flattait un peu le mal de Celadon, il perdrait peu à peu la dévotion et la volonté d'y travailler, il nomma le temple du nom de la déesse Astrée. (II, 327)

Ultimately, Celadon's subjective identification with the social occurs not in the Temple d'Amitié which still resonates with the echoes of the traditional ontology, nor in the hamlet where erotic energy continues to militate against determinate representation, but in a third and final phase of narrative development which occupies the last episodes that come to us from d'Urfé's hand. When Astrée is kidnapped and taken by force from her bucolic retreat toward the end of the fourth volume (IV, 747), Celadon finds himself implicated, in spite of himself, in a struggle for political power centered at Marcilly, the capital city, seat and symbol of secular social authority. Henceforward, the personal erotic concerns of the hamlet, and the theological metaphysical concerns of the Temple, become increasingly intertwined with the affairs of state. This segment of the narrative's development culminates in the famous "siege of Marcilly"—a battle between the legitimate forces of Queen Amasis and the usurper Polemas. And, although the account stops short before the outcome and its consequences for the lovers have been revealed, ample evidence may be adduced from the extant passages to support my thesis that through participation in the siege, Celadon advances rapidly toward the moment when his identity as Astrée's lover and his representation as a social subject will be finally reconciled. The siege itself is a magnificently choreographed ritual process whose symbolic universe brings competing ideologies and cultural values into play. When Celadon is drawn by love to take his place in the battle, he becomes, as it were, a subject of its discursive structure, and assumes an identity imposed by its inscribed alternatives. The erstwhile unbridled and unrepresentable energies of the self cease to be a *locus* of inward resistance, and become instead a force that motivates his self-identification within an external order. By taking arms in defense of Astrée he also upholds the legitimate social and symbolical regime of Amasis, thereby establishing the truth of his love and his public identity with a single gesture. The sign and the self are one.

***

The suspension of the symbolic order between two incompatible horizons of reference elicits, as we have already indicated, both progressive and conservative responses from d'Urfé's characters. On the one hand there are those who affirm the epistemological priority of subjective consciousness only to find themselves among the first casualties of unforeseen pitfalls in a mode of self-representation which, however alluring, had yet to be established on the firm foundation supplied by the transcendental ego. On the other, there are those who advocate a return to a metaphysical conception of identity and meaning only to discover that new aspects of human experience—the subjective interiority associated with the birth of love—cannot be represented within the structures provided by the old paradigm. This double response, and the double impasse to which it leads, informs the narrative at every level, and provides its developmental logic. The following chapter will further specify this logic as an open-ended process tending toward the authentication of discourse not only for d'Urfé's characters, but for the author and his readers. Subsequent chapters will explore, first, the juxtaposition of the objectivist and subjectivist modes of conceptualization in the love debates which compose a large portion of *L'Astrée*'s voluminous bulk; then, the alternative responses to the semiotic crisis which are exemplified by Astrée's autobiographical discourse and by Celadon's spiritual re-education under the guidance of Adamas respectively. Finally, a few reflections, offered in an epilogue, will call attention to the historical continuity that links the seventeenth-century crisis of meaning with the relativization of discourse that haunts postmodern culture in the present day.

Notes

1. According to Bernard Germa, "nul livre ne peut lui être comparé et ne contribua avec plus d'efficacité à l'organisation de la société polie." [*"L'Astrée" d'Honoré d'Urfé, sa composition et son influence* (Paris: Alphonse Picard, 1904), p. 238.] For O.-C. Reure, d'Urfé was "l'interprète d'abord, le directeur ensuite des sentiments publics." [*La Vie et les oeuvres de Honoré d'Urfé* (Paris: Plon, 1910), p. 276.] For Maurice Magendie, *L'Astrée* is "le roman d'une société qui s'organise." [*Du Nouveau sur "L'Astrée"* (Paris: Champion, 1927), p. 463.] Recent critics continue to reiterate these opinions. In the eyes of Henri Coulet d'Urfé, having produced in *L'Astrée* "la somme d'un monde et d'une époque," enjoys a stature comparable to that of Rabelais and Balzac. [*Le Roman jusqu'à la Révolution* (New York: McGraw-Hill, 1967), p. 145.] Jean Starobinski finds in *L'Astrée* "le modèle qui inspira un style de vie et de passion." [*Un Paradis désespéré: l'amour et l'illusion dans "L'Astrée"* (New

Haven: Yale University Press, 1963), p. xiii.] For Jacques Morel, it is "l'oeuvre majeure d'une époque." ["Honoré d'Urfé," *Littérature française*, Vol. 3, La Renaissance, 1570–1624 (Paris: Arthaud, 1973) p. 232.]

2. I am using the term "symbolic order," derived from structural anthropology and psychoanalysis, in its broadest possible sense to refer to all of the signifying structures that constitute a culture, and of which language is but one example. The symbolic order includes all of the collectively ratified, and subconsciously internalized, codes of interpretation within which, as Clifford Geertz has said, "all of our acts are signs." It will become clear in the subsequent development of the current essay that the justification for lumping such apparently disparate things as ritual performance and speech together in the single category of the symbolic lies in part in the fact that the structure of signifying relations—the nexus of linkages among subject, sign and referent—which pertains in the one sphere of symbolizing activity also pertains in the other.

3. For a summary of these views see Christian Wentzlaff-Eggebert, "Structures Narratives de la Pastorale dans *L'Astrée*," *Cahiers de l'Association Internationale des Etudes Françaises*, No. 39 (May 1987), pp. 63-64.

4. Jacob Burckhardt's *The Civilization of the Renaissance in Italy* (1908; London: Phaidon Press, 1965) provides one of the earliest expositions of Renaissance individualism. Ernst Cassirer's *The Individual and the Cosmos in Renaissance Philosophy* (1927; New York: Harper & Row, 1964) analyzes the transition from a psychological paradigm in which the individual's identity is determined by his place in an objective order, to one in which it is a function of his own, self-creative action in the world. C. B. MacPherson's *The Political Theory of Possessive Individualism: Hobbes to Locke* (London: Oxford University Press, 1962) contrasts "customary status societies" in which the individual is defined by his place in a larger social whole, with the "market society," already fully operative in the early seventeenth century, in which the individual is "the proprietor of his own person or capacities, owing nothing to society for them," and in which "society becomes a lot of free equal individuals related to each other as proprietors of their own capacities and of what they have acquired by their exercise" (3).

5. Studies devoted to the analysis of this epochal reversal of priorities and its consequences for theories of knowledge and meaning are numerous. I am particularly indebted to those of Anthony Kenny, Richard Rorty, Timothy Reiss, Hiram Cotton and Michel Foucault. In general, their arguments support the view that philosophers from Plato through the Middle Ages had granted epistemological priority to the objective

order, whether conceptualized in terms of transcendent ideas as in the Platonic tradition, or material forms as in the Aristotelian. In either case, the mind was assumed to acquire its contents and structure from something outside itself and not to begin with the certainty of its own existence in order to analyze the world according to the principles of its own intrinsic and self-enclosed logic, or, even more radically, to refashion it in the image of its own desires. Anthony Kenny credits Descartes with having "created a new philosophy of mind" which reverses the traditional relation between the external and public as opposed to the internal and private. While Aquinas and other medieval Aristotelians had believed that knowledge of the human mind "must be secondary to, almost parasitic on, knowledge of the external world" (113), Descartes was the first to assert that "the internal is more certain than the external, the private is prior to the public" (114). [*The Anatomy of the Soul: Historical Essays in the Philosophy of Mind* (Bristol: Basil Blackwell, 1973).]

Richard Rorty contrasts a "hylomorphic conception of knowledge" with a "representative" conception. For the former, knowledge is dependent on "the subject's becoming identical with the object." For the latter, it is dependent on "the possession of accurate representations of an object" (45). [*Philosophy and the Mirror of Nature* (Princeton: Princeton University Press, 1979), pp. 45–61.] Reiss employs a series of contrasting terms to distinguish between medieval and modern "modes of conceptualization." In the former, the subject participates in "a conjunctive manner of being," while in the latter he becomes "a disjunctive center of knowing;" in the former he understands by virtue of his "knowing participation in a totality" (31–32) which encompasses both the conceptualizing faculty and the world it contemplates, in the latter by virtue of "applying an abstract schematization to the concrete" in order to apprehend objects in their difference from the knower and from one another. [*The Discourse of Modernism* (Ithaca: Cornell University Press, 1982).]

Hiram Caton provides an extremely helpful synopsis of Klaus Oehler's essay on "Ancient and Modern Philosophical Self-consciousness" which reiterates the fundamental distinction between the object-centered and the subject-centered theories of knowledge. For the modern mind, he writes, "subjectivity is sovereign because its measure of truth is a design it projects on the world." [*The Origin of Subjectivity* (New Haven: Yale University Press, 1973), pp. 207–209.]

All of these, in my view, substantiate Foucault's well-known formulation of the problem in terms of his theory of "epistemes."

6. In *The Order of Things: An Archeology of the Human Sciences* (New York: Vintage Books, 1973), Michel Foucault develops his influential theory of "epistemes," according to which a transformation in the relation between signs and what they signify from inherent resemblance to arbitrary representation occurs simultaneously with a parallel shift affecting all domains of human knowledge in the early seventeenth

century. In *The Discourse of Modernism*, Timothy Reiss employs conceptualizations
of the sign initially proposed by Foucault to distinguish between a medieval "discourse
of patterning" and a modern "discourse of analysis and reference."

7. Rorty, 45. See note 5 above.

8. Laurence Gregorio has commented briefly on *L'Astrée*'s semiotic ambivalence,
although without reference to the epistemological issues we have outlined here. See
The Pastoral Masquerade: Disguise and Identity in "L'Astrée" (Saratoga, CA:
ANMA Libri, 1992), p. 12; and "Implications of the Love Debate in *L'Astrée*,"
French Review LVI.1 (October 1982), p. 38.

9. I have chosen this term because it seems to embrace both structuralist and poststructuralist theories of signification. Both schools of thought, and all of the minor
currents they encompass, deploy a textual metaphor according to which social and
cultural phenomena may be analyzed as compositions of signs within self-enclosed
relational structures. The crucial difference between structuralism and post-structuralism lies in whether or not one believes that structure can be analyzed from an
extra-structural, or meta-discursive point of view. The affirmative answer offered by
the founders of the movement upholds a subject-object dualism according to which
"objective" knowledge is possible precisely because of the self-presence of the
conceptualizing faculty. The negative answer offered by their poststructuralist heirs
implies a prior structuration of subjectivity by discourse which renders objectivity
impossible, and announces the end of the Cartesian epistemological tradition.

10. The question of causation is at issue even among those who share the conviction
that cultural history is punctuated by global paradigm shifts. Michel Foucault's
insistence on the logical priority of symbolic structures to thought leads him at least
provisionally to deny the possibility of discovering a cause for cultural change:
"Ultimately, the problem that presents itself is that of the relations between thought
and culture: how is it that thought has a place in the space of the world, that it has its
origin there, and that it never ceases, in this place or that, to begin anew?" (*The Order
of Things*, 51).

      Others have attempted to rectify this extremely difficult aspect of his theory by
suggesting that an "episteme" or "mode of conceptualization" possesses, as part of its
own structure, a negative or "occulted" underside which provides both the motiva-
tional energy and the conceptual raw materials for the creation of a new dominant
model. Timothy Reiss adheres to this view: "The dominant theoretical model is
apparently invariably accompanied by a dominant occulted practice. This is composed
of widespread activities (though the phrase is awkward) that escape analysis by the

dominant model, that do not acquire 'meaningfulness' in its terms, that are therefore in the strictest sense unthinkable." The passage from one dominant theoretical model to another, he continues, takes place "when internal contradictions of the [current] dominant model begin to prevent its effective functioning, when it begins to produce strong alternative elements of discourse [. . .], and when the dominant occulted practice begins to become conceptually useful" (*The Discourse of Modernism*, 11).

11. Thomas S. Kuhn, *The Structure of Scientific Revolutions*, Second Edition Enlarged (Chicago: University of Chicago Press, 1970), p. 77.

12. Kuhn, 53.

13. I am not alone in this view which, as we shall see, is imposed upon us by the sequence of events in *L'Astrée*. Cassirer argues that the emergence of a transcendental *cogito* was anticipated by Petrarch's highly personal and affective celebration of individuality. The poet's struggle against Averroism "concerns something more than mere speculative, theoretical discussion. Here, we have a highly gifted personality; by right of its original feeling for life, it rebels against conclusions that threaten to limit or to weaken this right. The artist and virtuoso who rediscovered the inexhaustible wealth and value of 'individuality' now sets up his defenses against a philosophy that considers individuality to be something merely casual, something purely 'accidental'" (*The Individual and the Cosmos*, 128-129).

14. The first reference in each citation refers to *Essais*, ed. Alexandre Micha (Paris: Garnier-Flammarion, 1969). The second refers to *The Complete Essays of Montaigne*, trans. Donald M. Frame (Stanford: Stanford University Press, 1965). For a helpful analysis of Montaigne's role in the evolution of early modern subjectivity see "From Self to Subject: Montaigne to Descartes," in Dalia Judovitz, *Subjectivity and Representation in Descartes: The Origins of Modernity* (Cambridge: Cambridge University Press, 1988). My only difference with Judovitz is that her account exhibits the bias typical of cultural materialist analyses of early modern subjectivity. She insists upon passages in the *Essais* which call attention to the cultural determination of the self, but ignores those which invite us to marvel at its infinite, and uncontrollable, polymorphous mobility.

15. I am thinking of Jean Rousset's influential conception of the baroque aesthetic as being characterized by "metamorphosis" and "ostentation," Circe and the peacock: on the one hand a principle of mutability, and on the other a delight in appearances for their own sake. [*La Littérature de l'age baroque en France* (Paris: Corti, 1954).]

16. Subsequent references are to *The Philosophical Works of Descartes*, Volume I, trans. Haldane and Ross (Cambridge: Cambridge University Press: 1975).

17. Following Heidegger's "The Age of the World picture," Bernard Charles Flynn differentiates Greek skepticism, which "was possible only within a world where Truth was revealed as *aletheia*—unconcealment," from seventeenth-century skepticism which is possible only when "the subject, the I, becomes the transcendental ground of the known and the knowable." I agree entirely with this distinction, but question the accuracy of Flynn's historical claim that "the advent of subjectivity [and hence of Cartesian skepticism] is irreducible to pre-Cartesian philosophy." ["Descartes and the Ontology of Subjectivity," in *Man and World*, 16:003–023 (1983), pp. 3–23.] Much more satisfying is Cassirer's view, advanced in *The Individual and the Cosmos*, that Cartesian subjectivity has a long pre-history.

18. For a relevant discussion Shakespeare see Lionel Abel's *Metatheater: A New Vision of Dramatic Form* (Clinton Mass: Colonial Press, 1963). According to Abel, subjective self-awareness gives birth to a "metatheatrical" form in which tragic heroes stand both inside and outside of the ontologically determined roles they are forced to play. For a relevant discussion of Cervantes, see *The Order of Things*, 46-50. It is a remarkable testimony to the scholarly neglect of d'Urfé in French literary scholarship that Foucault relies exclusively on *Don Quixote* to illustrate the transition between medieval and modern epistemes while passing over *L'Astrée* in silence.

19. "It is well known that his [Augustine's] religious subjectivism led him directly to those basic conclusions that Descartes later formulated as a logician and as a critic of knowledge. His religious idealism and Descartes' logical idealism rest upon one and the same principle of interiorization, of reflection upon oneself" (Cassirer, 128).

20. Reiss demonstrates the interdependence of the act of naming with the act of taking possession in "analytico-referential discourse," and points out the explicitly "utilitarian" motivations of its early theorists and advocates. "Like Bacon, Galileo, and Hobbes, Descartes's avowed aim is possession and utility" (*The Discourse of Modernism*, 35).

21. These alliances owed their ultimate authority to an ontology that devalued the subject. C.S. Lewis tells us that "any idealization of sexual love, in a society where marriage is purely utilitarian, must begin by being an idealization of adultery." I would suggest, however, that the point is not merely that the marriages were "utilitarian," nor that love was "sexual," but that the marriages were intended to sustain a providentially established social hierarchy, and that sexual love was associated with the self-

affirmation of the individual as such. Behind the marriages which Lewis says were based solely on "interest" stands the justification provided by an objective ontological order, and behind the repression of sexual love which Lewis attributes to Christian morality lies a devaluation of all that pertains to the autonomous ego. While retaining the form of Lewis' statement, then, I would revise its theoretical emphasis as follows: To the extent that love is equated with that which is merely subjective in origin, it cannot be granted official recognition within an object-centered system of signifying relations where all social institutions, including marriage, are legitimized by their status as reflections of a supra-personal metaphysical reality. [*The Allegory of Love* (New York: Oxford University Press, 1958).]

22. Johan Huizinga traces the decay of chivalric idealism from the thirteenth through the fifteenth centuries, a period during which "the system is not given up; but its forms are filled by new values" (108). Already, the ethical precepts offered in the *Roman de la Rose* (begun at some point before 1240 and completed in 1280), he says, "are no longer so many perfections brought about by the sacredness of love, but simply the proper means to conquer the object desired" (115). The flowering of the pastoral genre toward the end of the middle ages marks a further phase in this "reaction against the ideal of courtesy. [...] The new, or rather revived, bucolic ideal remains essentially an erotic one" (128). [*The Waning of the Middle Ages* (New York: Doubleday Anchor Books, 1954).]

23. "Ideology 'acts' or 'functions' in such a way that it 'recruits' subjects among the individuals (it recruits them all), or 'transforms' the individuals into subjects (it transforms them all) by that very precise operation which I have called *interpellation* or hailing, and which can be imagined along the lines of the most commonplace everyday police (or other) hailing: 'Hey, you there!'

"Assuming that the theoretical scene I have imagined takes place in the street, the hailed individual will turn round. By this mere one-hundred-and-eighty-degree physical conversion, he becomes a *subject*. Why? Because he has recognized that the hail was 'really' addressed to him, and that 'it was *really him* who was hailed' (and not someone else)." [Louis Althusser, "Ideology and Ideological State Apparatuses," in *Lenin and Philosophy and other Essays*, trans. Ben Brewster (New York: Monthly Review Press, 1971), p. 174.]

24. Frances A. Yates provides a history of the Astraea myth which enlarges the significance of her subordination to the community beyond the scope of affectional life to include a secular and relativized conception of the foundations of imperial justice and rule. The myth makes its first appearance in literature in the *Phenomena* by Aratos, a Greek astronomical poet where Astraea is Justice who becomes the

constellation Virgo. Cicero, was responsible for one of several Latin translations of the *Phenomena*, and Roman poets perpetuated the myth. In Ovid's *Metamorphoses* the departure of Astraea from earth marks the close of the Golden Age; she becomes Virgo, the sign of the month of August. But "it is to Virgil that she owes her greatest fame" and in the *Aeneid*'s fourth eclogue that she becomes "the imperial virgin," associated by later readers of the poem in particular with the reign of Augustus, the golden age of empire. Christian writers such as Augustine and Dante, following the lead of the Emperor Constantine, reinterpret Virgil's fourth eclogue as a messianic prophecy and identify Astraea with the Virgin Mary. "Here the foundation is laid for the assimilation of the description of the golden age to the language of Christian mysticism." The golden age is the Christian era, the kingdom of God within. The return of the Virgin is a spiritual state. In England where the myth makes its appearance in works by Spenser and Shakespeare, Astraea becomes one of the central symbols of the Elizabeth cult, representing the queen as "the sacred One Virgin whose sword of Justice smote down the Whore of Babylon and ushered in a golden age of pure religion, peace and plenty" (47). In France Astraea also serves as "a symbol of the imperial justice of the French crown" (82), particularly associated with Henri IV. Yates points out that in his dedication to Henri IV, d'Urfé identifies his heroine with the justice that Henri's rule has restored to Europe. [*The Imperial Theme in the Sixteenth Century* (London and Boston: Routledge & Kegan Paul, 1975).]

25. Victor Turner and Clifford Geertz provide important indications as to the function of ritual in the interpellation of the psychological subject into the symbolic order. Turner says that ritual "makes desirable what is socially necessary by establishing a right relationship between involuntary sentiments and the requirements of social structure. People are induced to want to do what they must do." [*Dramas, Field, and Metaphors: Symbolic Action in Human Society* (Ithaca: Cornell University Press, 1974), p. 56.] Similarly, Clifford Geertz explains that religious ritual harmonizes the affective life of the individual with a culturally constructed model of reality: "It is in some sort of ceremonial form—even if that form be hardly more than the recitation of a myth, the consultation of an oracle, or the decoration of a grave—that the moods and motivations which sacred symbols induce in men and the general conceptions of the order of existence which they formulate for men meet and reinforce one another." [*The Interpretation of Cultures* (New York: Basic Books, 1973), p. 112.]

2

Narrative as a Quest for Meaning: The Mythopoeic Journey of the d'Urféan Subject

As the preceding chapter has already made clear, d'Urfé was chiefly oncerned with the problem of symbolic reference as it relates to self-representation. With this in mind we can restate and expand our thesis as follows: the inner logic of the narrative inheres in an interrogative process through which various epistemological alternatives are tried and rejected as the lovers search for an intersubjective criterion of truth in self-representation. The process is inconclusive not in the sense that it precludes the possibility of a *dénouement*—I believe the narrative projects a conclusion in which Astrée and Celadon marry—but in the sense that resolution is predicated on interpretive norms which are recognized as being relative. The "true" representation of identity is determined by its adequation to collective agreement rather than to metaphysical absolutes, or to psychological authenticity. Other characters might have joined other communities with other criteria for determining personal worth and relationships. The process can continually be renewed.[1]

The structure of this process, which we have already presented in broad outlines in the preceding section, may be made more specific by a close analysis of two discrete narratives in which we find an encapsulation of the whole, one inserted at the beginning and the other at the end of the opening volume. The first is an historical exposition that establishes the dramatic situation of the main plot, centering on the affairs of Astrée, Celadon and the deceitful rival, Semire. The second is an intercalated tale entitled the "Histoire de Damon et de Fortune." It is presented as an interpretive commentary on six paintings which portray, in a series of densely significant images, the lives of two lovers who succumb to the deceitful machinations of the magician Mandrague. Whereas the exposition at the beginning of the first volume purports to deal with actual events and projects us into the unresolved "middle of things," the tale is complete in itself, and establishes the entire structure of the plot from its beginning to its interminably deferred end, in the static and timeless form of a myth. It might almost be said that the "Histoire de Damon et de Fortune" functions as a master narrative in the sense of providing the code that governs the author's imaginative construction of the "real" or "historical" events represented in the frame.[2]

The quest for an intersubjective criterion of truth in self-representation at every level of the narrative—from the largest global patterns to the most local and narrowly circumscribed episodes—is always characterized by the same four phases in the relation between the subject and the objective symbolic order which I will designate with the following terms: metaphysical complementarity (the ontological unity of self and sign), disintegration (the conflict of self and sign), experimentation (the juxtaposition of progressive and regressive responses), and re-inscription (the reassimilation of the subject into the collective symbolic order). Both of the miniature plots we are currently considering record the disruption of an object-centered paradigm of self-representation by an experience of subjective interiority. The characters begin in a state of idyllic repose in which desire is perfectly harmonized with the external conditions of existence, and self-representation is a function of the subject's participation in an objective ontological order. They progress to a period of isolated inwardness coincident with the birth of love which engenders an acquisitive war of all against all, and an awareness of interior distance or estrangement from the traditional means of self-representation. Both aspects of the crisis of subjectivity are provisionally resolved by formulas of reciprocity which anticipate a neo-classical conception of order predicated on subjective interiority and discursive transparency. The lovers find temporary respite from agonistic desire in an ethic of equitable exchange, and an assurance of interpersonal knowledge in a discourse of objective reference. The tenuous balance established at both affective and cognitive levels of experience, however, cannot withstand the pressures brought to bear against it at once from private and public points of origin. The dissolution of metaphysical complementarity that constitutes the self and the sign as two competing *loci* of truth also bequeaths to posterity the twin perils—private irrationality and tyranny of inauthentic symbolic forms—which in the modern episteme militate against the possibility of transparent representation. As self-enclosed individuals defined by their interiority rather than by their participation in an objective hierarchy, the lovers become helpless victims of intra-psychic passions on the one hand, and of the imposition of arbitrary conceptions of personal identity on the other. Equitable exchange degenerates once again into mutual exploitation, while the transparency of the arbitrary sign proves to be an illusion that does little more than lend a specious appearance of epistemological validity to either solipsistic or collectively generated fantasy. The deconstruction of objective reference as a means of self-representation dominates both plots. Semire's report to Astrée, the testimony of the magical "fontaine de la vérité," the paintings on the lovers' tomb, and even, at last, d'Urfé's own narrative, are all revealed to be unreliable or indeterminate, rather than transparent and objective, representations.

Whereas the pre-history of the frame narrative concludes with the estrangement of the lovers, leaving the resolution to be worked out in the course of the subsequent thousands of pages, the "Histoire de Damon et de Fortune" foreshadows the historicist foundations upon which interpersonal knowledge will be restored and the lovers reconciled. As specimens of baroque *trompe-l'oeil*, the paintings exemplify an aesthetic which is at once realistic, and fanciful—a playful mode of realism which calls attention to the priority of art to life, and of cultural forms to reality. Realistic painting at this moment of transition between two discursive paradigms, although it detaches its objects from an ontological scheme in order to present them as though they indicated nothing beyond themselves, cannot yet be construed as a transparent representation of a self-subsistent reality. The images that adorn Damon's and Fortune's tomb therefore share the fate of all signs in *L'Astrée*. Suspended between alternative—objective metaphysical and subjective empirical—horizons of reference, they possess a determinate meaning only by virtue of collective assent to an authoritative commentary, in this case provided by Adamas.

By subjecting the absolute foundations of discursive reference—both the ideal and the empirical—to a decisive, skeptical critique, d'Urfé inevitably calls attention to the liminal status not only of the signs of love, but of his own discourse, and raises the question of literary meaning. The historicist resolution to the problem of symbolic reference exemplified *within* the narrative would seem to suggest that meaning does not exist inherently in the text itself, but must instead be added by the reader, and that the criterion of intersubjective truth which arrests "interpretive anarchy" lies neither in metaphysical nor in empirical horizons of reference, but in the imposition of collectively ratified norms of interpretation. Before exploring the epistemological foundations of literary meaning implicit in d'Urfé's conceptualization of the sign, however, we must turn our attention to the quest for a criterion of truth in self-representation undertaken by the characters in the two brief narratives at hand.

L'Astrée's first two paragraphs describe a mythical past in which personal identity and self-representation are functions of a metaphysically assured complementarity between the subject and an objective order of being. Affective life is characterized by "repos" because inward longing, rather than initiate an inconclusive quest or fruitless toil, finds a perfect complement in a world "capable de tout ce que peut désirer le laboureur" (I, 9). The point is not so much that desires are immediately satisfied, as that they are perfectly harmonized with the inherent resources of the external world, confirming the subject's place in an objective totality rather than signifying his separateness from it. By the same token, if the soil of the Forez yields whatever the "laboureur" desires, the Forezian landscape bespeaks, like a concrete discourse or network of symbols, the collective identity of its human inhabitants. The transformation of geography into sacred topography is effected by a double movement of empirical de-realization and discursive re-inscription. On the one hand, d'Urfé's idealizing mode of description—the mountains and plains are "fertiles," the air "tempéré," the central river "doux et paisible," and the waters of its tributary streams "claires" (I, 9)—empties landmarks of their concrete specificity. On the other, place names—Forez, Gaule, Loire, Lignon, Cervières, Chalmasel and Feurs—enmesh the landscape in an esoteric discourse of origins in which the properly initiated are able to read a history of the region's political and religious institutions. We say "properly initiated" because the link between a landmark and its meaning is not "transparently" indicated in its name, but rather must be recovered by virtue of the science of etymology which restores to language its original purity.[3] "Forez," d'Urfé eventually tells us, derives from the Roman word "forum" (I, 45), identifying the founders of secular institutions. "Gaule" on the other hand, the larger region of which the Forez is but a microcosm, is said to derive from "galère," referring to the ships in which the progenitors of the race arrived at the time of the great flood, bearing the teachings of the true religion (III, 477).

The first tableaux of the "Histoire de Damon" represents the complementarity of self and world visually in the image of a shepherd playing his pipes at the center of a bucolic scene. The shepherd's state of mind, the world of which he is a part, and his mode of activity are perfectly harmonized. Damon is not yet estranged by egocentric desire from the objective order.

Although his face, we are told, "représente bien naifvement une personne qui n'a souci que de se contenter," his is a desire, like that of d'Urfé's mythical "laboureur," that confirms his place in a supra-personal totality: "vous y voyez je ne scay quoi d'ouvert et de serein, sans trouble ny nuage de fascheuses imaginations" (442). And the scene of which he is the center, though not without moral and physical danger, represents a homeostatic universe whose internal checks and balances contain occasional violence within larger patterns of order. A group of astonished lambs observe "deux belliers qui se viennent heurter de toute leur force," and three dogs keep watch at the edge of the woods "pour s'opposer aux courses des loups." But while the fighting rams exemplify the violence that accompanies courtship, the lambs suggest the promise of regeneration. And while the wolves intimate the ever present threat of death, the watch dogs who keep high ground "à fin de voir plus loin" not only safeguard the mortals in their charge, but exemplify a moral vigilance informed by a sense of providential design. Finally, the shepherd's music, as a self-referential structure, provides an aesthetic corollary of both the self-completeness of a being at one with himself, and the self-regulating harmony of the natural order, and like the discourse of origins concealed in the Forezian place names, reveals their essential commonality.

This idyllic existence is lost in both the frame narrative and in the tale when an experience of affective interiority, associated, as we have seen, with the advent of a new and tyrannical form of desire, disrupts the metaphysical complementarity between the subject and the objective order. In his exposition of the main plot, d'Urfé writes: "Mais endormis en leur repos ils se sousmirent à ce flatteur [Amour], qui tôt après changea son authorité en tyrannie" (I, 9). What distinguishes this new and dangerous love from the desire of the mythical laborer who wants nothing that cannot be immediately supplied, and from that of the piping shepherd who seeks nothing but to "se contenter"? What makes it "tyrannical" rather than "authoritative"? The first is an expression of the lover's place in an objective, supra-personal order, while the second is a self-affirming expression of the individuated ego. *L'Astrée*'s polemical disputes, which I will examine more closely further on, establish the distinction in metaphysical terms. The desire of the piping shepherd, like his music, is self-completing because its object is nothing other than the plenitude of being that the shepherd always already possesses by virtue of his participation in a providential order. "Amour," Silvandre will say, "est un si grand dieu, qu'il ne peut rien désirer hors de soi-même: il est son propre centre, et n'a jamais dessein qui ne commence et finisse en lui" (II, 262–63). The desire of the smitten shepherd, by contrast, arises from the ontological incompleteness of an ego whose autonomy is bought at the price of an exile from transcendent sources of being. "Qu'est-ce qu'amour?" Hylas will ask rhetorically. "N'est-ce pas un désir de beauté et du bien qui deffaut?" (II, 383)

At the opening of his narrative, however, d'Urfé chooses to illustrate the effects of the new and destructive form of love rather than examine its metaphysical causes. Courtship proceeds as a negotiation between individuals seeking an equilibrium of interests. Loss and acquisition, service and payment, are the operative terms in a process that tends toward the establishment of reciprocity:

> Il est vrai que si en la perte de soi-même on peut faire quelque *acquisition*, dont on se doive contenter, il se peut dire heureux de s'être *perdu* si à propos, pour *gaigner* la bonne volonté de la belle Astrée, qui asseurée de son amitié, ne voulut que l'ingratitude en fût le *paiement*, mais plutôt *un réciproque affection* avec laquelle elle recevait son amitié et ses services. (I, 10)

A similar experience of disjunctive identity and strife provisionally resolved by means of reciprocal desire is recorded in the second tableaux of the "Histoire de Damon" which portrays the birth of love. Adamas opens his commentary on the scene by describing it as "bien contraire au precedent, car si celuy-là est plein de mespris, celuy-cy l'est d'amour." Repose gives place to agitation. An atmosphere of gentle madness prevails under the influence of the "petits Amours." Subverting the providential harmony of the pastoral world, they ruffle Fortune's hair "à l'envie de la nature." As they manufacture an archery bow to the measure of her eyebrows, and string it with her hair, they engage in grotesque contortions to which Adamas calls our attention. The conventional neo-Platonic image of Eros and Anteros represents the achievement of reciprocity, containing disorder. When Cupid, who dominates the upper portion of the panel, releases his arrow, Damon suffers the wound of erotic desire: "son coup ne fût point en vain, car le pauvre berger en fût tellement blessé que la mort seule le peut guerir" (I, 444). At the same time, Anteros binds the arms and neck of Fortune with a chain of flowers and places it in Damon's hands "pour nous faire entendre que les mérites, l'amour, et les services de ce beau berger, qui sont figurez par ces fleurs, obligerent Fortune à une amour réciproque envers luy" (I, 444). Like Celadon, Damon realizes an equitable "acquisition" (a desirable object) in compensation for his "loss" (transcendent sources of being).

With the birth of love, the transition from repose to agon in affective experience is paralleled by a transition from transparency to opacity in the domain of signs that forecloses the traditional path to interpersonal knowledge. Because the structure of symbolic reference as signification inscribes that which is merely subjective as the very antithesis of meaning, the reconceptualization of the individual as the autonomous, self-determining proprietor of his own identity not only initiates an acquisitive 'war of all against all,' but invalidates the metaphysical guarantees of truth in self-representation. Whereas the pre-lapsarian subject finds his identity illuminated by institutions and by a language that reflect the universal order inscribed on the face of the landscape itself, and of which he is both part and microcosm, the victim of love's tyranny conceives pre-existing symbolic structures as artificial accretions behind which the inner truth of the self resides, unspoken and unseen. Threatened with an enforced separation which would thwart the fulfillment of their desires, Astrée and Celadon effect a break with the traditional symbolic order in both its institutional and linguistic dimensions. They defy the authority of their parents, and embark on a career of deceit to ensure the success of their "desseins amoureux" (I, 10).

Omitted from d'Urfé's extremely truncated synopsis of the narrative's pre-history is the positive attempt on the part of the lovers to establish a new mode of self-representation predicated on signs that refer transparently to the inner truth of the self, rather than inscribe the self within an overarching cosmos. I will therefore defer my own examination of these discursive strategies, and merely note that the quest for possession is duplicated by the quest for objective knowledge, and that while the first is resolved at least provisionally by a formula of reciprocal desire, the second is resolved at least provisionally by a formula of reciprocal self-disclosure. The narrative projects an ideal situation in which two individuals, motivated by mutual love, agree to represent themselves transparently to each other. Insofar as they have become self-creating and self-determining individuals, they assert themselves as authors of meaning and manipulators of signs, rather than as passive recipients of the meaning that signs bestow. Although they deceive the world, they have no secrets in their private lives. Here, however, d'Urfé permits us to witness only the negative effects of the loss of metaphysical guarantees of meaning occasioned by the individual's awareness of his autonomy from the symbolic order.

Although the disintegrative effects of autonomous subjectivity are provisionally overcome by means of equitable exchange at once erotic and discursive, the resolution thus achieved contains within itself the seeds of its own destruction. The trend toward dissolution in *L'Astrée* is signaled by a general mutability whose sources are to be sought in the baroque conception of the self-enclosed ego as a *locus* of ceaseless change, and of the arbitrary sign as an instrument of subjective appropriation. In the frame narrative, d'Urfé declares that "rien n'est constant que l'inconstance, durable même en son changement" (I, 10). Similarly, the third tableau of the "Histoire de Damon" calls attention to the mutability of the real landscape which bursts the illusion of stability and balance artificially imposed by an aesthetic of transparent mimesis. Trees have died, new ones have grown up in their places, and the river has changed its course, since the artist's rendering. The lesson to be learned with respect to the quest for truth in self-representation is that reciprocity cannot, by virtue of an equilibrium of favors, satisfy the limitless desire of the self-enclosed, possessive ego, nor can confessional discourse, however transparent seeming, assure that reality will be perceived objectively. Desire re-emerges in a destructive negative form as a fear of dispossession, while the discourse of objective reference delivers the world up for subjective interpretations, or appropriations, precisely by positing its autonomy from an objective ontological order. Far from giving access to reality as such, the arbitrary sign becomes a vehicle for, and a surface upon which the lovers project, their irrational desires and fears.

The failure of objective reference to yield an unmediated apprehension of truth is the central point in Semire's successful plot to separate the lovers in the frame narrative. Celadon's deceit (he pretends to love Aminthe in order to conceal his love for Astrée from his parents) provides Semire with the means to make Astrée believe that he has truly been unfaithful: "Ruse vrayement assez bonne," d'Urfé says of Celadon's ploy, "si Semire ne l'eut point malicieusement déguisée, fondant sur cette dissimulation la trahison dont il deceut Astrée." At the most superficial level of the plot, we are faced with a simple case of villainy which is made the more poignant by an element of poetic justice. Astrée's susceptibility to deceit, however, is not an effect of providential, or even authorial, guarantees of moral order, but of the subjective self-enclosure and the indeterminacy of signifying reference inherent in the mode of representation upon which the lovers have chosen to predicate their knowledge of each other. While the subject's autonomy from an objective ontological hierarchy unleashes a destabilizing play of desire and doubt, the discourse of objective reference permits the referents of signs to be woven all the more easily into the warp and woof of subjective fantasy precisely because it functions as a simple substitution, or "representation," of objects rather than as a gloss on their providentially determined meanings. It is as though by detaching objects from their metaphysical frame of reference, representation eliminates a barrier which within the traditional epistemological paradigm had forestalled the threat of solipsism, and suddenly exposes the lovers to the unattenuated violence of their private passions.

Semire's ruse is hardly a ruse at all. It consists merely in a discourse, perfectly transparent on its own merits, by which he represents to Astrée Celadon's actual behavior with Aminthe. But it is the very transparency of his discourse that makes it effective as a ruse. By absolving Astrée of the responsibility of looking beyond appearance for a hidden metaphysical truth, it encourages her to believe that the subjective interpretation she places on the empirical events she observes is objectively true. The cautionary message conveyed by Semire's method of deception is that objects never appear to us as such. They are always embedded in a context that bestows upon them a supplemental value or meaning. They are always, in other words, signs inscribed within a signifying system which may be alternatively grounded in an objective metaphysical order, a subjectively generated fantasy, or a collectively ratified and historically relative vision of the real. For that reason, the most dangerously deceptive discourse of all is the one which encourages us to forget that such a contextualization has taken place, and which reassures us in the complacent and mistaken belief that the meanings we project upon the world are attributes of the world as it really is.[4]

The four final tableaux of the "Histoire de Damon" record the consequences for self-representation of the advent of subjective interiority in strikingly similar terms. Once again, the lovers are ensnared in self-deception precisely because they voluntarily enter a symbolic universe in which signs purport to represent the world objectively. This time the role of tempter-deceiver is played by the magician, Mandrague. The third tableau not only records the birth of Mandrague's erotic infatuation for Damon, but also calls attention to the egotism inherent in the desire to which the lovers themselves, no less than their archenemy, have succumbed. Leering at Damon's naked form from a place of hiding in the trees, Mandrague personifies the erotic voyeur appropriating others as objects of subjective fantasy, while Damon stands waist deep in the Lignon whose symbolical double source suggests the ambiguous suspension of the signs of love between subjective and objective centers of meaning which corrupts and ultimately destroys the reciprocity established in the previous scene. Here, as in the frame, the estrangement of the lovers results from dangers inherent in the mode of representation on which they rely for their knowledge of each other, and which are merely exploited and brought to fruition by the machinations of a jealous rival. If Astrée and Celadon succumb to the lure of objective knowledge promised by Semire's discourse, the catastrophe that befalls Damon and Fortune results directly from their reliance on the "fontaine de la vérité d'amour," an enchanted spring that reveals the inner truth of the beloved to lovers who peer into its depths. Tableaux four through six depict, first, Mandrague's sub-version of the fountain by magic, then, the dreams of betrayal which, by means of further enchantments, she causes the lovers to have, and finally, the false disclosures of the fountain which confirm the lovers' suspicions, and cause their deaths.

Created by a magician to memorialize his daughter who died from unrequited love, the "fontaine de la vérité" provides a means of representation intended to mitigate the ontological isolation suffered by lovers as a conse-quence of their self-enclosed interiority. It is a precise metaphorical equivalent of the confessional discourse employed in private by the lovers in the frame narrative—prefiguring a discourse of objective reference toward which seven-teenth-century sign theory had begun to move, but which it had not yet entirely succeeded in imposing as a theoretical possibility. As a transparent surface above a well of impenetrable depth, it functions as a simple mental representa-tion of a person's inner truth, rather than as a gloss on the person's place in an objective order. The fountain's mode of functioning, in other words, is not that of the inherent sign by which the self is providentially revealed to interpreters whose insight depends upon their participation with the object of knowledge in a metaphysical totality, but that of the arbitrary sign, by which the reality is rendered fully present to a knower who stands apart from objects as a self-enclosed center of consciousness.

Adamas explains the error to which Damon and Fortune succumb in a brief digression which, because it demystifies the "fontaine de la vérité" as a discourse of truth, proves to be the defining moment for the epistemology of signs not only in the "Histoire de Damon," but in *L'Astrée* as a whole. Adamas himself calls attention to the pivotal importance of this passage in his commentary by insisting that it is necessary "pour vous faire mieux entendre le tout" (I, 448). The key to explanation is a distinction between "love" and "magic" where love corresponds to a mode of knowing predicated on the underlying metaphysical unity of differentiated beings revealed in providentially given signs, and "magic" to a mode of knowing predicated on the autonomy of the knower from the known, and the mediation of arbitrary signs. Because the two modes of knowing are incommensurate, they have no power to interfere with each other. Magic, we are told, has no power over love: "les charmes de la magie ne puissent rien sur les charmes d'amour" (I, 448). It is only by voluntarily crossing over in the act of consulting the fountain that the lovers expose themselves to both the particular advantages and the characteristic dangers of magical representation.

At the most superficial level of the plot the lovers are victims of Mandrague's magic conceived as an arbitrary, external force which inspires dreams of betrayal, and alters the testimony of the fountain. The true cause of their estrangement, however, is to be found in the inherent features of a mode of self-representation for which magic and the fountain it produces and controls are but metaphors. Magic evokes at one and the same time the power of the arbitrary sign to render the inward truth of the self-enclosed individual fully present to another, and the equally extra-ordinary power of subjective consciousness to appropriate others for its own purposes when they have become detached from their places in an objective ontological structure. Tormented by dreams of betrayal, the lovers each consult the fountain in order to lay their doubts to rest, but find that the fountain merely confirms, and lends a semblance of objective validity, to their fears. Their dreams are less an effect of magic than of the anticipation of deceit with which lovers, as self-enclosed individuals, are habitually plagued: "Suivant l'ordinaire des amants, [Damon] était toujours en doute" (I, 449). And the fountain's treacherous confirmation is less an effect of Mandrague's controlling intelligence than a projection of those fears. Although Fortune had never loved Damon's rival, "amour qui croit facilement ce qu'il craint, persuada incontinent le contraire à Damon" (I, 449).

In addition to showing that the transparency of the arbitrary sign is subverted by subjective fantasy, Adamas' digression also locates the fountain, and the mode of representation it exemplifies, in an historical narrative, implying a second source of unreliability. Although we learn that a magician created the fountain in memorial to his daughter who died from unrequited love, the empirical details of the account are less important than the simple fact that it reveals, by its very existence, the historicity of the "transparent" sign, and thereby exposes its claim to objectivity as a fraud. The fountain of truth which presents itself as a mirror of history is in fact embedded in a history of its own which shapes and predetermines the 'reality' it represents. Its origins are indissociable from its current unreliability. Because it was created by a magician, Adamas explains, it is susceptible to the designs of Mandrague whose magical powers are greater than those of her predecessor. "Et d'autant que la vertu de la fontaine lui venait par les enchantements d'un magicien, Mandrague qui a surmonté en cette science tous ses dévanciers, la lui peut bien ôter pour quelque temps" (I, 448). The arbitrary sign is once again shown to be enmeshed in a play of competing interests which prevent it from functioning as a representation of objects as they really are. Instead, it becomes the vehicle of all that the subject brings to bear, and all that discourse itself, as a historically embedded medium, imposes on the world.

Recent theorists have told us that claims for transparency in discourse, even as an ideal, have been challenged since the end of the nineteenth century by the twin pressures exerted by psychology and ethnology. The first reveals the degree to which discourse is a projection of suppressed eroticism reducing knowledge to mere subjective fantasy, and the second, the degree to which it is a cultural artifact constraining thought within the predetermined patterns of an historically relative tradition. In the light of the foregoing analysis, it should be clear that both of these dangers were foreseen by those who lived at the moment when the discourse of objective reference had just begun to establish itself, and had still to struggle against the objections of its detractors. While d'Urfé, like Montaigne and other baroque writers, rejects the metaphysical criterion of truth that undergirds symbolic reference as "signification," his skepticism extends as well to the emergent paradigm in which signs will be posited as transparent representations of objective psychological and empirical facts. For d'Urfé, the escape from the baroque paradox of personal authenticity and determinate self-representation does not lie in the direction of a "Cartesian" discourse of confessional self-disclosure. Transparency falls prey to the twin epistemological perils—private fancy and arbitrary custom—precipitated out of the dissolution of the medieval synthesis of self and sign. The obstacle to knowledge initially posed by conventional codes of speech and behavior whose historical relativity had been recognized has given place in the modern subject-centered episteme to the double subversion of objective reference by the proliferation of discourses which, though presenting themselves as objective presentations of fact, are vehicles of subjective desire on the one hand, and collective opinion on the other.

The narratives we have just examined both lead to a seemingly insurmountable epistemological impasse. In the frame narrative, a lie "disguised" as truth by a second act of deceit doubles back to shape the self-perceptions of its authors. The suggestion that representation precedes and shapes our perceptions is even more pronounced in the "Histoire de Damon" where the identification of the fountain of truth with magic forces us to wonder whether all representation is in some way transformative of its objects, and whether there is truth beyond appearance, or whether appearance itself, governed by a play of competing interests, is the only truth. In a discursive universe where representation precedes reality *ad infinitum*, all we can know of the human heart, our own as well as others, are masks.

Nevertheless, because the narrative offers the reader the illusion of a privileged vantage point external to discourse, the subversion of the arbitrary sign would seem to stop short of challenging the distinction between representation and reality. We not only know that both the dreams and enchanted images that give them "objective" validity are false, but we also know *why* they are false because we are made privy to the mechanism of deceit. We are shown, as it were, both subjective psychological, and historico-ethnological sites of discursive production. Although Semire encourages Astrée to misinterpret Celadon's behavior, we have a sense that beneath deception and self-deception truth remains untouched, awaiting rediscovery. Similarly, although Mandrague plays on the fears of Damon and Fortune to create an appearance of infidelity, we are never permitted to doubt that the images in the fountain are false—a perception reconfirmed when the lovers recognize their error in the end. D'Urfé's deconstruction of objective reference, however, encourages us to examine, and expose as illusion, the final feat of magic by which he, as author, projects the transparency of his narrative, and imparts a sense of epistemological security to his readers.

It is particularly significant in this regard that the lover is not the only figure who serves to exemplify in *L'Astrée* the characteristics of the modern psychological and epistemological subject, affirming the individual's powers of self-determination and relying on the direct testimony of subjective experience as the measure of truth. The image of man as an artist, maker and molder of his own identity, capable of transforming the world for his pleasure and use, conveys a similar exaltation of the individual as the self-sufficient center of identity and meaning.[5] The figure of the artist, moreover, illustrates more clearly even than that of the lover the relation between the appropriation of others as objects of desire, and the subjective control of representation. The artist not only conceptualizes the world according to a self-interested bias, but reifies that subjective vision in discourses and visual representations—in narratives, sculptures and paintings—that subsequently have the power to influence the perceptions of others.

It is, in fact, precisely through an examination of the role of man as artist in the "Histoire de Damon" that d'Urfé carries his skeptical critique of a subject-centered theory of knowledge to its logical extreme and indicates the manner in which *L'Astrée* moves beyond it. One of the central lessons of the tale is that every "ouvrier," and by extension every artisan's "oeuvre"—his conceptual universe—is also an "oeuvre" of other and more powerful "ouvriers." It is as though the very rejection of an *a priori* criterion of truth that precedes and undergirds the artist's freedom to become the maker and molder of himself also renders him vulnerable to the influence of representations that emanate not from his own subjectivity, but from the subjectivities of others, and which threaten to impose upon him an inauthentic role, whether as an unwitting tool, or as an object of desire. The egocentric 'war of all against all' manifests itself not only in the competition to possess desirable objects, but in the struggle to subjugate the consciousness of others by means of aesthetic images and discourses that project the artist's particular, self-interested vision of 'the real.' Artifice supersedes artifice until standards of truth and reality disappear by which we might hope to uphold the simple dichotomy of art and nature, representation and referent, and we are forced to recognize the futility of any attempt to establish a vantage point for subjectivity outside the play of mediating discourses. The only relief from a radical skepticism engendered by what might be described as a state of discursive anarchy lies not in the perception of nature-as-such beyond or beneath the deceptive appearances of art, but in the acceptance of a 'normative artificiality' legitimized by an authoritative commentary.

D'Urfé's examination of the artist's creative power begins immediately prior to the tale in a conversation between the princess Galathée and Celadon. In the course of a tour of the garden of the Palais d'Isoure which contains the "Grotte de Damon et Fortune," the princess elicits the shepherd's admiration for the artisan as a quasi-godlike being, and sets the tone of naive wonderment which Adamas' commentary on the six tableaux will systematically deflate. As they progress through the garden toward the grotto's entrance, and from the entrance to the interior, Galathée identifies a hierarchy of creative powers, each of which supersedes and determines the subjectivity of those preceding. At the lowest level we find the shepherdess, Fortune, whose love for Damon conforms to the laws of the objective natural order, followed by the sorceress Mandrague, who creates the fabulous garden and the grotto. She, in turn, is superseded by Cupid whose spectacular actions the grotto's decorations depict, and finally by the spirits or demons who construct the lovers' tomb and the paintings from which we have our account of the love affair.

The exchange begins when Celadon asks his companion to tell him about the grotto which "semblait belle et faite avec un grand art." Galathée's reply, which represents Mandrague's one-sided and destructive love for Damon as "une des plus grandes preuves qu'Amour ait fait de sa puissance il y a longtemps" (I, 440), and dismisses Fortune's faithful and fruitful love as "chose ordinaire," reveals not only her infatuation with those who re-fashion the world in the image of their autocratic desires, but her contempt for those who remain obedient to the laws of nature. For Galathée, Mandrague merits praise because of the extravagance with which her artificial creations supervene upon the natural order, and the degree to which her enchantments represent the triumph of an independent subjectivity over *a priori* constraints:

> Si l'on connait à l'oeuvre quel est l'ouvrier, dit Galathée, à voir ce que
> je dis, vous jugerez bien qu'elle est une des plus grandes magiciennes

de la Gaule; car c'est elle qui a fait par ses enchantements ceste grotte,
et plusieurs autres raretés qui sont autour d'icy. (I, 440)

When they progress from the entrance of cavern to its interior, Celadon stands
as though transfixed—"ravy en la considération de l'ouvrage"—by the
evidence of the magician's virtuosity. The autonomous, polymorphous subjectivity of the artist has created an empirical universe in its own image—a world
entirely subordinated to the forms imposed by her "bizarre imagination."
Illuminated by an opening in the ceiling, and dripping with saltpeter, the cavern seems to be torn between darkness and light, earth and water, an image of
the natural world in change, while the statuary, decorative columns, garlands,
and fountains, create an impression of phantasmagoric movement. Mandrague's art, moreover, is itself a celebration of the autonomous creativity of
Love personified as an artisan of still greater power. The figures that flank the
entrance of the grotto—Syringue partially transformed into a reed on one side
while fleeing the love-smitten Pan who seems to pursue her from the other—
and all of the other images "représentaient quelque effet de la puissance
d'Amour."[6]

Finally, the highest rung of creative freedom is occupied by "les esprits
de Mandrague," the magician's familiar spirits or demons. If previous artifacts
have amazed us by fabulous subversions of nature which demonstrate the
autonomy of the creative subject from an objective ontological order, the
paintings which dominate the chamber, "si bien faites que la vue en decevait
le jugement," would seem to demonstrate the artist's power in another way. By
creating a likeness of nature so perfect that the viewer mistakes imitation for
reality, the artist attains near equality with God. It would seem that the chaotic,
polymorphous "baroque" subject has given place at last to the transcendental
ego which will permit intersubjective reference to be re-established as representation. In fact, however, the "realism" we witness here is not yet the kind
that takes for granted the subject's possession of reality-as-such through the
mediating agency of the arbitrary sign. Rather it is that playful variety of realism known as *trompe-l'oeil* which effects a de-realization of objective
reference no less decisive than the subjective de-realization of the providentially established "book of nature" that precedes it. Just as the lover who
declares his autonomy from the conventional symbolic order is permitted to
declare his true feelings only *as though* he were feigning, the creative artist at

the dawn of the modern era may only be permitted to practice realistic representation in the visual arts *as though* it were an optical illusion. Far from proclaiming themselves as a representation of objects as they are in truth, the six paintings merely seem to display the artist's technical virtuosity at a previously unmatched peak of extravagance. Entranced by the illusion of reality, Celadon "louait l'invention et l'artifice de l'ouvrier." This immensely peculiar, and typically baroque, double movement which simultaneously asserts and retracts the epistemological priority of the subject is a strategy for preserving what little credibility continues to cling to the now decayed edifice of symbolic reference as signification.

The first words of Adamas' commentary dampen the atmosphere of exaltation established by Galathée, and announce the deconstructive, or deflationary, movement of the tale. Every artist's power is limited, if not by an objective *a priori* order to which he or she must submit, at least by the will of still other, more powerful craftsmen. Man is not a godlike creator, but a toy of the gods:

> Tout ainsi que l'ouvrier se joue de son oeuvre et en fait comme il luy plaît, de mêmes les grands dieux, de la main desquels nous sommes formés, prennent plaisir à nous faire jouer sur le theatre du monde, le personnage qu'ils nous ont esleu. (I, 11,441)

As Adamas proceeds with his commentary, he calls our attention to the fact that Mandrague's subjectivity is determined by that of Cupid, and that Cupid's, in turn, is circumscribed by that of the demons who represent both the sorcerer and the god, in the transparent-seeming glass of their six tableaux, as authors of *mis*representation. And finally, because the paintings deconstruct their own claim to objectivity, we are forced to recognize the relative and artificial status of even this last and most compelling vision of the real. In the governing subject position we find neither the two deceivers (Mandrague or Cupid), nor the spirit-painters, but an aesthetic interpreter, who in turn derives his authority not from an ontological or epistemological criterion of truth, but from the collective assent of his audience. Thus, while Adamas exposes derogations from the objective order as solipsistic projections on the part of Mandrague and Cupid, he re-establishes truth in representation on neither objective-metaphysical nor subjective-empirical grounds, but as a function of the interpellation of individuals into an historically relative community.

The deconstruction of Mandrague's subjective autonomy takes place in the third tableau where, succumbing to the power of erotic desire, the enchantress reveals the limitations of her power. Adamas makes a point of contrasting her former autonomy with her present helplessness: "Je crois qu'elle vient de faire quelques sortilèges, mais jugez ici l'effect d'une beauté" (I, 446). She whose magical skills we have been led to believe are limitless becomes an "oeuvre" or artifact produced by the bizarre imagination of a greater craftsman visible in the upper regions of the painting: "Or haussez un peu les yeux, et voyez dans cette nue Venus et Cupidon, qui regardans cette nouvelle amante, semblent éclatter de rire" (I, 446).

If Mandrague alters the "fontaine de la vérité" upon which Damon and Fortune rely for their knowledge of each other, she does so only because love, personified as Cupid, has similarly transformed her perception of Damon. Like magic, moreover, which is associated with both the inward psychological and the outward historical subversions of objectivity, Cupid is at once the embodiment of an aspect of Mandrague's inner life that escapes her control, and the governing intelligence of an external design in which she is forced to play a part. Adamas at first attributes love's victory to the Mandrague's subjective response to the sight of Damon in his bath: "jugez ici l'effect d'une beauté" (I, 446). Her gaze subverts the signs by which the innate "sympathies" and "antipathies" that govern the natural order are disclosed: "Si l'amour vient de la sympathie, comme on dit, je ne sçais pas bien où l'on la pourra trouver entre Damon et elle" (I, 446). Far from apprehending the shepherd as he really is, she appropriates him as an object of desire, projecting upon him a purely subjective value, just as Damon and Fortune project their fears onto the surface of the fountain. At the same time, Cupid intervenes as an external agent. Although depicted as the god of love, he stands at the farthest remove from the immanent divinity who, in Adamas' mystical theology, sustains the differentiated order of nature while at the same time drawing all things together toward a unitive consummation. Rather he embodies, like the Cartesian evil genius, a self-enclosed subjectivity defined in opposition to the objective order, and effecting gratuitous transformations and deceptions for reasons of his own. Adamas enumerates: "Pour quelque gageure peut-être qu'il avait fait avec sa mère;" or "pour faire voir en cette vieille que le bois sec brule mieux, et plus aisément que le verd;" or merely "pour montrer sa puissance sur cette vieille hôtesse des tombeaux" (I, 446). Whether Mandrague's failure to recognize her objectively ordained relation to Damon is a function of her own subjectivity or that of another, however, the central point remains. The rejection of *a priori* constraints that underlies her own creative power also renders her subject to arbitrary forces which, whether they emanate from an unbridled, and polymorphous, inner world, or ensnare her from without, ultimately undermine her status as a unified and self-determining center of consciousness.

At the center of the layers of illusion—the magical appearances created by Mandrague, and those to which Mandrague herself falls victim—the elevated bodies of the lovers Damon and Fortune would seem to reassure us of the existence of an inviolable substratum of reality or truth, and the paintings adorning their tomb to exemplify an ideal of objective representation of historical events as they actually happened, free at once from the false projections of the inner psyche, and from deceptions perpetrated by external agents. But transparency itself proves to be a specious appearance sustained by means of strategic exclusions and specifiable artistic techniques. On the one hand, the spirit-painters assert their objectivity by removing themselves from the field of representation, and on the other, they lend an air of factuality to their canvases by practicing a rigorous attention to empirical detail.

The spirits implicitly claim for themselves a "meta-discursive" status by representing the two principal illusion-makers—Cupid and Mandrague—in action, while concealing themselves from view. At various moments, we witness Cupid shooting his arrows, and Mandrague subverting the native virtue of the fountain. The demystification effected by the spirits reaches a climax in the final scene in which Damon and Fortune discover that the fountain has deceived them, and Mandrague and Cupid implicitly acknowledge the moral perfection of love they have destroyed, and hence the existence of an objective standard of value from which their bizarre imaginations have led them to depart. Mandrague renounces her art and curses her demons. Her contorted gestures are signs "de son violent desplaisir et du regret qu'elle a de la perte de deux si fidelles et parfaits amants" (I, 452). We see Cupid, likewise, his arrows broken and his torch extinguished, weeping "pour la perte de deux si fidelles amants" (I, 452). The claim to moral authority cannot be more pronounced than when representing not only the defeat, but the repentance of one's rivals. Only the demons themselves are absent from the general remorse with which the tale concludes, and it is by this strategic self-exclusion that they establish themselves as the *locus* of the controlling subjectivity which, from a privileged vantage point external to the play of competing (mis)representations, grasps the story's final moral, its kernel of objective truth. They create the paintings, Galathée tells us, in order to leave posterity a moral exemplum in the form of a touching tale: "pour temoignage, que l'amour ne pardonne non plus au poil chenu qu'aux cheveux blonds, et pour raconter à jamais à ceux qui viendront ici les infortunes et infidelles amours de Damon, d'elle et de la bergère Fortune" (I, 441).

The illusion of objective reference is an effect not only of the effacement of the artist from the scene of representation, but of the deployment of specifiable aesthetic techniques and procedures. Adamas devotes as much of his commentary to artistic style as to historical content. The descriptive epithets he employs with reference to the former define an aesthetic diametrically opposed to the individualistic self-assertion that informs the spectacle of Mandrague's art, and the equally capricious creativity of Cupid, and which announce, as it were, the creative agency of the artist. At variance with the godlike "ouvrier" who "se joue de son oeuvre et en fait comme il luy plait," and with the anthropomorphic deities who "prennent plaisir a nous faire jouer sur le theatre du monde le personnage qu'ils nous ont esleu," the ideal painter whom Adamas holds up for admiration submits to the rules of his craft, and by his obedience achieves a "naive" or natural portrayal of the external world. We are no longer in the world of baroque distortion, but in that of 'preclassical' or *trompe-l'oeil* realism.

"Prenez garde," Adamas says of the first tableau, "comme l'art de la peinture y est bien observé, soit aux raccourcissements, soit aux ombrages, ou aux proportions" (I, 442). With "soigneuse industrie" (I, 443) the artist captures the lifelike attitudes of the watchdogs. He faithfully represents even the irregularities of nature, such as the obscurity of the stars in the big dipper on a cloudy night: "Voyez comme le judicieux ouvrier, encore qu'elle ait vingt-sept estoilles, toutesfois n'en représente clairement que douze" (I, 446). He employs the laws of perspective to lend an impression of depth to the cavern depicted in the fifth scene (I, 448), and is "diligent" to the point of rendering the nails in the handle of Damon's blood-smeared knife (I, 450). He merits the ultimate praise: "Je crois que la nature ne sçaurait rien représenter de plus naïf" (I, 450).

By a final twist of reflexive self-consciousness, however, the spirit-artists deconstruct their own claim to objectivity by depicting the history of the "fontaine de la vérité" in the receding perspective of the fourth tableau, which reveals the psychological and historical agendas that cloud the transparency of representation. The very demons who created the fountain at the behest of a prior magician, and whose aid Mandrague invokes to alter its testimony, are those to whom Galathée attributes creation of the paintings, and to whom she asks us to turn for a morally instructive account of the love affair. All of the unreliability we have learned to attribute to the fountain, and to the mode of representation it exemplifies, we are constrained by the logic of this revelation to attribute to the paintings. The objectivity the spirits seem to possess by virtue of their absence from the scene of representation is a measure of the subtlety with which they would impose their view of reality as "truth," and their accuracy at the level of empirical detail merely lulls us into forgetting that the artist's canvas is in fact an indeterminate and corruptible surface upon which the artist and the viewer project the images of their fantasy. Like Semire's discourse in the frame narrative, and the fountain of truth in the tale, the paintings interpose themselves between subject and object, as a construction of reality rather than as an image of reality itself.

We know, moreover, that the relation between the paintings and a real, extra-representational signified, is indirect at best by the very fact that they require interpretation. Galathée refuses Celadon's request that she explicate the paintings because she lacks the insight or "esprit" to unlock their concealed meanings, and defers to the authority of Adamas. The ensuing discourse is an act of interpretive imagination exercised upon paintings which in turn portray the "oeuvres" of other "ouvriers." The commentary, in other words, is art about art about art. We reach the logical limits of the Montaignian dictum that the authors of his day do nothing but "s'entre-gloser." In a mental universe where illusion supersedes illusion endlessly, the only escape from infinite regress is that provided by a normative, as opposed to an absolute, truth. Reality becomes a function of art. We accept the paintings as "verisimilar" on the authority of the aesthetic commentary rather than upon that of an immediate, and unmediated, awareness of their relation to the real. In the final analysis, it is only the institutional authority vested in Adamas, the "grand druid," counsellor of conscience to the queen and celebrant of communal rituals, that arrests the play of illusion.

The intensive interrogation of symbolic structures in *L'Astrée* inevitably calls attention to the problem of literary meaning, and leads us to wonder whether a psycho-cultural quest for meaning may perhaps have motivated both the creative production of the narrative, and its enthusiastic reception by seventeenth-century readers. I would like to suggest that the indeterminate status of the symbolic structures in *L'Astrée*—Semire's discourse, the fountain of truth, the paintings on the tomb of Damon and Fortune, for example—parallels the indeterminacy of *L'Astrée* as a whole which is, itself, suspended between objective ontological and subjective empirical horizons of reference. In consequence, the narrative functions as a liminal space, analogous to the liminal space in ritual processes where, poised betwixt and between fixed positions in the established social structure (in this case between two discursive paradigms) the ritual subject encounters the revered *sacra* of his or her culture, unhinged from their conventional signifying contexts, and participates in the projection of new interpretive norms.[7]

We would then be able to conclude that the four modalities of the self/sign relation through which d'Urfé's characters progress in the journey toward authentic self-representation—complementarity, disintegration, experimentation and re-inscription—models a process of meaning-making in which author and readers were alike engaged. Both were living through a period in history characterized, above all else, by the *absence* of a dominant semiotic model, and they found in the activities of writing and reading *L'Astrée*—a narrative that by its sheer density and length tended to draw all of the fragments of the culture into its creative vortex (philosophy, poetry, music, theology)—an aid in the construction of provisional communities of discourse in which meaning could be determined by consensual agreement. One might even speculate that the enactment of processes of this nature through *narrative* is in part a reflection of the declining relevance of conventional communal rituals in a culture increasingly founded on the prerogatives of the individual and the autonomy of subjective consciousness. The notion I am putting forward therefore implies, in a larger cultural historical context, a possible reason for the "rise of the novel" as a literary genre at the dawn of the modern period.

The prefatory letters which appear at the front of the first three volumes, and are addressed to Astrée, Celadon and the river Lignon respectively, explicitly outline d'Urfé's conception of the epistemological status of his narrative, substantiating a claim we might otherwise have been forced to leave in the realm of speculation. Throughout these ancillary texts which would normally be devoted to establishing the subservience of the main body of discourse to a particular modality of the Real or the True, d'Urfé astonishingly maintains that *L'Astrée* refers neither to an external world of objective fact (he disposes of this notion in his letter to Astrée), nor to a metaphysical order disclosed in material signs (he demonstrates the obsolescence of this view in his letter to Celadon), but to a prior text.

In the "Lettre à la rivière Lignon," written in reply to critics who deplore *L'Astrée* as a retreat from reality into a world of fantasy and chimera, d'Urfé recapitulates these ideas and carries them to their logical extreme. Instead of vindicating himself by offering proofs of mimetic accuracy, he openly embraces the self-referentiality of his narrative, and by implication of discourse in general. Indeed, in the course of the letter, the river emerges as an image of absolute textuality inscribing the referent, the audience and the author of narrative as interdependent functions of discourse, rather than as various *loci* of an extra-discursive reality. Apostrophizing the Lignon, d'Urfé says, "je ne te donne, ni t'offre rien de nouveau, et qui ne te soit déjà acquis" because "tes bords ont été bien souvent les fidèles secrétaires de mes imaginations." But the river is not only witness and scrivener, but source and inspiration of d'Urfé's thoughts. The passions and desires recorded in *L'Astrée* were engendered by "la beauté qui te rendait tant estimé par dessus toutes les rivières de l'Europe." All avenues to an extra-discursive ground are foreclosed by the reciprocal referentiality of text to text. Finally, the purpose of writing, at least as it is articulated in the letter to the Lignon, is neither to delight nor to teach, but merely to perpetuate textuality itself. Pronouncing the futility of all disciplines—philosophy, theology and science—that purport to represent Truth (412), the author of *L'Astrée* entrusts his thoughts to his "secrétaire," the Lignon, in order that "les conservant, et les publiant, tu leur donnes une seconde vie." The reader's response to *L'Astrée*, then, according to the author's own prescription, takes place under conditions of representation in which the signifier reigns supreme, and discourse extends infinitely in all directions without edges.

D'Urfé's creation of a liminal text that models a process of meaning-making may well have been motivated by a need that arose from a poignant personal experience of dissociation from "structure." By evoking an image of the author as a young lover confessing his anguish privately in the solitude of nature, the prefatory letters have helped to fuel speculation about the autobiographical inspiration of *L'Astrée*. In particular, d'Urfé's tormented love affair with Diane de Châteaumorand, his sister-in-law, has frequently been regarded as a source for the unrequited love of the fictional Silvandre for Diane. Whether these claims may be true or false, however, I would like to propose that the narrative achieves its deepest autobiographical significance not as a record of external events in the author's life, but as an embodiment of the structure of his quest for meaning. He himself was a "liminal character"— a personality formed at the threshold between two cultural worlds—and his life history may be analyzed in terms of the four stages of integration, crisis, experimentation and re-inscription that define the development of his characters.[8]

The pastoral ideal in which shepherds and shepherdesses enjoy at once a pre-lapsarian repose and an intuitive knowledge of personal identity mediated by providentially established signs, would seem to correspond to d'Urfé's monastic period. In 1580, at the age of thirteen, he was forced by his father to enter the religious order of the Knights of Malta. Although his biographers have found reason to believe that d'Urfé's submission to the order was less than complete (his vows were in fact annulled in 1592), the fact remains that *as an ideal*—and a paradigm is never more than an ideal—the complete self-emptying and abnegation of the individuated ego implicit in the taking of religious vows renders the subject transparent to a metaphysical *a priori*, and exemplifies in its most extreme form the relation between self and sign presumed to exist in an object-centered structure of signifying relations.

The events that open the space of an autonomous interiority may in turn be identified at the romantic level with the inception of his love for his brother Anne d'Urfé's wife (1585), and at the political or public level with the inception of Henri IV's prolonged struggle to accede to the throne of France (1589). Many pages have been written about d'Urfé's life-long infatuation with Diane de Châteaumorand which began, according Reure, when d'Urfé graduated from the Collège de Tournon at the age of eighteen and concluded in marriage in 1600. Nevertheless, it has not been observed that the psychocultural value of his incestuous passion would have been to effect a rupture at once with the traditional metaphysical conception of personal identity, and with any determinate structure of social relationships at all. His illicit love cuts to the root of the very possibility of kinship in human society. Henri's victory over the Valois effects a similar displacement of the conventional symbolic order at the political level. Although d'Urfé himself remained faithful to the Catholic cause and was an active *ligueur*, Henri's "conversion" in 1594 ("Paris vaut bien une messe"), and the religious wars that preceded it, forever altered the metaphysical status of orthodox belief, even for the faithful, by exposing it as a manipulable fiction. Whether locked in open conflict, or reconciled by means of Machiavellian subterfuge, Church and State no longer function as parallel and mutually reinforcing reflections of a supra-personal reality. It is a remarkable testimony to d'Urfé's own ambivalence that, although he was never able entirely to reconcile himself with a protestant king who wore the mask of Catholic piety for pragmatic purposes, he aligned himself with a Catholic Cardinal who virtually invented modern political realism for France. In 1625 he died fighting in the campaign of the Valteline which was even then understood to be a master stroke in Richelieu's design to assert the prerogatives of the absolutist nation-state at the expense of those of Rome.[9]

Displaced from within the social structure by an incestuous passion, and within the metaphysical and symbolic order of medieval Catholicism by his complicity with Richelieu's statecraft, d'Urfé must have found it difficult to assign the defining episodes in his own life a determinate meaning in terms of interpretive norms indigenous to either side of the cultural divide. He exemplifies a perfect chivalric regard for a mistress who happens to be his sister-in-law, and lends political support to a Catholic Cardinal who undermines the authority of the Roman church. Under conditions such as these, the composition of *L'Astrée*, which preoccupied him sporadically throughout most of his adult life, permitted him to experiment in the medium of fiction with alternative semiotic systems, and to project the emergence of a culture in which the free play of the signifier would be arrested by a collective determination of "the real." Such a vision must have afforded provisional respite from an experience of life in which every action, suspended between alternative centers of meaning, is doubly and paradoxically inscribed. It is as though the fictional Forez, d'Urfé's imaginative recreation of his actual place of birth, became a conceptual space in which he was able to bring into being a community where discourse could at last become authentic.

Insofar as d'Urfé was a representative subject of the early seventeenth century, his psyche was implicated in, and informed by, the semiotic upheaval of his time. Consequently, both the crisis of meaning and the provisional solutions projected in his fiction are expressions of an evolutionary process that was not only biographical but cultural. If the experience of dissociation from a fixed ground of meaning provides the psychological context for the narrative's creation, it also provides the historical context of its reception by seventeenth-century readers. In particular, the liminal status of the narrative— the fact that it creates a conceptual space between two discursive paradigms— may help to explain, in a manner more satisfying perhaps than has yet been done, certain peculiar features of reader response: namely, that the work's popularity transcended national and cultural boundaries; that reading was frequently accompanied by quasi ritualistic and cult-like practices which helped promote the formation of miniature societies or coteries; and that these readers typically regarded the work as a model of thematic and formal coherence in marked contrast with moderns who are apt to be impressed instead by its intractable polyvalence.

Two explanations for the enthusiastic reception of *L'Astrée* by d'Urfé's contemporaries have predominated to date. The first is the traditional claim that the narrative appealed to the tastes of a society which, exhausted by the violence of the civil strife of the previous century, had begun to long for a more genteel train of life—one which gave less prominence to heroic action, and greater honor to the cultivation and analysis of the sentiments. Mlle de Gournay remarked in the 1620s that the work "sert de bréviaire aux dames et aux galands de la cour,"[10] establishing the tendency to regard *L'Astrée* as a "textbook of refined manners." Most of the nineteenth- and early twentieth-century historicists subscribe to this view.[11] A second, more pessimistic current of opinion attributes the popularity of the narrative to escapist tendencies on the part of the French nobility who sought respite from various aspects of contemporary culture. Georges Molinié regards aesthetic form in general, and the baroque novel in particular, as an imaginary alternative to the painful chaos of historical experience, and, perhaps, as a domain in which we vicariously live out repressed fantasies of adventure.[12] Jacques Ehrmann argues that d'Urfé's readers were attracted to neoplatonic metaphysics because, as unwilling heirs to the Renaissance, they were loath to live sensibly among things. Taking a sociological approach to a similar thesis, Marxist scholars have argued that the French nobility under Louis XIII found in *L'Astrée* the idealized image of a feudal past when they had enjoyed class prerogatives now threatened by the simultaneous encroachment of the central monarchy on the one hand, and the wealthy and highly educated bourgeoisie on the other.[13]

With the exception of Ehrmann's, however, these versions of the "textbook of refined manners" and the "escapist fantasy" theories are all dependent on cultural conditions specific to the French aristocracy at a particular historical juncture and cannot, for that reason, adequately account for the enthusiastic reception of the narrative by audiences throughout Europe living under a wide variety of specific political and social conditions over a period of some 50 years. Reure tells us that *L'Astrée* was translated into Italian (1637), English (1620 and 1657), German (1620), Flemish (1644), Dutch (1625, 1634 and 1670) and Danish (1645). It would seem that the narrative's broad appeal must be explained in terms of criteria that transcend national, theological and class distinctions to touch upon something shared by all educated and culturally aware participants in the events of the first two-thirds of the seventeenth century, the period of *L'Astrée*'s overwhelming international acclaim.[14]

The crisis of symbolic reference effected by the transition from an object-centered to a subject-centered epistemology provides just such a transnational, trans-theological and trans-social experience. Proponents of a feudal, metaphysical world view could no more take the conventional symbolic order for granted as the only natural and obvious representation of reality than could middle class, protestant individualists complacently presuppose the epistemological and ethical pre-eminence of subjective consciousness. It mattered little whether one were an habitué of the Hôtel de Rambouillet, a Calvinist convert to Catholicism, a German prince, or a protestant refugee from the Restoration of Charles II, all of whom read *L'Astrée* with equal enthusiasm. Sensitive individuals everywhere were equally disquieted by the emergence of elements of experience, tending toward the emancipation of the subject, which could not quite be assimilated into, or even adequately represented within, the traditional semiotic model.

It is at least possible, given the historical juncture in which *L'Astrée* appeared, that many of d'Urfé's first readers were compelled to see themselves and their world through the conceptual grid of the narrative because they, no less than Celadon and Astrée, had to navigate the difficult terrain between medieval and modern semiotic systems. Rather than champion one extreme or the other in the "culture wars" that inaugurated modernity, d'Urfé created a narrative whose intrinsic structure models a process by which they could be reintegrated into communities united by a shared ideology, and in which discourse would be authenticated with reference to collective agreement, rather than to objective-ontological or subjective-empirical absolutes. Moreover, the narrative itself tended to become a focus of cult veneration and ritual behavior that facilitated the induction or "interpellation" of individual readers into precisely such communities in the domain of actual, historical experience.

An air-tight demonstration of such a thesis would require research beyond the scope of the present work. My purpose at present, however, is not to provide definitive "proof," but to suggest a plausible explanation for phenomena with which we are all already perfectly familiar. Throughout the seventeenth, and even the eighteenth, centuries, *L'Astrée* served as the catalyst for the formation of reading communities which collectively engaged in strategies of interpretation that stand in stark contrast to those elicited by either allegorical or realistic modes of fiction, both of which inscribe a determinate ground of meaning, and elicit a passive readerly response. We have already mentioned the privileged position *L'Astrée* occupied at the Hotel de Rambouillet. At least two groups of readers beyond the borders of France are easy to document. We know, from surviving correspondence, that a number of German princes (presumably protestant) met regularly during d'Urfé's lifetime to discuss *L'Astrée*. Even more curiously, in England the work inspired the formation of a "lovely society" of middle class Puritans led by Peter Sterry, an Independent minister and son of a London merchant, who, having served as a preacher to Oliver Cromwell, retreated with his followers from the political dangers and the licentiousness of the Restoration court.[15]

The degree to which aristocratic readers under Louis XIII, and later under the Cardinal Mazarin and the young Louis XIV, entered into the narrative's symbolic universe and interpreted their experience through fictional prototypes is well documented in the non-fictional literature of the time, and summarized by Reure, Magendie, and other commentators. They were not content merely to read and discuss the work, but rather, felt compelled to memorize the argumentation, to master the sacred topography, to assume the names and play the parts of the characters, and to read the text on location in the Forez. A citation from Reure will convey the general tenor of seventeenth-century, *Astrée* mania in France:

> Il suffit de parcourir la littérature, pour voir à quel point *L'Astrée* a
> pénétré dans les idées et dans les habitudes. Les conversations, les
> livres, les modes même—car il y a des 'jarretières Celadon' qui un
> moment ont fait fureur—tout, plus ou moins, s'inspire des souvenirs de
> *L'Astrée*. Noirmoutier, en pleine Fronde, entrant dans la chambre de
> Mme de Longueville qu'il trouve pleine de cuirasses et de dames en
> écharpe bleue, pense de suite au siège de Marcilly [the final battle
> which resolves the political intrigue in d'Urfé's narrative]. [...] Chez le
> cardinal de Retz, on s'amuse à s'écrire des questions sur *L'Astrée*, par
> exemple à quelle main est le couvent des vierges de Bonlieu au sortir du
> Pont de la Bouteresse, et qui repond mal paie pour amende une paire de
> gants de frangipane. [...] Les compagnies n'étaient pas rares où, comme
> à l'Académie des Parfaits amants, on prenait les noms et quelquefois les
> habits des heros de *L'Astrée*. De grandes dames étaient représentées en
> costume de bergères.[16]

Equally cultish behavior prevailed among *L'Astrée*'s readers abroad. The
German princes who wrote to d'Urfé, requesting the speedy publication of a
sequel, signed the names of his fictional characters and dated their letter from
the "Carfour de Mercure."[17] Peter Sterry was endearingly known by his friends
as Adamas, and used the name in personal correspondence.[18] The desire to
participate in, and as it were to become subjects of, d'Urfé's fictional universe
reached an extreme when the Bastie d'Urfé (the author's family home) became
a place of pilgrimage. D'Ecquevilly, Reure tells us, "alla lire *L'Astrée* dans le
pays même de M. d'Urfé," as did many others throughout the seventeenth
century. Even d'Urfé's most famous eighteenth-century admirer, Rousseau,
aborted such a journey only upon learning that the Forez had become a center
for iron works and could not be assimilated to a pastoral paradise inhabited by
"de Dianes et de Silvandres."[19]

    The ritualistic quality of the reading response—the tendency to conflate
d'Urfé's imaginary universe with empirical reality by re-enacting, as Reure
puts it "dans une vie moitié réelle et moitié idéale, les scènes du roman"[20]—
strikingly parallels the mental stance assumed by participants in sacred rites
and games in which the goal is the subject's total absorption into the cosmic
scheme of which the rite or game is but a model. But in this case, the order in
question is manifestly social, not metaphysical. We have already noted that
Astrée, the fictional heroine, accepts the foreclosure of both metaphysical and

empirical origins of identity and meaning in order to assume her role as embodiment of the collective perceptions of the community into which Celadon will be "interpellated." In much the same way, the narrative that bears her name—the reader's "Astrée"—functions as a floating signifier which lends itself to interpretive appropriations by historically situated communities, and assists in the ideological interpellation of the individual readers of which such communities are composed. In short, I am giving a somewhat specialized meaning to Reynier's claim that d'Urfé's narrative served as a medium in which seventeenth-century society "s'est en quelque sorte définie."[21] Animated by the discovery that they were both artifacts and artisans of discourse, *L'Astrée*'s readers, no less than its characters and its author, were engaged in a process of mythopoeisis. As writer and readers of *L'Astrée*, they became agents in creating normative representations of private and social identity through the reconstruction of cultural myths.

If *L'Astrée*'s hold on the imaginations of early seventeenth-century readers may be attributed to its function as a polymorphous and highly adaptable cultural icon, we can assume that the unity it seemed to possess was not entirely a property of the narrative itself, but was at least in part a projection of the collective consciousnesses of the various societies *into* which it was received, *and for* which it became functional. It was precisely by becoming an embodiment of the collectively and provisionally determined ideologies of each of these miniature societies that *L'Astrée* aided in the creation of a shared intellectual context for a world that had lost faith in its overarching master-narratives.

Notes

1. Our view of unity-as-process may, perhaps, bear comparison with the approach to literary meaning elaborated by Stanley Fish in "Literature in the Reader: Affective Stylistics" [reprinted in *Reader Response Criticism: From Formalism to Post-Structuralism*, ed. Jane P. Tompkins (Baltimore: Johns Hopkins University Press, 1980) pp. 164–84]. Fish developed his method of reading in order to address internal contradictions in seventeenth-century texts not unlike those we find in *L'Astrée*. Otherwise intractable ambiguities melt away as we learn to follow the sinuous

maneuvers of the dialectical method employed by poets who thought of their works as heuristic instruments capable of transforming the reader's inner life. Whereas Fish refers the coherence of the text to the process it induces in the reader's mind, however, I am interested in the process to which d'Urfé subjects his fictional characters.

2. I am thinking of Hayden White's argument that "interpretation in history consists in the provision of a plot structure for a sequence of events so that their nature as a comprehensible process is revealed by their figuration as a story of a particular kind." ["Interpretation in History" in *Tropics of Discourse: Essays in Cultural Criticism* (Baltimore: Johns Hopkins, 1978), p. 58.]

3. Ernst Robert Curtius attributes the importance of etymology as a "category of thought" throughout the middle ages to the influence of Isidore of Seville's *Etymologiarum libri* which, by advancing the Cratylist view of language, bestows upon the study of lexical origins an importance it could not otherwise have enjoyed. Cratylism holds that words designate the metaphysical natures of the objects to which they refer, and are therefore inherently, rather than arbitrarily, associated with them. In Curtius words, Isidore of Seville "chose the road from designation to essence, from *verba* to *res.*" As a consequence etymology comes to be regarded one of the many providentially established paths by which man is able to attain an understanding of the universal order of being. [*European Literature and the Latin Middle Ages*, pp. 496–97.]

4. Iago's deception works in precisely the same manner as Semire's. Villains of approximately the same historical moment, their methods illustrate the dangers attributed to a discourse of objective reference by skeptical thinkers of the early seventeenth century, to whom Descartes provides an influential response. Like Semire, Iago accomplishes his purpose not by telling lies but by employing a mode of representation which, because it points toward nothing beyond the objects themselves, implicitly equates empirical appearances with reality as such, and thereby fails to elicit from its audience an attitude of spiritual introspection, or interpretive probing. Othello, like Astrée, becomes vulnerable to his enemy because he voluntarily forsakes a mode of knowing predicated on an intuition of metaphysical truth reinforced by signs that require interpretation, in favor of a mode of knowing predicated on "ocular proof" mediated by signs that purport to be transparent. As a result, empirical reality becomes pliable to Othello's creative imagination, and he is able to fashion appearances, precisely because they are construed to be what they are and nothing else, into a subjective fantasy of betrayal.

5. An important current in Renaissance philosophy made man a demigod by virtue of his creative freedom, and found in the artist an archetypal figure of mankind. The *locus classicus* for this view is to be found in Pico's *Oration* which proclaims that man's dignity consists in his "indeterminate nature" and in his power to fashion himself "in whatever shape thou shalt prefer." By contrast to other creatures whose existences are governed by an inviolable inner law, man is the "maker and molder" of himself. D'Urfé paraphrases the *Oration* extensively in the third volume of his *Epitres morales*, written some years prior to *L'Astrée*: "Mais à l'homme seule, il [Dieu] a laissé ceste prérogative qu'il est l'artisan de soi-même: et se peut donner telle forme qu'il luy plaît." [Quoted in Maxime Gaume, *Les Inspirations et les sources de l'oeuvre d'Honoré d'Urfé* (Saint-Etienne: Centre d'Etudes foreziennes, 1977), p. 402).]

Pico's work provided a bridge between a traditional metaphysical conception of personal identity, and a modern, subjectivist view. For Pico, man's mobility is confined within the limits imposed by an objective scale of being. One can either move upward and become a demigod, or downward and become a beast. His successors in the sixteenth and seventeenth centuries, by contrast, enlarged the scope of man's self-creative freedom to imply a complete detachment from an objective order and the possession of unregulated powers of self-determination.

In *L'Astrée*, both the conservative and the progressive views are represented. Silvandre condemns Hylas, a self-avowed sensualist, for having forsaken his humanity and become beast-like, while Hylas, scoffing at the notion that man is bound by an objective hierarchy, insists that he constructs his own identity precisely by pursuing objects of pleasure. Overall, the narrative tends toward the conclusion that man is limited in his mobility by an historical *a priori* embodied in the customs of a particular time and place, rather than by a metaphysical one reflected throughout creation.

For a helpful explanation of the manner in which Pico's work foreshadows later conceptions of subjectivity while remaining itself committed to a traditional view, see Jonathan Dollimore, *Radical Tragedy: Religion, Ideology and Power in the Drama of Shakespeare and his Contemporaries* (Brighton, England: The Harvester Press Limited, 1984), pp. 169–181.

6. The subjects are derived from Ovid's *Metamorphoses*, a work that held a particular fascination for the baroque imagination.

7. The original analysis of the liminal, or threshold, experience in ritual processes is to be found in Arnold Van Gennep's *The Rites of Passage* (1909; Chicago: University of Chicago Press, 1960). More recently, Victor Turner has defined liminality as a provisional loosening of culturally fixed meanings, including those associated with social status and role, which occurs not only within ceremonial rites, but on a much larger scale in social evolution. "History itself," he writes, "seems to have its

discernible liminal periods" when "a society takes cognizance of itself" (240), and men achieve "their highest pitch of self-consciousness" (255). At such moments, the symbolic structures by means of which a society projects significance onto the raw data of experience are created anew. [*Dramas, Fields, and Metaphors: Symbolic Action in Human Society* (Ithaca: Cornell University Press, 1974).]

8. Reure's is the most complete biography of d'Urfé. Jean Lafond provides a helpful chronology in his *L'Astrée: textes choisis* (Paris: Editions Gallimard, 1984), pp. 391–96.

9. For an account of Richelieu's Valteline policy and its significance see William Church, *Richelieu and Reason of State* (Princeton, N.J.: Princeton University Press, 1973).

10. See Magendie, 406; Adam, 133.

11. Gustave Reynier, O.-C. Reure, André Le Breton, and Maurice Magendie are representative.

12. The baroque novel "sert [...] de refuge, et de subterfuge, pour les imaginations libres qui trouvent là un aliment à leur envie d'action, de passion et de vagabondage" (Molinié, 369).

13. Monique Hinker describes *L'Astrée* as a symbol of a glorious past in which the aristocracy "retrouvait ses aspirations et ses rêves." ["La Préciosité," in *Manuel d'histoire littéraire de la France*, Vol. II (Paris: Les Editions Sociales, 1975), p. 146.] More recently, Erica Harth has written that "in the face of economic displacement and loss of prestige, the nobility's strategy was necessarily regressive. [. . .] *L'Astrée* offered its noble readers satisfactions that an outworn ideology could provide only with increasing difficulty" [*Ideology and Culture in Seventeenth Century France* (Ithaca: Cornell University Press, 1983), pp. 46–48.] Daniel Jourlait finds that "la mythologie et les mythes dans *L'Astrée* ont pour fonction sociale de ratifier un certain statu quo, de renouveler le vieux contrat féodal du vassal et du suzerain." ["La Mythologie dans *L'Astrée*," in *L'Esprit Créateur*, 16 (1976), p. 135.]

14. Reure divides the history of *L'Astrée*'s reception into four periods: "admiration presque universelle [1607–1660], estime respectueuse [1660–1735], dédain [1735–1839], réhabilitation [1839 au présent]" (*La Vie et les oeuvres*, 303).

15. Matar, N. I. "Peter Sterry and the 'Lovely Society' of West Sheen." *Notes and Queries*, 227 (February 29, 1982), pp. 45–46. Matar literally does nothing more than

note the society's existence. A wonderful research opportunity awaits the comparatist who will analyze the reception of *L'Astrée* by this unlikely enclave of disenfranchised co-religionists.

16. Reure, 277–78. He provides several other equally revealing examples. See the entire chapter, "L'influence de *L'Astrée*," 275–323. Also see Magendie, 424–28.

17. This remarkable letter is reprinted in *L'Astrée*, ed. Hugues Vaganay (Lyon: Pierre Masson, 1926).

18. For a detailed account of Sterry's life which includes references to *L'Astrée*, see Vivian de Sola Pinto, *Peter Sterry: Platonist and Puritan*, 1613–1672 (Cambridge: Cambridge University Press, 1934). Regarding Sterry's use of Adamas as an alias in personal correspondence, Pinto comments: "It would appear that it was a name given to Sterry by his intimate friends. [...] It is strange to find that these Puritans were readers of the same high-flown courtly and pastoral romances that were fashionable among the cavaliers. It would seem that there was a point of contact between the 'enthusiasm' of mystical religion and the 'enthusiasm' of the heroic school of Love and Honor" (56–57).

19. Reure, 278, 318.

20. Reure, 281.

21. Reynier, 176.

Part Two: Negotiating the Liminal Sign

3

Love Sickness and the Metaphysical Doctor: Subjectivity and the Idealist Dialectic in d'Urfé's Polemics

Although *L'Astrée* begins with an awakening of subjective consciousness associated with the birth of love, the affective and perceptual experiences of individuals do not enjoy official recognition as a new foundation of intersubjective knowledge. Instead, they present the established system with an "anomaly" which (and I say this in the light of T. S. Kuhn's theory of paradigm shifts)[1] had either to be discounted as meaningless, or explained in a manner that preserved the coherence of the normative paradigm at the expense of the experimental evidence. The first approach, with which I will deal only briefly, takes the form of comic dismissal. Like Montaigne who depreciates his private reflections as "chimères et monstres fantasques" worth writing down only in order to make his mind ashamed of itself, those to whom d'Urfé entrusts the defense of chivalric love regard the advocates of egocentric pleasure as comic figures unworthy of serious intellectual consideration. Silvandre introduces Hylas, the Forez's incorrigible inconstant, to Leonide as one who justifies an "agreable humeur" with "extravagantes raisons" (I, 245), warning us in advance that his disposition will be comical, his arguments a burlesque of logic. In fact, the narrative contains numerous love debates that Hylas invariably loses, greatly amusing the community of faithful lovers in the process.

At the same time, the dominant paradigm exhibits the capacity to appropriate anomaly as a negative confirmation of its own intrinsic logic rather than as a contradiction, or as a newly perceived and incommensurate reality. An extensive analysis of the polemical machinery by which this appropriation occurs (and ultimately fails) will enable us to place the narrative in the structure of the paradigm shift as a liminal text, committed neither to the old nor to the new, but suspended ambiguously between them. Because the object-centered paradigm contains a place for subjective experience at the lowest rung in a cognitive ascent toward metaphysical enlightenment, those who affirm the autonomy of the subject may be "diagnosed" as victims of a spiritual illness to which lovers are particularly susceptible. Enamored of corporeal beauty rather than the highest good of which beauty is but a dim reflection or sign, they prefer the lower to the higher, the physical to the spiritual, and the merely subjective to the suprapersonal. Spiritual invalids are subsequently "healed" by means of a dialectical process of dispute which leads the soul by an inexorable heuristic logic away from the lower toward the higher, and finally permits subjective experience to be resituated in the context of an objective, suprapersonal order. Operative in the opening chapter where Lycidas recognizes Astrée's jealousy as symptomatic of a "maladie," and in each of the many debates between inconstant and constant lovers, the idealist dialectic is one of the narrative's most pervasive organizing structures.

The hegemony of the dominant paradigm, however, has been irreversibly destabilized by an anomaly which refuses to be either dismissed or reappropriated. In spite of an association with playful greenworld hedonism and with lingering intimations of ethical malaise, d'Urfé's inconstant lovers emerge as a powerful independent ideological voice denouncing the metaphysical and symbolic order of chivalric love as a cultural fiction rooted in disguised self-interest and imposed by arbitrary social authority. As incorrigible egoists for whom speech and action find their meaning in the progressive fulfillment of the self-determined ends of the individual rather than in the articulation of a teleological design, they foreshadow the subject-centered paradigm of identity and meaning for which the transcendental *cogito* will provide the ultimate theoretical justification.

In *L'Astrée,* however, as in the *Essais,* the polemics of subjectivity conclude in an unresolvable paradox precisely because of the impossibility of imagining a seat of consciousness that escapes at once the distorting prism of private fancy and the deceptions of arbitrary custom. While chivalric idealism can no longer accommodate the lived experience of the individual, the "Hylasian" ego cannot provide an epistemological foundation for an intersubjective rational and social order. The lover is either an idealist alienated from the irrepressible testimony of his inner life, or an egoist isolated in the impenetrable uniqueness of his private perceptions and desires. This dilemma accounts for the fact that Hylas, though never permitted to win his disputes with Silvandre, earns the affection of the inhabitants of the Forez, while Silvandre, though winning every argument on logical grounds, secures little more than their amazed and obsequious admiration. At this early moment in the evolution of modern self-consciousness, the hearts of the Forezians belong to Hylas, but their heads continue to lean toward Silvandre.

I. The Idealist Ladder of Knowledge

For *L'Astrée*'s idealists, subjective consciousness is not altogether excluded as a source of understanding. Rather, it occupies the lowest level in a three-fold cognitive process that begins with the ideas, emotions and sense perceptions of the individual, but ascends by degrees toward an apprehension of the objective order within which they acquire a supra-personal meaning. Taking the raw data of subjective experience as its point of departure, the mind or soul progresses to an apprehension of rational forms derived from the intra-mental inscription of the *Logos*, and concludes with an intuition of metaphysical ideas. The final goal of the process, far from affirming the subject as an autonomous center of identity and meaning, is precisely the proper orientation of the affections, or the will, within a hierarchical cosmos, such that all things—inanimate, rational and divine—are esteemed according to their intrinsic merit. Shunning the lower in favor of the higher, the soul not only fulfills its destiny as a rational being superior to the beasts, but transcends itself by actualizing a latent potential for union with God.[2]

In *L'Astrée*, this cognitive model emerges from three polemical discourses—the first on the supreme good, and the second and third on the doctrine of sympathies—in which Adamas, the narrative's chief religious authority and counsellor of conscience, describes the process by which the soul comes to recognize its true soul-mate and, beyond that, the divine fountainhead of beauty and goodness. The earliest discourse, located at the beginning of the second volume, establishes a three-tiered ontological hierarchy among the objects of thought: matter, reason and idea. The rational soul, Adamas says, exists at an intermediate level of being between angelic intellect above and matter below. Above man the pure intellects of the angels, gazing upon the "souvéreine beauté," "sont embellies des idées de toutes choses" (II,78). Below man, matter possesses a beauty peculiar to itself which, though available to man via sense perception, is an inferior object, and unworthy of the lover's devotion. The providentially intended sphere of human knowledge is the middle region occupied by the faculty of understanding and its objects, which are identified simply as "reasons," imparted to it by the light of divine goodness.

While the discourse on the supreme good compartmentalizes the three levels of being, insisting upon their incommensurateness with one another, the theory of sympathies, elaborated in discourses which appear in the third volume, clarifies the function of each level of reality in an integrated process of cognition which moves from the lower to the higher. The first advances a metaphysical teleology according to which love is the transcendent unifying principle that draws all creatures—insensible, sensible, rational and divine—together as one, and provides the inner motivation and final purpose of human thought: "Le grand Tautates, qui, par amour, a fait tout cet univers et par amour le maintient, veut non seulement que les choses insensibles, encores que contraires, soient unies et entretenues ensemble par liens d'amour, mais les sensibles et les raisonnables aussi." Whereas insensible elements and the animals manifest love in the form of innate "sympathie" and "le désir de perpétuer leur espèce" respectively, human beings are drawn toward God, and toward all creatures in God by reason, the function of which is not to project a mathematical scheme on the empirical universe as in the Cartesian paradigm, but to permit the just estimation of all things according to their providentially ordained merit—the beauty and goodness each possesses: "Cette raison nous enseigne que tout ce qui est aimable se doit aimer selon les degrés de sa bonté." Finally, reason itself is but a stepping stone toward a state of being in which the soul, fully aware of its true identity in God, loves love itself without the aid of a mediating object. As the highest good of each creature, and of all creation, it must be loved for its own sake: "Puisque Dieu a fait toute chose pour l'amour, et que la fin de quelque chose est toujours plus parfaite, nous pouvons aisément juger que [...] nous sommes plus obligés par les lois de la raison d'aimer l'amour que toute autre chose" (III, 217–18). The objectivist paradigm ultimately leads to the sacrifice of individuation in an experience of unity not only with a beloved individual, but with all beings at the point where they converge in the divine ground.

The final discourse clarifies the role played in the soul's ascent not only by reason but by the other cognitive faculties—the senses and the memory. Although material objects are ontologically inferior to intelligible ones, the soul "n'entend ni ne comprend chose quelconque [...] que par des représentations corporelles, quoi qu'elle contemple les substances incorporelles" (III, 267).

And while human thought is largely constrained within limits prescribed by discursive reason, it nevertheless possesses a measure of supra-rational knowledge by virtue of mnemonic traces retained from a prior existence (III, 263). We are endowed, Adamas explains, not only with a "rational form," but with "participation intellectuelle"—an irradiation of divine ideas associated variously with "les entendements angeliques" (II, 78) and with the "pures intelligences" of the planets (III, 263). Thus, the conceptualizing faculty, or "entendement," is assisted at the low end of the journey by the senses, which extract from material forms an impression or "species" which becomes the basis for a mental image or concept, and at the high end, as it approaches the divine, by the memory which retains the imprint of angelic ideas received prior to its corporeal embodiment.

The cognitive journey outlined in Adamas' discourses provides one of the most pervasive organizing structures at both diegetic and polemical levels of d'Urfé's work. My analysis will accordingly turn first to the frame narrative where Lycidas presents the estrangement of Celadon and Astrée as the effect of jealousy which, symptomatic of a soul inappropriately attached to material forms, prevents the heroine from recognizing Celadon's apparent infidelity as a sign of love. The restoration of interpersonal knowledge therefore requires not merely an objective representation of empirical data—she already possesses that—but a process of spiritual healing that rectifies her ability to interpret appearances with reference to metaphysical meanings. I will then examine a similar process at work in the love debates where Silvandre, the idealist, engages his interlocutors dialectically in order to reawaken their intuitive apprehension of the metaphysical *a priori* which undergirds both a coherent theory and an ethic of love.

II. Astrée's Journey of Remembrance

Because the neoplatonic process of cognition predicates the possibility of knowledge on the immanence of being in the realm of material forms, all of the misunderstandings, unrequited passions, and delayed consummations that torment lovers are attributed to the difficulty of perceiving, through the medium of sensible signs or "preuves" the essential, spiritual nature of the beloved. On the one hand, having lost its immediate link with subsistent being, the soul

tends to appropriate material forms as affective and cognitive ends in themselves. In the discourse on the supreme good, Adamas argues that all of the
painful "dénouements d'amour" are effects of the lover's desire to possess the
lower in place of the higher, the sensible and the particular in place of the
intelligible and the universal, and that all of these torments will disappear the
moment the soul lifts its gaze to worthy objects.[3] On the other hand, the senses
are inherently fallible because they operate exclusively in the world of
becoming. In the second discourse on the sympathies, Adamas enumerates the
conventional *topoi* of the "ontological" variety of skepticism: a material substance may be of so crude a nature that it distorts the indwelling formal
principle beyond recognition; the sensory apparatus may fail by reason of
intoxication or bodily illness; the "milieu" or phenomenological field within
which an object is perceived may interpose an obstruction between the subject
and the object, such as when an oar appears to be curved because it is viewed
through water (III, 267). The soul recognizes its predestined partner as soon
as the disorder in the senses has been cured or the external obstacles removed
(III, 268).[4]

It is Lycidas who applies this explanatory model to the case of Celadon
and Astrée. Encountering the heroine on the banks of the Lignon shortly after
Celadon's desperate, suicidal leap, he refutes her charge of infidelity on the
ground that Celadon's actions, however culpable in appearance, must be
interpreted in the light of his previous "preuves d'amour":

> Vous avez peu croire celui inconstant, à qui le courroux d'un père, les
> inimitiés des parents, les cruautés de votre rigueur n'ont pu diminuer la
> moindre partie de l'extrême affection, que vous ne sauriez feindre de
> n'avoir mille et mille fois reconnu en lui trop clairement. Vraiment celle
> ci est bien une méconnaissance, qui surpasse toutes les plus grandes
> ingratitudes, puis que ses actions et ses services n'ont peu vous rendre
> asseurée d'une chose, dont personne, que vous, ne doute plus. (I, 18)

In keeping with the notion that the visible world must be understood with
reference to the invisible, and the sensible with reference to the intelligible, he
attributes Astrée's unjust suspicions to an egocentric possessiveness which
prevents her from recognizing Celadon's "extreme affection" even in his
relations with Aminthe. Through Lycidas' analysis, we are able to discern a

degenerative process, divisible into three phases, at work in Astrée's conduct of her affairs with Celadon long before the catastrophe occurs. Beginning with the inversion of ontological priorities implicit in her command that Celadon pretend to love other mistresses, it proceeds to a failure of inferential reason manifest in her irrational doubts and suspicions, and concludes in a hopeless attempt to re-establish the truth with reference to empirical evidence alone.

Although she rationalizes her command as an "épreuve" of his love—a means of apprehending a spiritual truth—it is at bottom a transparent stratagem for securing the "commodité" of Celadon's uninterrupted physical presence (I, 19). The egocentric motive, in turn, undermines the quest for "vérité" by alienating Celadon's actions, and Astrée's understanding, from transcendent sources of identity and meaning. He experiences his obedience as a cancellation rather than as a fulfillment of his true self and predicts that it will cause his death, while Astrée falls victim to a fear of dispossession that prevents her from interpreting appearances as signs.

The second phase of her decline is therefore marked by the onset of jealousy: "Je ne demande plus la cause de la mort de mon frère," Lycidas exclaims in a moment of sudden insight, "c'est votre jalousie, Astrée, et jalousie fondée sur beaucoup de raisons pour être cause d'un si grand malheur" (I, 19). Throughout the narrative, jealousy, which afflicts not only Astrée but all of the central couples—Lycidas is jealous of Silvandre (I, 268), Silvandre of Paris (II, 122–23), and Diane of Madonte (III, 610), and so on—is invariably symptomatic of a love attached to ontologically inferior objects. In the trial of Palemon and Adraste, where an egocentric and an altruistic lover each plead their right to the love of Doris, the former argues that jealousy proves the sincerity of his affection no less certainly than his sighs and his tears, while the latter counters that love and jealousy are mutually exclusive emotions. Pronouncing her verdict, however, Leonide expresses the third, intermediate, position. Jealousy,[5] she says,

> [...] est bien signe d'amour. Mais comme la maladie est signe de vie, car non plus que sans la vie on ne peut être malade, sans amour aussi on ne peut être jaloux, toutefois, comme la maladie est témoignage d'une vie mal disposée, de même la jalousie rend preuve d'un amour malade. (II, 378)

Finally, as though trapped in a vicious cycle, Astrée attempts to resolve the doubts engendered by her excessive attachment to objects of sense perception by means of empirical evidence alone, offering, in response to Lycidas' request for proof of Celadon's infidelity, an eyewitness account of his tryst with her alleged rival: "Hier j'ouis de mes oreilles mêmes les discours d'amour qu'il tenait à son Aminthe, car ainsi la nommait-il" (I, 18). Here she reaches the lowest rung in her spiritual descent. Lycidas marvels at corrosive effects of jealousy on the cognitive faculties: "Est-il croyable," he asks, "que cette maladie ait été si grande qu'il vous ait fait oublier les commandements que vous lui avez faits si souvent?" (I, 19) Detached from their metaphysical context, empirical facts serve merely to confirm the suppositions imposed by jealousy, trapping Astrée in a self-generated fantasy from which it becomes increasingly difficult to escape.

The mental journey toward recognition and insight simply reverses the process. After a degeneration from the higher to the lower, the soul is led along a path from the lower to the higher that begins with a full presentation of empirical data (an account of the visible proofs of Celadon's character), proceeds to a refresher course in logic (a series of dialectical arguments presented in Celadon's posthumous letters), and concludes with the restoration of metaphysical insight (foreshadowed throughout by her instinctive desire for truth). At the end of the process, Astrée at last achieves a contemplative awareness of perfect love with reference to which both objects of sense and discursive rationality acquire their ultimate meaning.

The necessity of initiating the process of correction with a presentation of verifiable, empirical facts is implicit in the theory of cognition provided by Adamas. The soul knows nothing except by means of the senses and of corporeal representations, even though, ultimately, it contemplates incorporeal things. Lycidas proceeds as an eye-witness reporting to Astrée only what he has seen and heard of Celadon's persistent but futile resistance to the stratagem of deceit which she had imposed upon him: "Je serais bien *témoin*," he says, "de cinq ou six fois pour le moins qu'il se mit à genous devant vous, pour vous supplier." His mode of presentation is strongly empirical in its appeal, as though to compete in sensory intensity with Astrée's still vivid memory of the incriminating tryst: "Dedans ce rocher [...] souvent je vous veis ensemble," he recalls. And again, "je me ressouviendrai toute ma vie des mêmes paroles" (I, 19). The villagers, whose conversation Astrée overhears, add the weight of collective memory to Lycidas' account. Gathering to lament their bereavement, "il n'y eut un seul qui n'en racontast quelque vertueuse action" (I, 21).

Astrée's progress is punctuated by her encounters with a series of posthumous texts written by Celadon—the "Madrigal" engraved on the bark of a tree (I, 20), the letter entitled "Réponse de Celadon à Lycidas" (I, 20), and the "Lettre de Celadon à la Bergère Astrée" (I, 22)—which invite her to consider, beyond the empirical facts of the case, the consequences of her command as a subversion of discursive reason. In sequence, they describe Celadon's mental journey from an anguished experience of paradox, to a carefully rationalized acceptance of Astrée's will as a law unto itself, to a reaffirmation of the priority of the universal order over the egocentric desires of his mistress.

In the "Madrigal," Celadon emits a lyrical cry of pain arising from the necessity of acting at variance with his essential nature, thereby establishing the existential context for the highly abstract analysis recorded in the two letters. He opens the first letter, the "Réponse à Lycidas," by reiterating the theme of the "Madrigal": "Aimer et ne l'oser faire paraître, n'aimer point et jurer le contraire: cher frère, c'est tout l'exercice, ou plutôt le supplice de ton Celadon" (I, 20). Then, advancing from a merely subjective and sentimental to a rational mode of expression, he demonstrates that feigning violates the *a priori* structure of being itself, using, as his point of departure, the Aristotelian principle of non-contradiction: "On dit que deux contraires ne peuvent en même temps être en même lieu, toutefois la vraie et la feinte amitié sont d'ordinaire en mes actions" (I, 20).[6] In so far as the lover's words and actions are phenomenological reflections of his inner, spiritual nature, the double reference of his false professions of love undermines, at least at the level of logical analysis, the unity and determinacy of his identity. He is at one and the same time a faithful lover by virtue of his obedience to Astrée, and an unfaithful lover by virtue of his deceit. The balance of the letter seeks to harmonize this paradox with the traditional Aristotelian ontology by construing it as an effect of Astrée's divine authority over the rational order. "Mais ne t'en étonne point [his letter continues], car je suis contraint à l'un [i.e. la vraie amitié] par la perfection, et à l'autre [i.e. la feinte amitié] par le commandement de mon Astre" (I, 21). By virtue of her perfection, Astrée is the ground of Celadon's being and source of his identity, from which he comes and to which he strives to return.[7] At the same time, like a god, she transcends the supra-personal order of which she is, if not the author, at least the supreme achievement: "Que si cette vie te semble étrange, ressouviens toi que les miracles sont les oeuvres ordinaires des dieux et que veux tu que ma déesse cause en moi que des miracles?" (I, 21) There is something fideistic in a conclusion that permits the entire edifice of rational discourse built upon the law of non-contradiction to disintegrate in the face of a higher principle. Divinity reveals itself in contra-distinction to discursive reason and the laws of nature rather than within and through them. The recollective apprehension of a *Logos* informing visible things gives place to an obedient submission to divine *fiat* in an attitude of blind faith.

The second letter completes the logical analysis of feigning by returning from the fideistic acceptance of paradox to a reassertion of the dominance of a rational order that determines the lover's true identity. It is as though he recognizes the inappropriateness of the theological analogy applied to Astrée, and reconceives her command as the illegitimate expression of an individuated and finite will. He begins by refuting its four possible justifications. As a godlike display of omnipotence it is inefficient. If Astrée wishes merely to make him die of pain, he says, "vous le pouvez plus aisément d'une seule parole" (I, 23). Neither can the command be justified as a confirmation of the providential order. If she intends to punish him for "outrecuidance," or self-will, he deserves instant death, whereas if she merely wishes to test the authen-ticity of his love, which is to say, of his capacity for self-sacrifice, she could find a more expeditious "épreuve." Finally, he discounts even the motive of self-interested secrecy. By the inevitable working out of its own paradoxical logic, the command will provoke a full disclosure, permitting Celadon's actions once again to be recognized as proof of his fidelity: "Ne pouvant vivre en telle contrainte, ma mort sans doute en donnera assez prompte et déplorable connaissance" (I, 23). He concludes by beseeching Astrée, for all of these reasons, to permit him to "faire le personnage" of his true self, now that he has "représenté celui de la personne du monde, qui lui est la plus contraire" (I, 23). He strives, that is, to liberate his identity from the tyranny of Astrée's will, and requests that she, too, submit to the universal order that embraces them both and confers the final meaning on their actions.

Empirical proofs and rational demonstrations, however, do not in and of themselves have the power to restore Astrée's knowledge of the truth. The

external turning points in her progress are clearly marked in the text at those
moments when the empirical and the rational modes of awareness each reach
an impasse from which she is rescued by a supra-rational impulse that compels
her as it were in spite of herself to accede to the next higher mode of
consciousness. It is though an innate intuition of truth animates her journey,
and guides her like an inner compass.

Astrée's imperviousness to the testimony provided by Lycidas and the
villagers reveals the inadequacy of empirical evidence. As long as jealousy
"retenait quelque force en son âme," d'Urfé explains, external appearances
would always be interpreted to Celadon's disadvantage. "Suivant la coutume
de plusieurs personnes, qui veulent toujours fortifier, comme que ce soit, leur
opinion" (I, 21), Astrée merely entrenches herself more deeply in error. The
discovery of Celadon's hat by the villagers, however, provokes a supra-rational response—"un grand renouvellement d'ennui" (I, 21)—that propels her
onward to the next phase of her journey. Turning away from the plethora of
external evidence she enters a period of rational reflection symbolized by her
solitary walk in the forest: "Elle partit seule, et se mit à suivre le sentier par où
ses pas sans élection la guidaient" (I, 21). Rather than assure the vindication
of truth, however, reason leads only to an agnostic suspension of judgment:
"Si elle se ressouvenait de ce que Lycidas lui venait de dire, elle le jugeait
innocent; que si les paroles qu'elle lui avait oui tenir auprès de la bergère
Aminthe, lui revenaient en la mémoire, elle le condamnait comme coupable"
(I, 22). While her aimlessness prior to reflection suggests the inconclusiveness
of empirical data, the aimlessness that follows aptly suggests the impotence
of unaided human reason: "En ce labyrinthe de diverses pensées, elle alla
longuement errante par ce bois, sans nulle élection de chemin" (I, 22).

At the moment when empirical and rational modes of knowing have
reached an impasse in a kind of total "crise Pyrrhonnienne" a supra-rational
power intervenes once more, manifesting itself externally as providential
guidance and inwardly as a visceral yearning to verify Celadon's innocence.
On the one hand, she finds herself drawn imperceptibly "par fortune, ou par
le vouloir du Ciel" (I, 22) toward the grove where she discovers Celadon's
"Madrigal" and his "Lettre à la Bergère." At the same time, she exhibits an
instinctive will to truth in the form of an almost compulsive "curiosity."
Finding herself in the neighborhood of Celadon's verses, her desire to verify
Lycidas' testimony "eut bien eu assez de pouvoir en elle pour les lui faire

chercher fort curieusement" (I, 22). Similarly, seeing a tell-tale bulge in Celadon's hat band, "elle y porta curieusement la main" (I, 22) where she finds his letter. As Astrée's moment of recognition approaches, the supra-rational mode of knowing achieves total ascendancy. When she discovers Celadon's verses to have been authentic, "combien vivement," we are told, "lui touch-erent-ils l'âme" (I, 22). And his letter, exerting an immediate and decisive effect above and beyond the persuasive force of its arguments, puts Astrée "toute hors de soi" (I, 22). Its words are "couteaux trenchants [...] en son âme" which convince her of Celadon's innocence.

Recognition and repentance bring her to the threshold of enlightened vision in which empirical, rational and supra-rational modes of awareness confirm each other without contradiction. Not only do Celadon's words "lui remirent en mémoire le commandement qu'elle lui avait fait" (I, 23), but the elimination of jealousy permits her to recognize her former life with Celadon as an ideal in contrast to which the present is but a dim shadow:

> Elle se ramenteut la fidèle amitié qu'elle avait auparavant reconnu en ce berger, l'extrémité de son affection, le désespoir où l'avait poussé si promptement la rigueur de sa réponse. Et puis se représentant le temps heureux qu'il l'avait servie, les plaisirs et contentements que l'hon-nêteté de sa recherche lui avaient rapportés, et quel commencement d'ennui elle ressentait déjà par sa perte. (I, 23)

The past whose remembered plenitude reveals present emptiness, cannot be entirely reduced to an actual historical moment. In actuality, the love affair has been fraught with difficulties from the start. The "services" by which Astrée recognizes Celadon's fidelity consist largely of his willingness to endure long separations without complaint. Rather, the ideal evoked by the formulaic expression, "fidèle amitié" and "extrême affection," derives its force throughout *L'Astrée* from a conception of personal identity that grants prior reality to "pure intelligences," and regards the birth and progress of love as a consequence of the individual's journey toward a transcendent origin located not in time past, but beyond time altogether.

III. The Dialectical Structure of the Love Debates

The love debates between inconstant and constant lovers, which compose a large percentage of *L'Astrée*'s total bulk, originate in the first book of Volume I with the sudden appearance of Hylas, a foreigner hailing from Camargue. Introduced as "une autre voix qui semblait de s'approcher d'eux" (I, 25) immediately after Astrée's commemorative vision, he intrudes into discursive preserve of chivalric love in much the same way as desire itself intrudes upon placidity of pastoral life.[8] The disputes which follow pose a formidable problem of order both with respect to their status in the work as a whole, and with respect to their own internal structure. For the modern reader, they seem to disrupt unnecessarily the advance of the narrative, and to distract from the psychological interest of the characters. Considered in themselves, moreover, they draw upon a polemical arsenal of such bewildering variety, ranging from mundane analogies to metaphysical speculation, and from light-hearted jest to deadly earnest, that they seem at times to border on incoherence. Both problems, however, resolve themselves when we realize that beneath the complex rhetorical surface, the debates possess a uniform dialectical logic, modeled on a tripartite process of cognition, and universally applied, whatever the immediate topic happens to be. Far from distracting our attention from the "psychology of the characters" they perform a therapeutic operation carefully designed to exploit the structure of that psychology, and the contradictions they contain indicate not a slide into incoherence, but an orderly progress through divergent levels of truth which are reconciled only from the unifying perspective achieved at the end of the journey.

In this section, I will examine three debates whose centrality derives from the fact that they illustrate the interdependence of the soul's ontological orientation—downwards toward material forms, or upwards toward divine ideas—with two opposing ethical systems. An initial choice between *presence* (sensible objects) and *absence* (intelligible objects) imposes subsequent choices between *change* (a mode of action adjusted to the flux of temporal becoming) and *fidelity* (a mode of action adjusted to the permanence of transcendent being), and between *moderation* (love proportionate to objects of relative value) and *extremity* (love proportionate to the supreme good).

Although Adamas provides the abstract elaboration of an object-centered theory of knowledge, it is Silvandre, the former student at the "école des

Massiliens," who promotes the spiritual enlightenment of the shepherds of the Forez through a dialectical mode of dispute. He regards the error that gives rise to inconstant and moderate lovers as a transgression against reason, not in the modern sense as an eruption into the conscious register from the unconscious, but in the medieval sense as a dislocation of the psyche in an overarching cosmos. "Vous faites paraître que vous n'aimez point, ou que vous aimez contre la raison," he tells Hylas, "car l'âme ne se doit point abaisser à ce qui est moins qu'elle" (II, 263). Forfeiting his providentially established place within the scale of being, the sensualist seeks pleasures appropriate only to the beasts and to those depraved human beings who "s'abbaissant par dessous la nature des hommes se rendent presque animaux privés de raison" (II, 389). As a creature at odds with the immutable law of his own nature, he becomes a living paradox, a freak: "C'est en ce monstre, ô Hylas! que tu degenères, quand tu aimes autrement que tu ne dois" (II, 389). If at times Silvandre attributes the soul's misguided preference for the less real thing over the more real, and for the contingent over the subsistent, to a conscious act of the will, as when he says that "chacun qui le veut peut estre vertueux ou vicieux" (III, 41), he also concedes the depravity of the will itself is symptomatic of a deeper spiritual disorder, or "maladie de l'âme," afflicting the conceptualizing faculty itself. Hylas' error, he explains, "procède d'un jugement imparfait, qui lui empêche de discerner ce qui est bon ou mauvais" (III, 42).

In each of the disputes, Silvandre, or his counterpart as dialectician, addresses his interlocutors in the spirit of a metaphysical doctor whose purpose is to reorient the desires of the deluded soul away from the derivative and contingent realities of space and time, toward the subsistent realities of the metaphysical absolute. And in each case, the conversion of the mind from a common sense pursuit of the former, to an enlightened awareness of the latter, entails an orderly movement upward through the three modes of knowing propelled by an intrinsic heuristic and logical necessity.

The healer begins by provisionally accepting his opponent's frame of reference, limiting himself to arguments commensurate with a pragmatic materialism for which rationality is little more than a "reality principle" designed to assure the fulfillment of erotic desire. This act of conceptual bridging enables him to predispose the misdirected soul to accept a higher truth by showing that the defense of inconstancy fails on its on terms. Even within the conceptual framework provided by *a posteriori* reason, "presence" may be shown to vitiate rather than nourish passion; "change" to violate the principle of retributive justice; and "moderation" to be incommensurate with the mistress' infinite self-love.

But because the mode of awareness he has provisionally accepted denies the ontological priority of the ideal to which lovers are bound to submit, it does not allow the elaboration of the code of "parfaite amitié" in affirmative terms. To accomplish this, the dialectician advances to the next phase of presentation where the intrinsic coherence of a syllogism, or deductive chain, replaces adequation to experience as the criterion of truth in argument. Love, he argues, is a desire for that which the understanding judges to be beautiful and good, and since beauty and goodness are universals, and therefore intramental rather than empirical in nature, absence is more advantageous to lovers than presence. Finally, since universals are unchanging and infinitely worthy, it follows that "eternelle fidélité" and "extrême affection" are indissociable attributes of love. "L'amour consiste principalement en l'affection extrême, et en la perpétuelle fidélité. Si nous ôtons quelqu'une de ces parties, ce n'est plus amour" (II, 381).

The second phase of the idealist's presentation, however, reaches an impasse when the miscreant argues convincingly that an ethic of love extrapolated from the intrinsic structure of *a priori* reason is incompatible with human happiness. The triumph in the chivalric code of an impersonal logical machinery over the individual, and of the supra-personal order over subjective consciousness, imposes a life of misery and unfulfillment on "parfaits amants" which contrasts sharply with the sensualist's enjoyment of life. The necessity of resolving this conflict motivates the dialectical ascent beyond proofs dependent on discursive reason to those whose plausibility requires an intuitive apprehension of the highest "mystère d'amour"—namely, the metaphysical unity of the lover and the beloved—which enables us to see that to love the other is to love the self in its highest sense, and that the sacrifice of the ego and the attainment of bliss are one.

Although Silvandre regards the doctrine of metaphysical unity as a sublime mystery available only to the enlightened few, he never ceases to shore it up with rational or quasi-rational demonstrations, the most frequently repeated of which reflects the enduring influence in the early seventeenth century of a "hylomorphic" theory of mind according to which knowledge is a function not of mental representations, but of the presence in the mind of the essences of objects.[9] If the knower and the known are one, he explains, and knowledge precedes love, it follows that the lover and the beloved "ne sont qu'une même chose." Although Adamas takes issue with Silvandre's rationalism, he, too, exposes the contradiction between self-gratification and the sacrifice of the ego as an illusion in so far as he defines love as the expression of a metaphysical "conformité des êtres." Because the lover is drawn by metaphysical reminiscence (rather than rational understanding) toward objects that bear the imprint of its particular nature (rather than universal goodness and beauty), he affirms his truest self in self-effacing adoration of the other.

Presence and Absence

The question as to whether love flourishes in the presence or in the absence of its (material) object receives its most systematic treatment at the beginning of Volume II where Leonide asks Silvandre to explain "pourquoi vos pensées vous devraient être plus chères que la presence même de celle qui les fait naître" (II, 12). Leonide unwaveringly maintains the view, already implicit in her question, that love is a sensual desire consummated in the possessive enjoyment of the beloved. Because love is nourished by sexual favors and caresses, presence enhances love while absence kills it. Silvandre by contrast maintains the view that love is a desire for that which the understanding judges to be good and beautiful. Because love is nourished by the contemplation of an idea, rather than by the enjoyment of a material object, absence enhances love while presence destroys it. Throughout the dispute, Leonide plays the devil's advocate, reiterating her defense of presence with little variation. Silvandre's defense of absence, by contrast, unfolds in three phases, ascending from materialistic, to rational and supra-rational modes of argument. According to the first, absence enhances love by giving free reign to subjective fantasy; according to the second, by directing the mind toward universals; and according to the third, by fostering the soul's contemplative union with its metaphysical ground.

In the *a posteriori* phase of the dialectical presentation, Silvandre develops a preliminary version of his governing syllogism: since love is nourished by "la connaissance des vertus, des beautés, des mérites, et d'une réciproque affection" (I, 13), and since knowledge is intra-mental rather than sensory, absence is more favorable to love than presence. The knowledge to which he refers at this stage, however, is a fantastical extrapolation from sense perceptions (rather than a rational grasp of universals) which fades from memory when absence endures too long, and which may be empirically falsified. After receiving the evidence of the eyes and the ears, he explains, the soul turns inward, submitting sense impressions "à la preuve du jugement," from whence "elle en fasse naître la vérité" (II, 13). But the soul, afflicted by passion, generates an idealized image by means of selective memory and embellishment which thenceforth replaces the real mistress as the object of love: "Amour qui est ruzé et cauteleux ne lui a peint que ces images parfaittes en la fantasie" (II, 13). And while absence engenders love by permitting the free play of fantasy, presence destroys it either by cloying the appetite with an excess of sexual favors, or by exhausting patience with insufferable scorn (II, 14)—in one way or in the other, exposing the discrepancy between the reality and the imaginary ideal. Thus, Silvandre concludes, no one has truly loved who "n'augmente son affection, étant éloigné de ce qu'il aime" (I, 14).

The second phase of the demonstration, provoked by Leonide's continued objections, constitutes a dialectical advance over the first signaled by Silvandre's promise of "de plus claires raisons." He begins by reiterating the priority of "connaissance" to love, but gives the statement an entirely new meaning by eliminating objects of sense perception as the measure of truth. Instead, they are now considered merely to initiate the soul's awareness of universals, after which they need never again be consulted. The knowledge of beauty, he says "vient bien par les yeux, mais depuis qu'elle est en notre âme, nous n'avons plus affaire de nos yeux pour l'aimer à l'advenir" (II, 15). Similarly, the knowledge of goodness "est produite ou des actions ou des paroles, qui toutes deux ont bien besoin de présence pour être connues, mais après nullement" (II, 15). While the first demonstration suggests that the contents of memory are less real than the objects they represent, the second suggests the contrary view that they are more real, liberating knowledge from the flux of empirical experience, and the distortional influence of the passions: "Cette connaissance [i.e. of beauty and goodness] se conserve dans les secrets cabinets de la mémoire, sur laquelle notre âme se repliant apperçoit ce qu'elle y a mis en réserve" (II, 15). By the same token, objects present to the senses diminish or endanger love not because they expose the discrepancy between a self-generated fantasy and empirical reality, but because the "troubles mouvements des sens" interfere with the soul's contemplation of intelligible objects in which alone the truth resides, unchanging and eternal. The conclusion of this phase is neatly summarized in the following syllogism:

> Que si l'amour s'augmente par la connaissance de la perfection aimée,
> puis que nous l'avons beaucoup plus grande étant absent, c'est sans
> difficulté que nous aimons davantage éloigné que présent. (II, 16)

An apparent discrepancy remains, however, between Silvandre's explanation of love as an attraction to objects that reason determines to be good and beautiful, and the persistence of desires in excess of those which are satisfied by acts of cognition. It would seem that absence permits the attainment of truth, but not the consummation of love, and that Silvandre's position tends toward an unacceptable sacrifice of happiness for knowledge. It is Paris who voices the objection: "D'où procède que tous les amants désirent avec tant de passion la vue de celles qu'ils aiment?" (II, 16) Silvandre initially offers the Socratic argument that the love of inferior objects is an effect of ignorance. Lovers commonly reject "cette profonde connaissance" in favor of "celle que les yeux de moment à autre lui peuvent donner" (II, 16) only because they fail to understand that the true object of desire lies beyond the realm of sense perception. But this answer in turn proves insufficient when Paris points out that Silvandre himself, though endowed with "profonde connaissance," continues to value Diane's presence above all else. In fact, the polemical dispute itself functions as a substitute erotic gratification since Silvandre engages in the defense of absence precisely for the purpose of making the interval of separation seem to pass more quickly.

The reconciliation of absence with the fulfillment of desire cannot in the last analysis be achieved at the level of rational argument, but depends, rather, upon a final conversion of the soul to a mode of awareness which, though not at variance with reason, nevertheless transcends it. While acknowledging his own frailty, Silvandre concludes that were the soul to free itself from the tyranny of the senses, it would enter into the infinite joys of contemplation where knowledge and enjoyment are one and the same:

> La nature nous a seulement donné les sens pour instruments, par
> lesquels notre âme recevant les espèces des choses vient à leur connais-

sance, mais nullement pour compagnons de ses plaisirs et félicités comme trop incapables d'un si grand bien. (II, 17)

Change and Fidelity

Much of the polemical material in *L'Astrée* is devoted to elaborating the ethical tension between change and fidelity which, in turn, derives from the ontological dualism of sensible and intelligible objects. Because material forms are in constant motion, ceaselessly becoming other than they presently are, they elicit an ethic of pragmatic change on the part of the human subject who wishes to regulate his or her behavior according to their particular mode of existence. Intelligible objects by contrast participate in the permanence of absolute being and elicit an ethic of fidelity from those who wish to regulate their behavior according to a transcendent and changeless order.

The tension between the two alternatives receives its most complete examination in the series of disputes occasioned by the case of Tircis, Laonice and Cleon. Throughout the narrative, Tircis remains faithful to the memory of Cleon, a former mistress who has died of the plague, while ignoring the persistent entreaties of her unrequited rival, Laonice. His fidelity precipitates a dispute in which Laonice represents the allure of opportunistic change in response to the needs of the empirical present on the one hand, and Cleon the promise of an eternal spiritual love dedicated to an empirically absent object on the other. The clash between the two value systems brings Laonice and Tircis to the Forez where, in accordance with the predictions of an oracle, they expect to find a judge wise enough to resolve their disagreement.

The formal elaboration of the dispute unfolds intermittently over several hundred pages beginning in the opening chapter where the contrast between the fidelity of Tircis and the inconstancy of Hylas occasions the first of *L'Astrée*'s love debates. The case appears again in a trial sequence in which Hylas pleads for Laonice and Phillis for Cleon before Silvandre who rules, predictably, in favor of the latter (I, 245–268). It finally resurfaces as the occasion of a dispute between Hylas on one side, and Tircis and Silvandre on the other, regarding the ends of love (II, 262–63). Together, the trial and subsequent debate constitute a complete dialectical structure internally organized by a three-fold cognitive process.

Hylas undertakes the defense of change from an uncompromisingly ego-centered perspective. Although he invokes the laws of God, man and nature to support his views, the weight of his argument rests on a logic of retribution to which metaphysical realities are irrelevant. Because justice requires that debts be repaid and wrongs redressed, Tircis owes Laonice love in return for love, as well as compensation for the deceit he perpetrated when pretending to love her in order to preserve the secrecy of his affair with Cleon. And because an unbridgeable gap separates metaphysical from temporal orders of existence, the living are obliged to limit their aspirations to the world of the living, and to leave the dead alone. Tircis abdicates his humanity by chasing an inaccessible ghost rather than real and palpable satisfactions.

At the beginning of her refutation of "the false reasons of Hylas," Phillis signals the inadequacy of empiricist assumptions by invoking the aid of Cleon's spirit. Unlike Hylas who predicates his conception of justice on the rights of the individual, she proceeds deductively from the (now familiar) ontological definition of love as a "conformité des êtres," which implicates the individual in an objective order. If love is a spiritual transaction by which the lover irrevocably sacrifices his will to that of the beloved, it follows logically that eternal fidelity is one of its essential attributes. Tircis cannot love another without retrospectively invalidating the love he professed to Cleon. If he loves at all he loves eternally; if he changes, he never loved. She concludes by showing that Hylas' conception of justice is not only incompatible with love properly understood, but that its application in the case of Tircis is self-contradictory on its own terms. By asserting the immortality of the soul (a doctrine perfectly consistent with a subject-centered paradigm of personal identity), Phillis reinstates Cleon as a participant in the structure of retribution, and turns all of her opponent's arguments to her advantage. The requirement of equity has been fulfilled with respect to Laonice, she argues, but not with respect to Cleon: "Si chacun doit aimer ce qu'il aime, pourquoi veux-tu qu'il n'aime pas Cleon, qui n'a jamais manqué envers lui d'amitié?" (I, 265)

The refutation of Hylas' position complete, she then undertakes the positive defense of fidelity. Again, her argument proceeds deductively from a definition, rather than inductively from experience, but since her object is to persuade Laonice to relinquish her suit against Tircis, she begins with a mode of argument accessible to a mind motivated by empirical concerns, and ascends only by degrees to the higher reasoning predicated on the epistemological priority of a metaphysical order. Just as Laonice by her own admission would remain faithful to Tircis during a long and even interminable absence, she should accept Tircis' fidelity to Cleon whose death is but an extreme instance of separation. The analogy, however, is but a provisional move designed to enhance the empirical plausibility of an argument whose underlying supports are not empirical at all, but rational. Phillis concludes by restating her case as the consequence of a logical deduction. Since love is an irrevocable gift of the spirit, it must follow its object eternally: "Nul amant ne doit jamais se retirer d'une amour commencée" (I, 266).

The rational defense of fidelity, however, like the rational defense of absence, leads to an impasse born of the conflict between experience and reason, pleasure and knowledge. When, at the end of her oration, Phillis asks Silvandre to choose between "la pitié de Laonice" and "la raison de Cleon" (I, 267), she tacitly acknowledges that the ethic of change accommodates the desires of the finite ego, while fidelity, though correct according to reason, requires sacrifice and pain. In fact, Silvandre affirms reason over pity, the metaphysical absolute over the vicissitudes of empirical experience, and prefaces his verdict in Tircis' favor by reiterating the definition of love which serves as his criterion of judgment: "Une amour périssable n'est pas vraie amour, car elle doit suivre le sujet qui lui a donné naissance" (I, 267). But the contradiction, and the potential challenge to the justice of his verdict, remains. Eternal fidelity may be the inevitable decree of deductive logic, but how can one reconcile the cruel machinery of *a priori* reason with the lover's need for companionship here and now, in the empirical present?

It is only later, when Tircis and Silvandre reframe the case on suprarational grounds, that fidelity may be recognized as a fulfillment rather than as a denial of the lover's deepest longing. The sequence begins when Hylas once again questions the compatibility of fidelity with happiness: "Quel contentement, et quelle fin proposez-vous à votre amour?" (II, 262–63). Fidelity, he insists, lacks any discernible purpose, promises no reward, and is, in short, devoid of practical value.

Whereas Phillis had refuted Hylas by abandoning empirical arguments in favor of deductive reason, Tircis begins with a metaphysical assertion that radically alters the conceptual landscape once again, defying not only the pragmatic logic of experience, but straining the capabilities of discursive reason: "Amour est un si grand dieu, qu'il ne peut rien désirer hors de soi-même: il est son propre centre, et n'a jamais dessein qui ne commence et finisse en lui" (II, 262–63). At issue is the nature of love itself in its highest form. While the empiricist reduces the relation between lover and beloved to the desire of each to possess the other, and the rationalist asserts that love consists in the irrevocable sacrifice of each to the other, the contemplative asserts that love by its very nature eliminates the self-other dichotomy upon which both conceptions are founded. The one who loves and the object loved are one and the same, leaving only a radical unity of being with reference to which progress and linearity, whether conceived empirically as pragmatic design, or logically as deductive necessity, become impossible to sustain. Self-sufficient, and self-perpetuating, love always already possesses its object. It is "un cercle rond, qui partout a sa fin et son commencement, voire qui commence où il finit, se perpétuant de cette sorte, non point par entremise de quelque autre, mais par sa seule et propre nature" (II, 262–63).

Moderate Love and Extreme Love

The shift from an object-centered to a subject-centered epistemological paradigm was accompanied by a parallel shift in the determination of value. If the merit of any object had been considered to be intrinsic and providentially determined, it comes to be regarded as a function of market forces, or "exchange."[10] Thus, like change and fidelity, moderation and extremity and their corollaries, inclusiveness (the division of love among many partners) and exclusiveness (the indivisibility of love), reflect an attempt to ensure the adequation of desire to its object. Advocates of "presence" are champions not only of "change" because material objects are ceaselessly becoming, but of "moderation" and "inclusiveness" because their value is arbitrary (attributed by opinion) and therefore relative (contingent on a changing base of comparison). Advocates of "absence," by contrast, are champions not only of "fidelity" because intelligible objects participate in the permanence of being, but of "extremity" and "exclusiveness" because their value is intrinsic (providentially given) and therefore absolute (contingent only upon its identity with itself). D'Urfé introduces these alternatives in an early conversation between Hylas and Silvandre in which the former proposes to admire all mistresses neither too ardently, nor too indifferently, but in a manner proportionate to their relative merits, while the latter insists that a true lover must give himself completely and, as it were, infinitely, to the single mistress who most perfectly embodies the ideal he seeks, and provides the ontological complement of his essential nature (I, 287–90).

Hylas defends moderate affection and the plurality of partners as necessary pre-conditions for the determination and representation of personal worth through market forces. Moderation not only prevents the compromise of personal freedom—an extreme affection smothers its object with importunate and oppressive attentions (I, 288)—but more importantly, it preserves the autonomy of judgment which permits individuals to pursue whichever objects promise the highest degree of pleasure. The moment anything, or, more particularly, anyone, comes to be regarded as *intrinsically* worthy, all values are instantly fixed in relation to an absolute standard, and market relations cease to function as a value-creating mechanism. The multiplication of partners, on the other hand, is not only a logical consequence of the self-interested quest for increasingly desirable objects, but the means by which personal worth may be represented to others. A dearth of paramours diminishes the reputation of the lover by leaving his prowess, or "courage," open to question. His mistress, "pensant estre aimée à faute de quelqu'autre," will hold him in contempt (I, 288). By loving in all quarters, however, he not only increases pleasure, but enhances the opinion each mistress has of his desirability, and hence of her own. Seeing herself selected by one who has proven his ability to win whomever he pleases, she will not suspect "quand vous venez à elle, que ce soit pour ne savoir où aller ailleurs, et cela [Hylas concludes] l'oblige à vous aimer" (I, 288).

Silvandre's refutation ascends through appeals to the three modes of awareness, beginning with pragmatic empiricism, progressing to deductive rationality, and concluding with a metaphysical affirmation that provides the ultimate ground for the conclusions reached in the other two. The pragmatic, empirical appeal hinges on Hylas' admission that when in love he wishes "que la personne que j'aime fasse plus d'état de moi que de tout autre" (I, 289). Armed with the fact that each individual in the market system applies the principle of exchange-value only to others and never to himself because each insists upon being valued absolutely, Silvandre is able to demonstrate the implausibility of the psychology of love to which Hylas adheres. Far from assuring the mistress of her value, the inconstant lover's promiscuity offends the desire for distinction that Hylas himself concedes to be inescapable, by placing her on a level with all of womankind and rendering her value contingent on an external mechanism of comparison. The second phase in the dialectical presentation, by contrast, begins not with the self and its needs, but with the supra-personal order of *a priori* reason. The criterion of truth is no longer subjective experience, but the internal coherence of a syllogism. Because love is numbered among those things "qui n'ont point d'extrémité, de milieu, ni de défaut," "celui qui peut la mesurer, ou qui en peut imaginer quelqu'autre plus grande que la sienne, il n'aime pas" (I, 289–90). Extreme devotion is, by definition, an essential attribute of love. Moderate love is therefore a contradiction in terms. Although the strategic necessity of ascending to the final phase of the dialectic is not immediately apparent in this early dispute because Hylas, at variance with the pattern that later emerges, concedes defeat at the intermediate stage, Silvandre nevertheless concludes with an appeal to metaphysical intuition which establishes extreme and exclusive devotion as external signs of the lover's spiritual unity with the beloved:

> Savez-vous bien que c'est qu'aimer? c'est mourir en soi, pour revivre
> en autrui, c'est ne se point aimer que d'autant que l'on est agréable à la
> chose aimée, et bref, c'est une volonté de se transformer, s'il se peut
> entièrement en elle. (I, 290)

Had Hylas chosen to insist upon the conflict between the ethic of extremity and the happiness of lovers, his objections would have been vanquished by the claim that the services performed by even the most importunate lover are rendered acceptable because they demonstrate his desire to submerge his identity into that of the beloved, and, by achieving a total self-effacement, to reveal the spiritual conformity by which they are joined at the level of their essential beings.

The alternatives of moderate and extreme love are also at issue in the dispute between Hylas and Silvandre over the justice of Leonide's verdict in the trial of Adraste, Palemon and Doris. The central facts of the case are as follows: Doris is courted by Palemon and Adraste, the first of whom exemplifies the possessive egotism of the sensualist, and the other, the self-sacrificial service that distinguishes "parfaite amitié." Initially preferring Palemon to Adraste, Doris renounces him when jealousy and neglect render him unworthy. Instead of transferring her affection to the faithful and selfless Adraste, however, she vows never to love either, complaining at once of "les mauvaisetiés et infidélités de l'un, et les indiscretions et importunités de l'autre" (II, 351). At this impasse, the three unhappy lovers encounter Astrée and her companions, to whom Doris tells her story in the form of a plea for justice.

Leonide's verdict is predicated on the laws of fidelity and extremity rationally deduced from the unity of souls. Doris, she concludes, must remain faithful to Palemon and indifferent to Adraste. To abandon Palemon on account of his jealousy would be to violate the law of fidelity for too slight a cause. "Celui serait injuste, qui jugerait que l'amour se deut perdre pour une chose qui lui est si naturelle" (II, 378). We have already witnessed this principle at work in Silvandre's arbitration of the case of Tircis: Love must continue eternally in adoration of its original object. At the same time, were Doris to return the affection of both shepherds she would stand in violation of the law of extremity. It is equally unjust, Leonide declares, for love to "se diviser à plusieurs, pour quelque considération que ce soit" (II, 378). A love divided among several objects is not true love: "Ce n'est pas aimer que de ne se donner tout entièrement à la personne aimée" (II, 378).

The verdict occasions a dispute which centers entirely on the second law. Hylas argues that by requiring Doris to return the affections of both suitors, Leonide would have made all three people happy (II, 380), while Silvandre avers that "en amour n'en avoir qu'une partie c'est n'en avoir rien du tout" (II, 381). The case for inclusive love divided among several suitors proceeds monologically as an analysis of love in terms of market relations, while the case for exclusive devotion to a single lover proceeds dialectically through ascending levels of argument.

Hylas establishes his case for promiscuity, even before the verdict has been delivered, on the basis of a theory of exchange-value. Mocking Doris for failing to recognize the advantages of being approached by two eligible shepherds at once, he argues that the more numerous her suitors, the greater both the public estimation of her personal value, and the measure of sensual enjoyment she receives: "C'est honneur à une fille d'être aimée et recherchée de plusieurs, outre la commodité qui s'en peut retirer" (II, 377). The discussion that follows reveals that Doris adheres to the notion that values precede and govern desire as in the idealist model, while Hylas assumes that desire precedes and produces value by means of exchange relations. When Doris insists that she cannot possibly satisfy the desires of several suitors at once, he replies that like the gods, her resources are always equal to the demands placed upon them: "Les dieux ne se sentent point importunés que plusieurs chargent leurs autels de sacrifices" (II, 377). Under market conditions, her capacity to please is not a function of her intrinsic and finite worth, but of the very desires she fears she will be unable to satisfy. The more numerous her lovers, the greater her perceived value, and the greater the pleasure her favors afford. And when she objects that even if she were able to keep them happy she would be incapable of returning the love of more than one suitor, he assures her that desire is free, and can extend to as many objects as exist: "La volonté s'étend à tout ce qu'il lui plaît" (II, 377). She may love as many suitors as present themselves precisely because her will is free from the tyranny of the supreme good. Within the system of exchange-value, desire emerges as a new divinity, creating value and procuring infinite pleasure, without the necessity of acknowledging any *a priori* constraints whatsoever.

Silvandre's defense of exclusive love begins with an appeal to practical reason according to which love is a proprietary relationship rather than a metaphysical one. Common sense teaches us, he says, that since one person cannot possess that which another already has, love cannot be consummated except on exclusive terms: "Le sens commun nous apprend que ce que plusieurs possèdent n'est à personne entièrement. Si plusieurs possèdent la bonne volonté de Doris, ni Adraste ni Palemon n'en auront que leur portion" (II, 381). He then embarks on a rational argument that rests on the intrinsic coherence of logical deduction rather than on the testimony of "le sens commun." Love by definition demands the total and undivided assent of the will: "Mais en amour, n'en avoir qu'une partie, c'est n'en avoir rien du tout" (381). If exclusiveness is an essential attribute of love, to love two suitors is to love neither.

Having reached an impasse, Hylas and Silvandre turn their attention to the alternatives of moderation and extreme devotion. Hylas begins with a deconstructive move aimed at the idealist notion that perfection consists in a being's "extreme" realization of its teleological purpose, which in turn renders it self-sufficient, complete, or whole (II, 383). Perfection in this sense, Hylas argues, cannot be considered as an attribute of lovers since love implies a deficiency by definition: "Qu'est-ce qu'amour?" Hylas asks. "N'est-ce pas un désir de beauté et du bien qui défaut?" (II, 383) He then introduces the alternative standard of perfection upon which he intends to establish his own status as an exemplary lover. Perfection in love, he says, consists in the proportion that obtains between a man and a woman who are equally imperfect: "Tout ainsi que je ne vaux pas tant qu'un autre ne puisse valoir davantage," Hylas explains, "aussi n'est-elle pas [referring to Phillis] si belle qu'une autre ne la puisse être plus" (II, 384). Although he doesn't use the term "moderation" at this juncture, his argument clearly implies the arbitrary and relative determination of value, and a corresponding ideal of "mesure" which regulates desire according to the relative merit of imperfect objects.

Silvandre's defense of extreme devotion, like that of exclusive love, proceeds through empirical and rational appeals. He begins by demonstrating that the materialist definition of love is paradoxical when considered on its own pragmatic terms: If love is a desire for the beauty and the good one lacks, consummation puts an end to love precisely by satisfying desire (II, 386). Moreover, insofar as love is reduced to possessive desire, it is not only destroyed by possession, but intensified by deprivation. Silvandre revisits the delayed gratification argument he used in proving that absence increases love. "Notre âme," he says, "pousse bien avec plus de violence les désirs dont les effets lui sont malaisés et deffendus, que ceux dont l'accomplissement est en sa puissance" (II, 386).

He then proposes a definition of love that places the soul's knowledge of ideal goodness and beauty in a position of logical priority to its desire for the material objects that embody them. Love, he says, is "un acte de la volonté qui se porte à ce que l'entendement juge bon" (II, 386). With this definition he ascends beyond the practical logic that regards value as a function of desire, to an *a priori* mode of reasoning for which an object's value is intrinsic and absolute because determined, not by public opinion, but by its status in a metaphysical order. The good the lover desires is not the relative good of material objects evaluated through a process of exchange, but the supreme good according to which all other values are fixed. "Ne faut il pas," he reasons, "puis que la volonté le porte toujours à ce que l'entendement lui dit être le meilleur, qu'il l'estime plus que toute autre chose?" (II, 388) On the basis of this conception of love, Silvandre proves that those who love are perfect in both senses Hylas proposed. They are self-sufficient because love is a state of being, an act of acknowledgement or even of surrender which depends on nothing outside itself (II, 386). They are proportionate to their (perfect) objects because if knowledge, which requires the unity of the knower and the known, precedes love, it follows logically that the lover and the beloved are one as well. No greater proportion can be achieved, he concludes, than complete ontological identity (II, 387).

There remains the apparent conflict between rational love and the quest for pleasure. The polemical discourse with which Hylas regales his audience is little more than an elaborate attempt to rationalize his fundamental objection that the ethic of extremity, like the ethic of fidelity, leads to unhappiness. He concludes his defense of moderation by painting a vivid and memorable picture of "ces mornes et pensifs amants qui vont continuellement serrés en eux-mêmes, se rongeant l'esprit et le coeur" (II, 384). Accordingly, Silvandre, in the final phase of his argument, demonstrates that the ethic of extremity is not only imposed by reason, but occasions man's greatest happiness. In contrast to Hylas' portrayal of the madness of lovers who abdicate their right to possess the objects they desire, Silvandre offers a vision of blessed madness, or "heureuse folie," in which the soul achieves its liberation not only from carnal desire, but from the constraints of reason itself, and thereby garners delights that transcend the reach of understanding:

> Si tu étais capable de la comprendre, tu ne me demanderais pas, comme tu fais, quels plaisirs reçoivent ces fidèles amants que tu nommes mornes et pensifs, car tu connaîtrais qu'ils demeurent de sorte ravis en la contemplation du bien qu'ils adorent, que, méprisant tout ce qui est en l'univers, il n'y a rien qu'ils plaignent plus que la perte du temps qu'ils employent ailleurs, et que leur âme n'ayant assez de force pour bien comprendre la grandeur de leur contentement, demeure estonné de tant de thresors, et de tant de felicitez qui surpassent la connaissance qu'elle en peut avoir. (II, 389)

Once again, the tension between pleasure and virtue is overcome not because obedience to the laws of love may be shown to lead to sensual satisfaction, but because at the level of metaphysical explanation the lover always already possesses the object of his desire.

In spite of the intrinsic coherence of its logic, the idealist dialectic does not succeed in reforming Hylas. By permitting inconstant lovers to escape the definitions, and to refuse to interpret their experience through the grid provided by the conventional ontological hierarchy, d'Urfé encourages us to examine the emergence of the autonomous ego on its own terms, and to take into account not only its official status within the dominant paradigm, but its irreducible otherness, and role in producing change.

IV. Hylas and the Temple d'Amitié

D'Urfé's critique of chivalric idealism, woven into the narrative in the character of the inconstant lover, exemplifies an intermediate position between Montaigne and Descartes in the evolution of a modern subject-centered episte-mology. Like Montaigne, D'Urfé denies the accessibility to human thought of a metaphysical *a priori*, and reduces traditional laws and icons (in this case, those of chivalric love) to the status of cultural fictions with origins in the concealed and/or forgotten interests of individuals. At the same time, by call-ing for the accountability of speech and institutions to empirical experience, he anticipates the moment when the subjective consciousness will replace the objective order as a new foundation of knowledge. Nevertheless, his tentative movement toward modernity stops short of establishing the individual as the *locus* of suprapersonal truths. On the one hand, we are never far in *L'Astrée* from the early baroque tendency to equate all that is merely subjective with chaos and impermanence. Separated from transcendent sources of being the world is a "grand branloir" and thought a fallow field bringing forth laughable chimeras and fantastic monsters. On the other, the self-determining, rational subject of modernity appears only in its negative form as the deceitful "evil genius." An emergent ideology of the individual increasingly supersedes and attenuates baroque mutability in the later volumes of the work, especially in three and four. But the rational pursuit of self-interest and naïve empiricism which are its central features lead only to a Hobbesian war of all against all. D'Urfé's position as one who anticipates a modern, subjectivist epistemology, while holding to skeptical arguments that prevent its emergence—the giddiness of the unbridled mind, and the impenetrable atomism of the individualist—vividly appears in the two episodes in which Hylas accompa-nies the shepherds of the Forez to the Temple d'Amitié (Book II and Book III). Defining himself in opposition to established social and religious authority, the most famous "inconstant" of seventeenth-century fiction posits his ego as a law unto itself only at the expense of psychological and social order.

Beginning with his first appearance in the narrative, Hylas denounces the metaphysical rationalization of the chivalric code as a fraud imposed by self-interested individuals. Convinced that pure ideas, first principles, the di-vine mind and other hypostatizations of being lie beyond the scope of human thought, he insists that the objects of love are empirical and transitory rather than spiritual and eternal. Time, he says, witnesses the origin of love and must therefore "triomphe de sa fin, et s'en nomme vainqueur" (I, 31). The rejection of metaphysical premises, in turn, leads to the conclusion that Silvandre's polemical defense of chivalry is—to paraphrase d'Urfé's more famous contemporary—"a tale told by an idiot, signifying nothing." "C'est bien druiser, dit Hylas, en se moquant," when Silvandre claims that love is a mystical circle that begins and ends in itself, "mais quant à moi, je crois que tout ce que vous venez de dire sont des fables, avec lesquelles les femmes endorment les moins rusés" (II, 262–63). Without metaphysical referents, his vocabulary is meaningless, and without a foundation in the *a priori logos* of being, his rationality is a fabulous display of creative imagination. Throughout the narrative, numerous characters suspect him of being a mere wordmonger, a "beau parleur" (IV, 258), employing a gratuitous, self-reflexive vocabulary, and owing his polemical victories to seductive eloquence.

The impediment to knowledge created by a language without referents in empirical or psychological experience is a central feature of the early modern critique of medieval philosophy. It appears not only in Montaigne's indictment of authors who "se communiquent au peuple par quelque marque particulière et estrangère" ("Du repentir," III, 20), but in Bacon's refutation in the *Novum Organum* of the "idols imposed by words on the understanding"—a category of discourse in which he includes the "names of things which do not exist": "Fortune, the Prime Mover, Planetary Orbits, Element of Fire, and the like fictions which owe their origin to false and idle theories."[11]

Although the vocabulary at issue in *L'Astrée* is psychological and social rather than cosmological in its applications, it is similarly (if one accepts the materialist premise) detached from reality. Silvandre apologizes for the necessity of using "quelques termes qui ne sont guères accoutumés parmi nos champs" (II, 386) before deploying propositions whose sense depends upon the prior acceptance of the metaphysical structure of cognitive and affective relationships: "l'entendement qui entend, et ce qui est entendu, ne sont qu'une mesme chose," "l'amant et l'aimée ne sont qu'une," and the like. Even common words have metaphysical meanings which require learned explication. When Phillis objects to an apparent logical contradiction in the claim that the lover is "in" his mistress' heart and she "in" his (how can both be true?), he elucidates the mystical reference of the preposition: "A parler, dit Silvandre, avec le commun, on l'entend comme vous le dites, mais quand on discourt avec les personnes un peu mieux entendues, l'un signifie l'autre," because, he continues, "être en quelque lieu, s'entend de deux sortes" (III, 50). Confronted with a discourse whose referents lie beyond the scope of subjective experience, the uninitiated find his doctrines incomprehensible. "Encore que j'aie long-temps été dans les écoles des Massiliens [...]" Hylas complains, "si avez-vous eu beau m'embrouiller le cerveau par vos discours" (II, 262). In one instance, Diane intervenes on his behalf: "Ne savez-vous, berger [she chides Silvandre], qu'il n'entend pas ce langage?" (II, 381).

At the same time, Silvandre's polemical brilliance elicits both admiration and dismay from those who not only recognize his breathtaking virtuosity, but who also suspect that logic itself is little more than an exercise in empty verbal play. As might be expected, Hylas accuses him of single-handedly bringing constancy into vogue with "false reasons" and "subtle wit" (III, 601), but many other characters express a similar sentiment. Leonide recognizes Silvandre as a masterful sophist— "[elle] loua en elle même beaucoup le gentil esprit du berger, qui soutenait si bien une mauvaise cause" (I, 241)—as does Paris who remarks on Hylas' behalf that "nous avons la raison de notre côté, mais que Silvandre par ses discours s'acquiert l'opinion de toute la troupe qui le favorise" (II, 382). Diane refuses to hear him defend himself against the charge of infidelity because, she tells Phillis, "ne sçavez-vous point encores que jamais personne qui ait escouté Silvandre ne luy donna le tort?" (III, 614). She reiterates this point on several occasions, until the very name "Silvandre" becomes synonymous with seductive discourse: "un Silvandre," she exclaims, "qui a opinion de pouvoir par son beau discours, éblouir aussi bien les yeux de nos esprits que les sorciers ceux de nos corps?" (IV, 85).

Finally, just as Montaigne attributes orthodox belief to the "gaillardise de ces esprits anciens," the partisans of experience in *L'Astrée* suggest that the laws of chivalric love are rooted in the subjective experiences of individuals which have been generalized by tradition, and imposed by force of habit. According to Hylas, inconstancy has been unjustly vilified by those who wish to secure by ties of duty the affection they can no longer hope to win by means of beauty and free choice: "C'est une imagination, ou plustôt une invention de quelque fine amante, qui se voyant devenue laide, ou prête à être changée pour une plus belle qu'elle n'était pas, mit en avant cette opinion, et la fit croire pour quelque chose de très-mauvaise" (II, 384). Galathée similarly denounces the "sottises de fidélité et de constance" as "paroles que les vieilles et celles que deviennent laides ont inventées pour retenir par ces liens les âmes que leurs visages mettaient en liberté" (I, 438–39).

Silvandre's own motives are open to question. Although events recounted at the end of the fifth volume reveal him to be the displaced son of Adamas, the mystery of his identity throughout the narrative undermines his credibility as a teacher and orator not only because it underscores the philosopher's lack of self-knowledge, but because opportunistic and even entrepreneurial motives may be imputed to a "raisonneur" who, as a foundling, has been obliged to survive by his wits. His autobiography in fact reveals a character who combines features of the picaresque hero with those of the itinerant sophist. Kidnapped while still an infant, and raised and educated by a rich bourgeois, he has acquiesced in his adoptive father's plan to disinherit Alzahyde, the legitimate son. Escaping an assassination attempt by his enraged rival, he travels to the Forez where, "ayant la cognaissance des herbes, et du naturel des animaux," he continues to thrive by private industry to the point that "à ceste heure il est a son aise et se peut dire riche" (I, 389). The ease with which he assumes alternative identities, his profit-seeking industriousness, and his love for a mistress (Diane) above his station all implicate him in an attempt to create an identity out of whole cloth rather than to disclose the qualities of a providentially determined self: "Il n'y a sous le ciel un berger," Diane declares, "qui désire plus de donner une bonne opinion de soi-même" (IV, 221). His agility in debate might easily be regarded as yet another entrepreneurial skill.

Late in the narrative, the imputation of conscious deceit to the advocates of chivalric love gives place to a more corrosive skepticism arising from an awareness of the self-deceptions by which we conceal the self-interest at the heart even of our most altruistic actions. Silvandre is made to overhear a conversation between two bothers in which one attributes the other's belief in selfless love to an ignorance of human motivation. Even his willingness to lay down his life for his beloved is nothing more than a displaced expression of the same "amour-propre" that engenders the lunatic possessiveness of a miser. The passage, which anticipates the ironic deflation of ethical idealism that gains momentum in the middle decades of the seventeenth century in such works as La Rochefoucauld's *Maximes* (1665), is one of d'Urfé's most beautiful and psychologically profound:

> Car si nous voulons en parler sainement, nous advouerons que c'est
> pour l'amour que nous nous portons que nous les aimons; et comme
> [l'avare] expose sa propre vie pour la conservation de l'or qu'il aime,
> que de mesme nous nous sacrifions pour le plaisir de ces belles que
> nous chérissons. [...] Et par la, mon frère, mon ami, avouons que tout le
> bien que nous leur désirons, c'est comme l'avare aime l'or, c'est à dire
> pour notre interêt particulier, quoi que l'excès de notre passion nous
> fasse juger au commencement tout le contraire. (IV, 246–47)

The constructive movement which accompanies the refutation of chivalric idealism is predicated upon the epistemological priority of experience to the conventional symbolic order. For Hylas, truthful discourse mirrors or represents the facts of experience, whether they be the extra-mental, empirically verifiable data of the senses, or the intra-mental thoughts and feelings of the private self. What one says must be verifiable either through empirical observation or self-examination.

> Quant à moi [Hylas declares], je sais bien que l'expérience est plus
> certaine que les paroles. Or Silvandre n'a que des paroles pour preuver
> ce qu'il dit, et moi j'ai les effets et l'expérience si familière, que je n'en
> veux point chercher de plus éloignée qu'en moi-même. (II, 382)

Unlike the constant lover who regards his mistress *a priori* as the embodiment of an ideal— "la plus belle, et la plus aimable bergère de l'univers"—Hylas defers to empirical evidence, telling Silvandre that ocular proof will be the measure of his words: "Si vos yeux ne me servaient bientôt de tesmoins contre vous-mêmes, je m'efforcerais de le vous tesmoigner par mes paroles; mais je me remets à eux, et au jugement qu'ils en feront" (III, 60).

The insistence upon the accountability of language to experience is a constantly reiterated theme in the love debates. The famous wooing contest in which Phillis and Silvandre each strives to prove "qu'il mérite d'être aimé" (I, 243) begins as an empirical test of Silvandre's words. "Mais à quoi servent tant de paroles," Phillis replies to his boasting, "S'il est vrai que vous soyez tel, venons-en à la preuve, et me dites, quelle bergère fait particulièrement état de vous? (I, 242). When Silvandre fails to produce examples she proposes an experiment: "Or bien, continua Phillis, quand les paroles ne peuvent vérifier ce que l'on soutient, n'est-on pas obligé d'en venir à la preuve?" (I, 243) The ensuing competition occasions several disputes in which Silvandre's abstract rationality and Phillis' experience come into conflict. When Silvandre proves by means of a syllogism that Phillis doesn't love Diane, she finds his logic unanswerable on its own terms but questions its relevance: "Si l'amour, répliqua Phillis, consiste en paroles, vous en avez plus que le reste des hommes ensemble: car je ne crois pas que pour mauvaise cause que vous ayez, elles vous deffaillent jamais" (I, 274). Dorinde concurs with Hylas and Phillis in affirming the epistemological priority of experience to formal logic which she regards as a verbal game. "Parce que j'ai une grande expérience de ce que je dis," she assures Silvandre, "il n'y a guères de raisons, pour bien desguisées qu'elles soient, qui puissent faire grand effet en moy." And although she assents to a series of logical deductions from "premiers principes" (IV, 112), she reverts in the end to her initial position: "Ah! s'écria Dorinde, j'avoue tout jusqu'à la conclusion que vous en tirez" (IV, 113).

Nevertheless, d'Urfé's polemics do not establish subjective experience as a *locus* of intersubjective truths, or truthful discourse as a transparent representation thereof. An "ontological" variety of skepticism preoccupied with the mutability of a world separated from transcendent sources of being exists side by side with a "representational" variety preoccupied with the impenetrable self-enclosure of consciousness.

The lingering influence of the "ontological" tradition may be observed in the fact that Hylas himself, no less than his opponents, continues to associate an epistemology of experience with the dispersion of personal identity in a flux of erratic impulses, and with a radical unraveling of social authority. The brief exchange in which Galathée attempts to dissuade Celadon from his love for Astrée on the ground that natural law "nous commande de rechercher notre bien" (I, 438) illustrates the general tenor of the objection. To her entreaties, the shepherd replies that the individual dedicated to the pursuit of pleasure gives himself over to a succession of unpredictable impulses: "Y a-t-il rien de plus leger qu'un esprit qui va comme l'abeille, volant d'une fleur à l'autre, attirée d'une nouvelle douceur?" The continuity of the psyche and the stability of social relationships depend upon the surrender of the ego to an objective order: "Madame, si la fidélité se perd, quel fondement puis-je faire en votre amitié?" (I, 439).

As though in confirmation of this view, Hylas emerges from many of his lyrics on the theme of inconstancy, including those with which he is first introduced (I, 27; I, 31), as the champion of "plaisir" against pain, unbridled "franchise" against "esclavage," temporal flux against eternal permanence, movement against stasis. His polemical discourse mirrors not the self-enclosed rational structure of the *cogito*, but the open-ended, searching movement of thought and the spontaneity of private feeling. He habitually confounds logical categories, and speaks in a precipitous and inconsequential manner, "s'étant tellement ému par ses propres raisons, qu'il en était tout en feu" (II, 385). Because polite dissimulation and artificial forms barely contain the volatile energy of his passions, his amorous discourse likewise is an uninterrupted confession of the chaotic changes that characterize his inner life. When he falls in love with Phillis he reveals his feelings "sans autre déguisement de paroles" (I, 285), and leaving her for Alexis he says simply: "C'en est fait, Phillis, je vous dis adieu" (II, 464). A woman can take him precisely at his word: "Et de fait," he tells Stelle, "ne voyez vous pas que soudain que je n'ai plus aimé Alexis, je le lui ai dit?" (III, 488).

The second "representational" variety of skepticism arises from the fact that the problem of mutability, though definitive for the early baroque mentality exemplified in the *Essais*, is counterbalanced in *L'Astrée* by claims for the intrinsic continuity of subjective consciousness. While the older writer posits the mind as a *locus* of chimera and grotesque monsters because he continues to regard permanence as a function of absolute being even while affirming its irremediable otherness, d'Urfé's inconstant lovers begin to formulate a theory of mind in which the stabilizing function performed by the objective metaphysical order under the old paradigm gives place to a unity of subjective intention or, to use Hylas' term, "dessein," under the new. Throughout the narrative, Hylas argues that "aimer en divers lieux, ce n'est pas inconstance" (II, 110), declaring, in one of his lyrics, that "l'expérience n'est que d'avoir epreuvé/Cent diverses humeurs, *et s'estre conservé*" (III, 229). [Emphasis mine.]

It is entirely consistent with the epistemological ambivalence of the text that Hylas should attempt on at least one occasion to prove his paradoxical claim that change is not inconstancy in terms provided by the traditional, object-centered paradigm. Those who love a mistress whose beauty has begun to fade, or in preference to a more beautiful rival, are inconstant by virtue of their love for divergent objects:

> Si aymer le contraire de ce que l'on a aymé est inconstance, et si la
> laideur est le contraire de la beauté, il n'y a point de doute que celuy
> conclut fort bien, qui soustient celuy estre inconstant, qui ayant aymé un
> beau visage, continue de l'aymer quand il est laid. (II, 127)

At the very least, the syllogism depends upon the assumption that the lover's
identity is a function of the object to which he devotes his affection, and not
of an intrinsic principle of private consciousness. Were we to trace the argument to its unstated major premise, we would find the hylomorphic theory of
knowledge according to which the unchanging love of a mutable object proves
the lover's inconstancy—the fragmentation of his identity—precisely to the
degree that love is a function of the unity of the lover and the beloved.[12] The
same premise underlies the Hylas' conclusion that those who love beauty
wherever it appears are constant in spite of their changes because the object
of their affection is always the same:

> Pour n'être inconstant, il faut aimer tousjours et en tous lieux la beauté,
> et que lors qu'elle se sépare de quelque sujet, on s'en doit de même
> séparer d'amitié, de peur de n'aimer le contraire de cette beauté.
> (II, 127)

From the idealist's point of view, of course, the argument is easily refuted
because it rests on a category mistake. What changes is only the body, while
love is an affair of the soul.

Hylas' arguments entail a "representational" mode of skepticism, however, only to the degree that they relocate sources of constancy from the being
of the beloved and the transcendent ideal she represents to that of the lover
himself. According to this view, the lover possesses an inward continuity of
consciousness that appears in two modalities: self-interest, and the capacity for
cumulative empirical knowledge. With regard to the first, Hylas repeatedly
tells the incredulous Forezians that it is precisely his willingness to abandon
a lesser for a greater beauty that signifies his constancy because, in his view,
such changes demonstrate not a displacement within an overarching cosmos
but a tenacity in the pursuit of self-chosen ends. Defending his position when
leaving Phillis for Alexis-Celadon, he asks rhetorically: "Appellez-vous inconstance de parvenir pas à pas où l'on a fait dessein d'aller?" Far from it, he

avers. The transfer of desire from one object to another is a necessary corollary of the unity of a subjective "dessein":

> Puis qu'ayant fait dessein de parvenir à la parfaite beauté, tout ainsi qu'en marchant on change d'un pied à l'autre, jusqu'à ce qu'on parvienne au lieu que l'on s'est proposé, de même ai-je fait, aimant les beautés que j'ai rencontrées jusqu'à ce que je sois parvenus à celle d'Alexis, que véritablement je reconnais être la plus parfaite de toutes. (II, 465)

Self-creating rather than objectively determined, the lover's ego provides the unifying thread through an endless series of changes in which every action finds its ultimate justification in self-preservation and self-advancement: "Nous voyons par l'effet que ce changement est bon et raisonnable, étant selon le loix de la nature, qui oblige chaque chose à chercher son mieux" (III, 39). Modelling his behavior on that of the merchant who posits himself as master of his own social and material fortunes, Hylas boasts of submitting all women to the "jeu de la plus belle," and sings, when leaving Phillis, of exchanging bad merchandise for good: "C'est grande prudence de savoir bien changer" (III, 36). Qualities such as beauty and love which had formerly served to reveal the essential identities of those in whom they appeared become commodities possessed by individuals whose identities are associated with the profit-seeking intelligence itself:

> Il faut que vous sçachiez que je m'y gouverne tout ainsi qu'un marchand bien avisé: lors qu'il fait dessein d'acheter quelque chose, il regarde combien elle peut valoir, et puis amasse de tous costez l'argent qui luy est nécessaire pour esgaler ce prix. J'en fais de mesme; car lors que j'entreprends d'aimer une dame, je regarde incontinent quelle est sa beauté, car, comme vous sçavez, ce qui donne le pris aux femmes, ce n'est que la seule beauté. [...] Et soudain, je fais un amas d'amour en mon âme, esgal au prix et à la valeur qui est en elle [...], si bien qu'en cela mon argent et mon amour se ressemblent bien fort. (III, 348).

In a dispute with Silvandre he effects a similar commodification of the "services d'amour." No longer signs of the intrinsic "sympathie" or "conformité des êtres," they function as sexual currency offered in exchange for favors of equal worth: "C'estait vivre en personne de peu de jugement, que de vivre sans conte" (III, 359).

The continuity of self-interest is doubled by a continuity of empirical experience. From his first appearance in the narrative we are assured that Hylas has learned the art of love from having plied the trade: "J'ai toujours cru que l'ouvrier se rendait plus parfait, plus il exerçait souvent le métier dont il faisait profession" (I, 28). Because he has successfully courted mistresses "de toutes sortes, de tout age, de toute condition, et de toutes humeurs," he assures Phillis, "je sais de quelle façon il le faut, et ce qui doit, ou ne doit pas vous plaire" (I, 287).[13] While the first installment of his autobiography identifies inconstancy as a trait of character bequeathed to him by the heavens, and unfolds as the progressive disclosure through a series of "preuves" of an innate identity (I, 294), later episodes abandon these vestiges of the traditional object-centered paradigm. Retrospectively, he rationalizes his behavior as a quest for practical knowledge—"Y a-t'il quelqu'un qui puisse blasmer l'expérience, puisqu'elle est mère et nourrice de la prudence?" he asks, as he begins his account of his courtship of Cryseide (III, 350)—and he reformulates his life story as an extended apprenticeship: "J'y commencai mon apprentissage auprès de Carlis, et le finis en Stiliane, qui me firent quitter le lieu de ma naissance, tant j'étais nouveau en ce métier" (III, 351).

In spite of the intrinsic continuity which sets the "Hylasian" ego apart from the protean, polymorphous mentality of the *Essais*, however, it cannot establish the subject as the *locus* of *intersubjective* truths. The Cartesian *cogito*, which ultimately provides the epistemological center of the emergent paradigm, does so precisely because it is not only private and self-enclosed, but shared by all individual minds. Self-interest and empirical experience, by contrast, are irreducibly private, and lead only to incompatible perspectives and self-interested deceit. Hylas himself remains a sympathetic character throughout the narrative largely because d'Urfé localizes the negative effects of his philosophy in deceitful villains such as Polemas, Climante, Semire and Laonice. The limitations attendant upon Hylas' position are dramatically illustrated in the two episodes in which he accompanies the community of lovers to the "Temple d'Amitié."

The temple concretely embodies in word and visual icon the doctrines of chivalric love, and functions both as a place of pilgrimage for the community of faithful lovers and as Celadon's place of retreat from the world. As pilgrims progress from the outermost to the innermost chamber, the objects they encounter are organized in an ascending pattern moving from those that represent the subjective experience of carnal love toward the symbol of divinity at its metaphysical and structural center. The outer chamber contains the image of Eros and Anteros, and the tablets inscribed with the twelve laws of love. If the icon represents the ontological conformity of the lover and his mistress, the laws permit that unity to be known through the evidence of the lover's obedience. The inner chamber, which bears the name "Temple d'Astrée," contains the high altar adorned with a portrait of Astrée placed near a tree whose three branches growing from a single root represent the persons of a divine trinity. According to the precepts of d'Urfé's religion of love, the mistress merits worship insofar as she embodies the lover's highest earthly good, and she, in turn, receives her goodness and beauty directly from the divine source. Although Hylas remains defiantly outside the temple in protest or in fear (both interpretations are possible) of the metaphysical and symbolic order it represents (II, 177; III, 438), he is unable to formulate a subjectivist alternative that doesn't either destroy the unity of consciousness, or initiate a Hobbesian war of all against all that precludes the possibility of harmonious collective life.

His protest in each instance centers on the laws of love which he subverts in two quite different ways. Entering the outer chamber secretly in the first episode, he erases the authorized version and replaces it with one consistent with his inconstant humour. The result, however, is not a code of ethics predicated on the principle of the mutual self-interest of self-determining individuals, but rather a comic parody of the chivalric code which stands its principal tenets on their heads. While the original begins "Qui veut être parfait amant,/Il faut qu'il aime infiniment" (II, 181), the forgery reads, "Qui veut être parfait amant,/Qu'il n'aime point infiniment" (II, 194), and so on with all twelve laws. The parody is inherently conservative. By affirming incessant change as the inescapable reality of the human condition, Hylas does not escape the fundamental assumption of the ideology he mocks. Order continues to be a function of immanence, or, to put the thing in the language of the religion of love, of "fidelity"—that relation by which the particular becomes transparent to the universal, and the contingent and transitory receive the imprint of the subsistent and unchanging. When his companions discover the fraud and force him to restore the original, Hylas merely rewrites the official code in the margins of his own, providing a visual reminder of the interdependence of the two sets of laws. Thenceforward both versions appear in the Temple, each logically and literally in the margins of the other because they reinforce a single epistemological paradigm.

The amorous contract between Stelle and Hylas, concluded in the field outside the temple on the occasion of the second collective pilgrimage, represents yet another subversion of the twelve laws: "Je désire," Stelle says, "que nous fassions des conditions ensemble, lesquelles nous serons obligés d'observer, et que nous appellerons loix d'Amour" (III, 488). By contrast to the inherent conservatism of Hylas' parody, however, the provisions the lovers now adopt are based on a subject-centered conception of personal identity. While the official code finds its justification in the metaphysical relation between lover and beloved, Stelle and Hylas evoke the authority of "l'expérience [...] qui rend les personnes prudentes, et qui apprend à mettre les remèdes nécessaires pour éviter les inconvénients, où l'on a vu que les autres se sont auparavant perdus" (III, 490). Drawn up by mutual consent, each clause of the contract affirms the ethical and epistemological priority of the individual. The first substitutes equality for hierarchy: "Que l'un n'usurpera point sur l'autre ceste souveraine authorité, que nous disons estre tyrannie: (III, 490). Reciprocal exchange replaces the unity of souls as an ideal of proportion: "Que chacun de nous sera en mesme temps et l'amant et l'aymé, et l'aymée et l'amante" (III, 490). Self-determination replaces teleology: "Que nostre amitié sera eternellement sans contrainte" (III, 490). And finally, experience replaces the metaphysical *a priori* as the horizon of symbolic reference: "Que pour n'être point menteurs, ni esclaves, en effect, ny en parole, tous ces mots de *fidélité*, de *servitude* et d'*eternelle affection*, ne seront jamais melés parmi nos discours" (III, 490).

Individualist ideology, however, dissolves into unregulated anarchy when Silvandre points out the contradiction in their attempt to establish liberty by contract. Logical coherence requires the addition of a thirteenth law which releases the litigants from the provisions to which they have agreed, and returns them to the state of impenetrable privacy in which they began (III, 493). Forced to choose between subjective "franchise" and determinate self-representation, Hylas and Stelle opt for the former. In the adventures of Astrée and Celadon, however, d'Urfé explores ways of passing beyond this dilemma.

Notes

1. See Chapter 1 (above) for an explanation of Kuhn's theory, set forth in *The Structure of Scientific Revolutions*, and its relevance to my analysis of the epistemic shift that occurred in the early seventeenth century.

2. According to David Knowles, the "triple process of cognition" prominent in medieval epistemology originates in the works of Plotinus and Augustine. For Plotinus, "life was an ascent of mind and soul, in which there were three degrees; that on which the reason dealt with the universe of sense, that on which the soul, now possessed of wisdom, saw the reflection of the divine ideas in itself, and that on which it had intuitional knowledge of God. Above this was the ecstatic union with the One above all differentiation. Augustine has a parallel ascent; the knowledge of creatures by science; the knowledge of Scripture and theology by wisdom; and the knowledge of the supreme, immutable Truth by intuition. Above all this is the mystical, ineffable union with God." [*The Evolution of Medieval Thought* (Baltimore: Helicon Press, 1962), pp. 46-47.] D'Urfé was familiar with this cognitive model through the writings of the Italian neoplatonists. Several passages in the *Epîtres Morales* echo Ficino's doctrine that "le visage unique de Dieu se reflète donc successivement dans trois miroirs placés en ordre: l'ange, l'âme et le corps du monde." [Maxime Gaume, *Les Inspirations et les sources de l'oeuvre d'Honoré d'Urfé*, p. 443.] The model persists in the later seventeenth century, although in a form radically modified by the influence of a subject-centered epistemology. Pascal's three orders of experience— "la chair," "l'esprit," and "la charité" (*Pensées*, #298 and #308)—are a famous case in point. Unlike his medieval and Renaissance predecessors, Pascal no longer envisions the intuition of divine love as the logical consequence of the soul's ascent through lower orders of being, but as a gift of grace utterly incommensurate with the intrinsic nature of the empirical universe and with human mental faculties: "La distance infinie des corps aux esprits figure la distance infiniment plus infinie des esprits à la charité, car elle est surnaturelle" (#308).

3. "Que si nos désirs ne s'etendaient point au delà du discours, de la vue, et de l'ouie, pourquoi serions-nous jaloux, pourquoi desdaignez, pourquoi douteux, pourquoi ennemis, pourquoi trahis, et en fin pourquoi cesserions-nous d'aimer, et d'être aimés, puis que la possession que quelque autre pourrait avoir de ces choses n'en rendrait pas moindre notre bon-heur?" (II, 79–80)

4. In the "Histoire de Celidée, Thamire et Calidon" (II, 27–72), the physician who diagnoses Calidon's love sickness shares the view that disordered affections are an

effect of sensory errors, and that the soul, properly informed by the senses, unerringly recognizes and loves the highest good: "Tout vice étant mal," he concludes, "et tout mal étant entièrement opposé à la volonté, il n'y a point de doute que tout vice reconnu ne soit haï" (II, 34).

5. D'Urfé develops the "ontological" view of jealousy reflected here on several occasions. In an early authorial interjection, he envisions the words and deeds of the lover as branches of a tree growing out of the soil of his love. As an unhealthy branch, jealousy increases in magnitude as the vitality of the ground permits, but robs the other branches of their nourishment (I, 291). Diane likens jealousy to a decayed monument which, though proportionate in size to the original structure, bears witness to a former glory: "La jalousie est sans doute signe d'amour, tout ainsi que les vieilles ruines sont témoignages des anciens batiments, étants d'autant plus grandes que les édifices en ont été superbes et beaux" (II, 95). For Celadon jealousy is a "dangéreuse maladie d'amour" particularly common to immature lovers (II, 294).

While d'Urfé's position reflects the lingering influence in the early seventeenth century of a medieval theory of the passions, later seventeenth-century moralist literature prefigures a more modern psychologistic view. Jealousy is regarded by some as an effect of the rational pursuit of self interest, and by others as the projection of an intra-psychic fantasy. Descartes epitomizes the first position in "The Passions of the Soul" (408). La Rochefoucauld and La Bruyère, while continuing to recognize in jealousy an element of rational self-interest, give greater emphasis to a purely gratuitous tendency to appropriate objects without consideration for intersubjective standards of value. For La Rochefoucauld, jealousy is an expression of "amour-propre"—the irreducible and irrational principle of self-love which lies at the core of personal identity, and governs human affairs (*Maximes*, #324). For La Bruyère, it is "un soupcon injuste, bizarre et sans fondement" ("Du Coeur," #29).

6. Aristotle's version appears in Book IV of the *Metaphysics*. "The same attribute cannot at the same time belong and not belong to the same subject and in the same respect." He offers the law as the foundational principle of the study of being as such, or, as he calls it, the "first philosophy," and its importance insofar as concerns us here is to establish the determinate and unified nature of any existing thing. [*The Basic Works of Aristotle*, ed. Richard McKeon (New York: Random House, 1942), p. 736.]

7. From the perspective of the doctrine of sympathies, Astrée is Celadon's "astre" in the sense that she embodies the ideal form of the planet in ascendancy at the time of Celadon's birth, and is therefore the governing influence in his life, controlling his destiny. This theory also gives rise to the compass metaphor employed by Silvandre who explains that the mistress is the pole star toward which the lover, like the compass

needle, gravitates by virtue of a "puissance naturelle qui fait que toute partie recherche de se rejoindre à son tout" (II, 98).

8. To the question of whether Hylas exemplifies a new or an old mentality critics have offered various responses. Le Breton sees in Hylas a last echo of the robust license that characterized "l'ancienne France" protesting against the philosophical idealism and refinement of manners associated with "préciosité" (19–22). Magendie, by contrast, regards him as "un parfait modèle d'honnête homme," fulfilling the social and intellectual ideals of early seventeenth-century salon culture rather than resisting or mocking them (281). Still others have recognized in Hylas the embodiment of a baroque "psychologie de l'intermittence et de la mobilité," neither ancient nor modern, but the function of the transition between them (Rousset, 44). My own view is most compatible with that of Bernard Germa who argues that Hylas rejects idealism from the perspective not of an ancient, but of an emergent, mentality. D'Urfé, Germa writes, "entr'ouvre lui-même la porte par où passeront les romans réalistes du dix-septième siècle. Sorel peut parodier *L'Astrée*, d'Urfé l'a mis en bonne voie, en se parodiant spirituellement lui-même" (80).

9. This notion has historical origins in the direct realism of classical philosophy according to which the mind knows only that with which it has been imprinted by the objective order. See Rorty, *Philosophy and the Mirror of Nature*, pp. 38–45.

10. Foucault attributes a revolution in theories of monetary value in the early modern period to this aspect of epistemic change. In the declining "episteme of resemblance," coins are considered to be valuable by virtue of the intrinsic worth of the metal of which they are made. In the emergent "episteme of representation," their value derives only from the fact that people will receive them in exchange for commodities which are valued. In the first instance, value is intrinsic. In the second, it is a function of market forces (*The Order of Things*, 168–180). A similar distinction may be observed in *L'Astrée* whenever the question of value arises as a topic of debate, whether with reference to the qualities that define personal merit, or to any other exchangeable "commodity," including ideas. According to Silvandre, "ce n'est pas l'opinion que l'on a de chaque chose qui met le prix à sa valeur, mais la propre bonté qui est en elle" (IV, 88). According to Hylas, by contrast, values are determined by collective "opinion," and conditions of supply and demand: "La quantité de quelque chose, pour bonne qu'elle soit, la fait être à vil prix" (IV, 465).

11. Francis Bacon, *Novum Organum*, from selections reprinted in *Seventeenth-Century Prose and Poetry*, ed. Witherspoon and Warnke (New York: Harcourt, Brace, 1963), 55–56.

12. The poems reiterate the same theme: "Ceux qui d'être constants se donnent la louange,/S'ils aiment longuement, sont eux-mêmes inconstants;/En laideur la beauté se change par le temps,/Et qui l'aime changée, il faut aussi qu'il change" (III, 229).

13. He repeats the argument to each of his new mistresses in turn. When Silvandre mocks him for abandoning Phillis in favor of Alexis-Celadon, "Comment, dit Hylas, voudriez-vous me conseiller de faire ici mon apprentissage? Il y a bien apparence qu'un apprentif du premier coup peut être digne serviteur d'Alexis" (II, 464). And he assures Alexis: "Je n'ai pas attendu jusques ici à faire mon apprentissage [...] car avant que d'aimer Phillis, j'avais trouvé belle Laonice, et auparavant Madonte, et avant que toutes ces deux Cryseide" (III, 237).

4

Self-interest, Deceit and the Voyeur: Subjectivity and Self-disclosure in Astrée's Confession

D'Urfé's polemics conclude in an unresolvable conflict between an intersubjective discursive structure which cannot be reconciled with private experience (Silvandre's position), and an epistemology of experience which leads to an impenetrable atomism (Hylas' position). As lines "so truly parallel, though infinite can never meet," these alternatives represent the epistemological impasse from which d'Urfé's narrative arises, pushing forward toward a resolution which lies beyond them. This project, as we have already observed, unfolds in two interlocking triadic structures. The first, dominated by Astrée, represents the impossibility at this moment in the history of early modern consciousness of establishing the subject as a self-sufficient center of identity and meaning, and via this failure, concludes in a recognition of the epistemological finality of the collective voice. The second, dominated by Celadon, represents an equally ill-fated attempt to return to a metaphysical conception of order which has been permanently foreclosed by the birth of love, and tends toward his acceptance of the social authority with which Astrée has become identified at the end of the first phase.

In the present chapter, I will discuss the "Histoire d'Astrée et Phillis" (I, 111–152), which contains the first of these two grand and interdependent movements in d'Urfé's work. Narrated in the first person by Astrée with interjections from Phillis, it offers an account, from the heroine's perspective, of the entire love affair up to the point of Celadon's disappearance. As a personal confession to her friends, it serves to reveal her position within the ethical and epistemological dilemmas of the work. Most importantly, it describes the failure of "representation" as a reliable avenue to interpersonal knowledge in the intertwined biographies of two of d'Urfé's principal couples, and establishes the collectivist resolution toward which the narrative tends.

Formally, the tale treats each of the love affairs in three phases—the birth of love, the declaration of love, and the trials of love—examining the relation between the subject and the symbolic order in each.

Astrée's view of the birth of love invalidates the metaphysical origins of personal identity without establishing the individual as autonomous and self-determining. Love is perceived to originate neither in a providentially determined "sympathy," nor in an authentic inner well of desire, but in a complex interaction between private inclination and arbitrary discursive structures which destroys the notion of a pre-discursive "authenticity," and shrouds the question of origins in doubt.

Astrée's analysis of the declaration of love illustrates not only the failure of the conventional symbolic order to represent the inner truth of the self, but the impossibility of establishing subjective consciousness as an alternative horizon of discursive reference. Rather than stand outside the conventional symbolic order where they might reveal themselves transparently in confessional speech, Astrée and Celadon engage in a process of "subversive play" within the ritual playing space of a public festival. Celadon discloses his subjective intentions by means of transgressive gestures in the midst of prescribed performance, and Astrée rigorously conforms to the established code only "par apparence" while concealing reserves of private interiority.

Finally, a series of four "travaux d'amour" test the lovers' ability to negotiate a stable representation of self in the midst of the illusionistic, textualized universe initiated by the invalidation of metaphysical sources of identity and meaning. Here again, we witness a fundamental ideological difference between Celadon and Astrée. Confronted with signs that contradict their mutual fidelity, the former strives to restore the lost continuity of a discursive universe in which everything conspires to speak the inward truth of his love, while Astrée seeks to verify the representational accuracy of discourse with reference to extra-discursive objects. All of the trials conclude in the same way, by demonstrating the failure of both preliminary solutions and by affirming instead the epistemological authority of an historically situated community. Truth resides in social consensus rather than in either the divine mind or in subjective consciousness.

Because Astrée's narrative exposes as an illusion the subjective self-presence upon which confessional speech depends, it deconstructs its own claim to truthfulness. It is nevertheless preserved from radical indeterminacy by the fact that confession, as practiced by Astrée and her companions, is less a disclosure of private truths than a ratification of collective opinion. The heroine's autobiography marks her re-entry into social life after an extended period of seclusion and mourning, signalling not only a personal rebirth, but the rebirth of community of which she is the most illustrious member. Moreover, it unites d'Urfé's three principal couples, or at least the three shepherdesses—Astrée, Phillis and Diane—in a relationship of mutual self-disclosure by virtue of which they become the nucleus of a privileged society of lovers predicated precisely on an exchange of autobiographical narratives. Thereafter, exiles and pilgrims come to the Forez from all corners of Gaul, and each new arrival establishes himself as a social subject by submitting his personal story for arbitration by the group whose ideals the shepherdesses, and most particularly Astrée herself, embody. The confession is not a self-validating form of speech whose author and object is the speaking subject, but rather an institutionalized rite of passage for membership in a community whose collective gaze legitimizes the identity of each individual.

I. Liminal Discourse and Decentered Origins:
The Ambiguous Birth of Love

D'Urfé's presentation of the "birth of love" throughout the work in the polemical discourses, intercalated tales, and the frame narrative, reflects a crisis of origins engendered by the liminality of the baroque sign. In the early modern period, an intensification of subjective self awareness invalidated the metaphysical adequation between the subject and the symbolic order before the theoretical formulation of the transcendental ego had established the subject as an autonomous horizon of discursive reference. If, in the traditional object-centered paradigm, signs disclose an ontologically real relation between lover and beloved; and in the emergent, modern view, they represent the irreducible will of the autonomous subject; in the intermediate or "baroque" view which predominates between about 1580 and 1660, they neither "signify" nor "represent," but constitute an arbitrary and self-reflexive struc-ture both determining, and determined by, subjective desire. Astrée's descrip-tion of the birth of love in the "Histoire d'Astrée et Phillis" is a paradigmatic case. She simultaneously rejects traditional metaphysical sources of identity, and deconstructs the emergent ideal of subjective self-presence. While the first negation reflects the intensification of subjective self-consciousness with which modernity begins, the second results from the fact that signs, suspended between objective and subjective horizons of reference—neither pheno-menological reflections of a divine idea, nor yet representations of private consciousness—emerge as a generative force with the power to construct their objects, including the primary object at issue in *L'Astrée*: personal identity.

A brief comparison of models of psychological causation developed in didactic discourses throughout *L'Astrée* will enable us to establish with greater clarity the peculiarly baroque features of the explanation of the birth of love in the "Histoire d'Astrée et Phillis." The traditional and the emergent modes of conceptualization are placed in opposition to each other in a passage which, though it appears late in the narrative, accurately reflects alternatives relevant to the whole:

> Quelques-uns soutiennent que l'amour ne vient pas de *sympathie*, ni de *destin*, mais de *dessein*, et de *volonté*, et que la naissance de cette affection ne se doit qu'à la violence avec laquelle la beauté tyrannise les puissances de notre âme. (IV, 490)

Sympathy and destiny evoke a theory of causation according to which personal identity is a function of an individual's location in an objective order. A crude form of the model appears in the myth of magnets, attributed by Celadon to Silvandre, which explains the birth of love as the consequence of a random distribution of magnetic stones among souls prior to their corporeal embodiment. Because each soul has been touched by a magnet possessed by another, and each possesses a magnet by which another has been touched, they are drawn by an intuitive attraction toward their divinely ordained partners (I, 387). The discourses on sympathies, which we have already examined in another context, develop a theory of psychological causation that replaces arbitrary fatality with a comprehensive theory of personal identity based on astrological influences. Adamas envisions character—all traits that compose an individual's personality, such as affinities, antipathies—as the consequence of a mark imprinted on the substance of the soul by the "pure intelligence de la planète qui domine lors qu'il est né" (III, 263-4). Literally inscribed or impressed upon it as a kind of metaphysical calligraphy, the soul's "caractère" functions as an indelible sign of its place in an objective order composed of the nine planets and the humors and dispositions associated with each. In this view, souls are drawn "par un instinct qui se veut dire aveugle" to others born under the influence of the same planet, and to whom they are bound by an inherent resemblance, or "conformité des êtres" (III, 264). Although love is predestined, it is not coercive in the sense of being imposed upon the lover from without, because the principle that determines amorous attraction is intrinsic, and to act upon it is to actualize a latent potential—to fulfill a teleological purpose. Like a compass needle drawn toward the north star because the needle and the star are composed of like substance, the lover yearns toward his mistress as toward the completion of his own being: "Toute partie" Silvandre says in a later discourse, "recherche de se rejoindre à son tout" (II, 98).

At the other extreme from teleology in its various forms, "dessein et volonté" encompass explanations based on a subject-centered psychology ranging from the merely irrational impulses of "volonté" as an irreducible, self-validating principle of identity, to the highly rational, but self-seeking consciousness required for the execution of a pre-meditated and self-serving "dessein." More perfectly exemplified in practice than formulated in theory, these alternatives presuppose the freedom of subjective consciousness from *a priori* constraints. We have already seen that Hylas asserts the priority of experience to words, and asserts control over discourse in the episode of his amorous contract with Stelle. Calling himself a "marchand de paroles," he views the lover's vow as the transparent representation of a subjective intention, offered in exchange for the vows of other equally free and self-determining individuals, and not, as in the traditional view, an acknowledgement after the fact of a metaphysically necessary, or ontologically real, relation.

Between an innatism which subordinates the subject to an objective metaphysical and symbolic order, and a contractualism which presupposes the autonomy of subjective consciousness—in short, between destiny and will—an intermediate position appears in which interior privacy and arbitrary (that is, historically contingent) symbolic structures are interdependent and reciprocal centers of causation. The lottery of love at the court of Marcilly captures the situation in a concrete image. In the "Histoire de Leonide," Silvie recalls that Clidaman, prince of the Forez,

> fit un serviteur à toutes les nymphes, et cela non point par élection, mais
> par sort; par ce qu'ayant mis tous les noms des nymphes dans un vase,
> et tous ceux des jeunes chevaliers dans l'autre, devant toute l'as-
> semblée, il prit la plus jeune d'entre nous, et le plus jeune d'entr'eux:
> au fils il donna le vase des nymphes, et à la fille celui des chevaliers.
> (I, 76)

At variance with both the calligraphy of "pure intelligence" in which
signs inherently reveal an essential and providentially determined self, and the
lover's contract in which they transparently reflect an autonomous and self-
enclosed intentionality, the decrees of the lottery compose an autonomous
structure without any extra-discursive referent whatever. Public identity becomes the function of a symbolic system in which the relation between the sign
(the names in the vase) and the self (the individuals whose social relations they
establish) is neither that of "signification," nor of "representation," but of
disjunction and paradox. It is precisely this feature of the lottery to which
Silvie calls our attention, and which we expect both delighted and tormented
the baroque imagination:

> Or de ceux qui furent ainsi donnés, les uns servirent par apparence, les
> autres par leur volonté ratifierent à ces belles la donation que le hazard
> leur avait fait d'eux, et ceux qui s'en déffendirent le mieux, furent ceux
> qui auparavant avaient déjà conçu quelque affection. (76)

Because the external marks that designate the subject's public identity are not
guaranteed to correspond to the inner truth of the self, many serve, in the spirit
of Montaignian expediency, "par apparence" alone, while retaining secret
reserves of inward freedom. When signs *do* express subjective reality, it is
either by coincidence, or because the sign itself engenders (rather than reflects
or reveals) desire. The first scenario approximates the structure of a discourse
of objective reference, but reduces it to the status of a game. Those who enjoy
an accidental accord between private desire and public appearance are able to
serve without revealing their personal emotional investment because in the
eyes of others, they are merely acting a part. As in *trompe-l'oeil* painting, the
most realistic presentation is equated with the very height of artificiality. The
second scenario is the most disturbingly subversive because it suggests that
signs which neither "signify" an *a priori* truth, nor "represent" a subjective

one, impose upon the subject an arbitrary, discursively constructed reality, undermining the possibility of personal authenticity.

The disjunction of sign and self is the central feature of Astrée's account of the birth of love. She announces at the beginning of her tale that her experience contradicts received opinion about the origins of love, and by implication, of personal identity as a whole. Hatred and love, she promises, will be quite unexpectedly individualized, and placed in opposition to an external order—in this case identified with paternal authority—which would traditionally be expected to direct the passions toward predictable objects.

> Ceux qui pensent que les amitiés et les haines passent de père en fils, s'ils savaient quelle a été la fortune de Celadon et de moi avoueraient sans doute qu'ils se sont bien fort trompés. Car, belle Diane, je crois que vous avez souvent oui dire la vieille inimitié d'entre Alcé et Hippolyte, mes père et mère, et Alcippe et Amarillis, père et mère de Celadon, leur haine les ayant accompagné jusques au cercueil, qui a été cause de tant de troubles entre les bergers de cette contrée que je m'asseure qu'il n'y a personne qui l'ignore le long des rives du cruel et diffame Lignon. Et toutesfois il sembla qu'Amour, pour montrer sa puissance, voulut expressement de personnes tant ennemies en unir deux si étroittement, que rien n'en peut rompre les liens que la mort. (I, 111)

Were we to read this passage anachronistically from the vantage point of a modern, subject-centered psychology, we might conclude that d'Urfé wishes to call attention to the redemptive and unifying power of romantic love in a society where possessive self-interest has destroyed communal values. In the midst of the early modern paradigm shift, however, Astrée's point is quite the reverse. Far from integrating the community, love occasions an experience of subjective interiority which invalidates the conventional symbolic order. The public roles Astrée and Celadon are expected to assume originate not in the authority of a metaphysical *a priori*, but in the amorous rivalries of the previous generation which longevity and force of habit have made a part of local tradition ingrained indelibly in the consciousness of the region's inhabitants. At the same time, their own experience of love would seem, by contrast, to provide an authentic center of identity and meaning in opposition to an official code whose arbitrary, and ultimately subjective, origins have been decisively exposed.

The claim that paternal authority has lost its relevance to the inward reality of the self does not entirely situate the principal love affair in the current of causal explanation that grants the psychological autonomy of the subject, and posits signs in a representational role. The balance of Astrée's account of the birth of love reveals that the invalidation of metaphysical guarantees of meaning not only constitutes a gain for self-determination, but renders the lovers vulnerable to the influence of discourses projected by the self-interested imaginations of others. The two currents of causation represented by subjective impulse and arbitrary discourse are intimately intertwined throughout Astrée's account of the "birth of love." Celadon and Astrée each desire to see the other long before the opportunity arises, inspired by rumors each hears about the other.

> [Celadon] en avait conçu le désir longtemps auparavant par le rapport que l'on lui avait fait de moi. [...] Et faut que j'avoue, que je ne crois pas qu'il en eut plus de volonté que moi; car je ne sais pourquoi, lors que j'oyais parler de luy, le coeur me tressaillait en l'estomach. (I, 112)

But the reports they hear and assimilate are not sufficient in themselves to engender love, but only to prepare the way for the visceral attraction that grips them both, and defies rational explanation, at their first encounter:

> Or soudain qu'il me vid, je ne sais comment il trouva sujet d'amour en moi, tant y a que depuis ce temps il se résolut de m'aimer, et de me servir, et sembla qu'à cette première vue nous fussions l'un et l'autre sur le point qu'il nous fallait aimer, puis qu'aussitôt qu'on me dit que c'était le fils d'Alcippe, je ressentis un certain changement en moi, qui n'était pas ordinaire. (I, 112)

On the one hand, a predisposition originating in rumors, or reports, and on the other, an inscrutable inwardness—a "volonté," a "désir," a "tressaillement du coeur," "un changement en moi"—leaving the question of causation permanently in doubt.

The decentering of subjective consciousness by discourse also figures prominently in the origins of Phillis' love for Lycidas. Phillis conceptualizes personal identity in terms of a deep interiority that cannot be fathomed or grasped, existing independently of any supra-personal order: "Mais voyez que c'est de notre inclination. Je reconnaissais bien que la nature avait en quelque sorte advantagé Celadon par dessus Lycidas; toutesfois sans en pouvoir dire la raison, Lycidas m'était beaucoup plus agréable" (124). "Inclination" is an irreducible inward impulse which stands in opposition to determining structures represented diversely by "nature," the socially imposed "parental enmities," or metaphysical forces such as the mythical "magnets," and "planetary intellects."

Astrée's recollection of the same events, however, leaves little room for an authentic, primordial "inclination," and suggests instead that Phillis' love for Lycidas, and his for her, are both engendered by the desires and strategic machinations of others. Admiring "deux belles et sages bergères," Phillis and Diane, Celadon encourages Lycidas to take one of them as his mistress (I, 124). Even the choice between the two, far from being a free expression of personal desire, reflects the imperative of preserving the integrity of a closed social group: "Et d'autant que j'avais encore fort peu de connaissance de vous, belle Diane," Astrée recalls, "je lui repondis, que *je désirerais plutôt qu'il servist Phillis*" (I, 124). Just as the birth of love is externally determined, so is the pace and progress of courtship. Astrée proceeds to create opportunities that bring the future lovers together, and takes full credit for the outcome: "Et *il advint ainsi que je le souhaitais*, car l'ordinaire conversation qu'il eut avec elle à mon occasion, produisit au commencement de la familiarité entr'eux, et en fin de l'amour à bon escient" (I, 124). Finally, Lycidas' declaration of love gains credence because others attest to his sincerity. Astrée elicits Phillis' promise that "puis que je voulais qu'elle receust Lycidas, qu'elle m'obeyrait lors qu'elle reconnaitrait qu'il l'aimerait *ainsi que je disais*" (I, 128). Phillis' eventual trust is an effect of her friend's deft mediation: "Après plusieurs repliques d'un côté et d'autre, *nous fimes de sorte que Lycidas fut reçu*" (I, 128). [Emphasis mine.]

II. Self-Disclosure and Subversive Play

Astrée's account of the second pivotal event in the *progrès d'amour*, the declaration, explores the tension between subjective interiority and conventional symbolic structures in the domain of self-representation. The episode may be divided into two parts. The first, dominated by Celadon, unfolds over the course of three consecutive days at the Festival of Venus, while the second, dominated by Astrée, takes place immediately following the festival in "un lieu écarté." That Celadon chooses to make his declaration in the ritual setting of a public festival, and Astrée to express her acceptance of his service in the unstructured setting of the forest, in itself reveals the central difference between their respective relations to the symbolic order. Although each experiences an "interior distance" from conventional institutions and modes of discourse, Celadon continues to apprehend and represent himself within and through them, while Astrée positions herself as autonomous author of her own identity, and the hidden manipulator of signs.

My analysis will demonstrate that neither Celadon's conservatism nor Astrée's modernity fulfill the requirements of a coherent epistemological paradigm. Although Celadon continues to interpret his experience through the grid of an object-centered structure of signifying relations—a structure in which self-representation requires the sacrifice of the ego to an ideal that pre-exists and predetermines the self—he establishes a limited autonomy within the conventional symbolic order by transgressing against prescribed forms of speech and gesture. Still more radically, he unhinges that order from its metaphysical foundations, making Astrée herself, rather than the transcendent goodness and beauty she embodies, the determining origin and teleological destiny of every act. The consequences of this permutation are far-reaching, and shall be examined in detail in due course. Astrée, for her part, expresses her inward "franchise" at this early moment in their affair not in terms of a discourse of transparent self-reference, but only by employing conventional symbolic structures as a means of self-concealment. Like the courtiers who participate in Clidaman's lottery, she either displays her subjective feelings *as though* she were feigning, thus reducing "representation" to the status of a game, or pays lip-service to authorities in which she no longer inwardly believes.

In order to situate Celadon's performances at the Festival of Venus in the context of an epistemological paradigm shift, it will be helpful to recall both the socializing function and the epistemological structure of ritual play in medieval aristocratic society—the entirety of which, Johan Huizinga tells us, was organized like a noble game.[1] In *Homo Ludens*, Huizinga's analysis of "the play element in culture" suggests that play, defined broadly to include all forms of ritual and ceremonial performance, is predicated on precisely the object-centered structure of signifying relations that d'Urfé's generation was at the point of leaving behind forever. Dances, games, religious ceremonies, and even war, are symbolic structures in which the relation between signs and what they signify is inherent rather than arbitrary, and in which the successful articulation of meaning requires the total sacrifice of subjective autonomy. At a purely practical level the rules of a game, or the ceremonial code, demand absolute obedience. At a deeper level, obedience signifies a sacrifice of the ego by which the player's identity becomes a function of social and cosmic order of which the game or rite is but a model. In ritual, Huizinga writes, "representation is really *identification*, the mystic repetition or *re-presentation* of the event. [...] The function of the rite, therefore, is far from being merely imitative; it causes the worshippers to participate in the sacred happening itself."[2] It is "through this playing that society expresses its interpretation of life and the world,"[3] and it is through play in its higher forms that "man's consciousness that he is embedded in a sacred order of things finds its first, highest, and holiest expression."[4]

At the Festival of Venus, Celadon's mode of self-disclosure exhibits not only the obedience to an objective order characteristic of play in the Middle Ages, but also the intensification of individual consciousness characteristic of early modernity. He faithfully executes his role as a ritual subject in three ideologically interdependent and interlocking performances (a dance, a foot-race and a beauty contest), which evoke three mutually reinforcing and progressively expanding horizons of meaning (the sentimental, the social, and the metaphysical) reinforced by three literary codes (Petrarchan, chivalric and mythical). Yet, the disclosure of personal identity entails at every moment a complex interplay between the ritual code—prescribed gestures and their collectively ratified meanings—and the idiosyncrasies of his performance. Minor, sometimes almost imperceptible transgressions permit Celadon's personal intentions to appear within the impersonal ceremonial machinery, attenuating the 'objective' status of social and metaphysical order it represents, while remaining within the boundaries it imposes.

Celadon's preliminary declaration of love situates the sentimental exchange between private persons (flirtatious gestures, a stolen kiss, a coy conversation) within the ludic space of a "branle," a medieval folkdance in which the entire community participates as a single body. Successive layers of structure impose a vast interpersonal distance between the lovers as private subjects. Their encounters occur, or at least appear to occur, as a consequence of the prescribed performance of impersonal gestures, and though the dance permits a brief exchange, it constrains them at last to "return to their places." Celadon initiates conversation indirectly, through Corilas, Astrée's official escort, and the content of his speech consists in the elaboration of the conceit of amorous combat, taken over from Petrarchan love poetry, which bestows upon the lover and the beloved pre-established roles: Celadon hazards his heart in combat with a cruel mistress whose divinity not only empowers her to reduce him to despair but to exercise clemency which, without compromising her claim to absolute power, constitutes a paradoxical victory for the lover. "En tel combat," Celadon remarks, "être vaincu c'est une espèce de victoire" (I, 114).

The second declaration takes place in the context of a festal athletic contest. Celadon wins in the category most appropriate to a faithful suitor, the footrace (his characteristic virtue is patience, and running is a feat of endurance), and presents his trophy, a garland of flowers, to Astrée. A contest of physical endurance, strength or agility is no less constrained by rules than a dance, but because it takes place in the public space of the sports arena, it intensifies the social, or collective meaning of every gesture. The conferral of "prix aux divers exercices" bestows a supra-personal social status upon the contestants by rendering individuals exemplary of a class. Astrée's account emphasizes the importance of the collective gaze as a ground of identity, and completely omits elements that would personalize the contest as an enhancement of an individual ego. The crown of flowers "lui fut mise sur la tête par toute l'assemblée, avec beaucoup de louange, qu'étant si jeune il eut vaincu tant d'autres bergers" (I, 114), and Celadon presents his trophy to Astrée in full view of the assembled spectators (I, 114). While the Petrarchan imagery informing the conversation at the dance reduces love to its sentimental dimension, the chivalric values that underlie Celadon's act of homage to his lady call attention to love's dependency on the collectively acknowledged worth of the lovers—Celadon "eut vaincu tant d'autre bergers"—and on the collective aspiration for social order. A union between Astrée and Celadon would put an end to "vieilles inimitiés" (I, 114).

The third day of the Festival of Venus centers around the dramatic re-enactment of the story of Paris and the apple of discord. Three shepherdesses (Astrée, Malthée, and Stelle) chosen to represent the goddesses in the myth (Venus, Minerva and Juno) enter the Temple de la Beauté to be judged by a fourth who plays the role of Paris. Mediated by the prescribed gestures of a ritual drama, Celadon's third and final declaration assimilates the lovers to mythical figures, and introduces a stratum of metaphysical meaning.

The divestment of individuating features of identity that enables players to accede to the place prepared for them within a supra-personal order finds its most vivid expression, perhaps, in the assumption of ritual disguise. Here, the lovers forego their private desires in order to take positions as exemplary subjects in a cosmic drama. Care has been taken to eliminate any appetitive or egocentric element from the performance: the contestants are chosen by a religious authority, "le grand Druide," and the judge is selected by that most depersonalizing of methods, the drawing of lots. Moreover, at least one autho-rized departure from the original story, the representation of Paris by a shepherdess, seems calculated to preclude erotic self-interest.

In contrast to the dance and the games which take place in public, the mythical drama unfolds in secret, in the sacred space of the Temple. Secrecy in this instance, however, should not be taken as an affirmation of private meaning, but as an indication that the true spectators of the drama are not mortals but gods. The *locus* of the gaze that confers identity and meaning is no longer to be found with the lovers themselves, as at the dance, nor with the assembled community as at the athletic contest, but in the heavens. Discourse in both its private and social modalities is ultimately grounded, under the traditional paradigm, in the structure of being itself.

Finally, the literary code that governs the intersubjective meaning of the performance is not to be found in a literal reading of the pagan legend, but in the allegorically mediated form it acquires within the neoplatonic thematics of *L'Astrée*. As Paris and Venus, Celadon and Astrée represent mortal and divine natures, matter and spirit. The reciprocal, interactive element of the adjudica-tory process that engages the judge in dialogue with the contestants inevitably suggests the metaphysical interaction of matter and spirit, body and soul—a tirelessly reiterated theme in *L'Astrée*'s polemical debates.

Each of the performances contains all three horizons of meaning—sub-jective sentiment, the social ideal, and the metaphysical tension between body and spirit, the erotic and the mystical polarities of love—but in each case, one of the three predominates, bringing the others into its sphere. At the dance, the "querelle des pères" and the putative divinity of the mistress serve only as supports to the development of the Petrarchan conceit of the combat of hearts. At the athletic games, the sentimental and metaphysical horizons of meaning are circumscribed within the social. The sentimental inflection Celadon gives his act of courtly homage—"Voici qui reconfirme ce que je vous ai dit," he says to Astrée in presenting the garland—is overshadowed by the social interpretation that preoccupies Astrée's aunt: "Artemis, qui désirait plutôt d'assoupir que de r'allumer ces vieilles inimitiés, me commanda de la recevoir" (I, 114). The metaphysical order figures only implicitly in the virtues and vices associated with the various contests: wrestling (moral struggle), running (endurance or fidelity), jumping (inconstancy).[5]

Finally, the sentimental, social and metaphysical currents converge and achieve their highest degree of integration in the enactment of the Paris myth where subjective and social experience alike find their ultimate justification in a conception of cosmic order. The sentimental horizon of meaning appears most forcefully in the overt eroticism of the scene in which Celadon contemplates his mistress clad only in a semi-transparent veil. At the same time, he has become an instrument by which the community will bestow a status distinction, the "prix de la beauté." Finally, a spiritual identity encompasses and harmonizes both his subjective desire and his social role. In the temple Celadon is neither the deceitful shepherd he objectively is, nor the exemplary shepherdess (Orithie) he pretends to be, but Paris, a representative mortal contemplating divine beauty.

The rules governing play in Huizinga's view are always "ready-made." They pre-exist the individual performer and command his or her total assent. The relation between the subject and the symbolic edifice is more ambiguous, however, in *L'Astrée*. By the mere fact of participation it would seem that the shepherds and shepherdesses subjectively ratify the rules or order that govern play, but Celadon also continually innovates in a manner that displaces structure ever so slightly in the direction of subjective desire. An expressive element in his manner of playing militates against the static, 'found' order and threatens to subvert it by shifting the horizon of symbolic reference from the suprapersonal to the private. Ritual playing—which composes a self-enclosed system of signifiers—oscillates ambiguously between internal and external, subjective and objective, centers of meaning.

Astrée's narrative continually calls attention to Celadon's employment of artifice in excess of the prescribed playing of ritual performance, enumerating transgressions or abuses that might seem to imply an appropriation of external structure for private ends. He manipulates the formalized movements of the dance with "tant d'artifice" that he gains Astrée as his partner "comme par mégarde." "Faisant semblant" to kiss his own hand (apparently a courteous gesture) he kisses Astrée on the mouth, and "feignant" to speak confidentially to Corilas he declares his love to Astrée (I, 113). Later, presenting the garland, he transgresses social expectation by paying homage to the daughter of his father's enemy. The most aggressive violations, however, occur in the temple episode, where Celadon subverts the intended, depersonalizing function of ritual disguise in order to step out of his prescribed role, and manipulate the other players from an undisclosed subject-position. Under the pretense of being a woman, he enters the Temple in flagrant violation of the law, and extracts the unsuspecting Astrée's promise to love and accept him as a suitor (I, 116). Celadon alone possesses a measure of identity in excess of that imposed by the drama. He alone has carved out for himself a niche of autonomy from which to regard the other players as objects. He alone has arrogated subjectivity to himself, setting himself up as an horizon of reality in competition with the gaze of the gods.

Celadon's double disguise is emblematic of his relation to the symbolic order in general. While his primary (authorized) disguise as Paris empties him of individuality, and marks his participation in an objective order of being, his secondary (unauthorized) disguise as Orithie establishes a degree of autonomy, and provides a position from which he can manipulate the culturally and metaphysically prescribed identity reflected in ritual action and speech. Having secured a kind of "interior distance" from the order of conventional signs, however, he continues to express himself through them so that the final relation is ambiguous and interactive.

Nevertheless, Celadon's subjective autonomy is constrained at every moment by the inevitable unfolding of the mythical narrative. His designs on Astrée and his role as Paris inter-penetrate each other at every point. As Paris, it is Celadon's role to gaze upon the naked beauties, and to demand a bribe: "Il fallait que chacune à part allast parler à lui, et faire offre tout ainsi que les trois déesses avaient fait autrefois à Paris" (I, 115). Moreover, it is precisely where the pagan myth seems to impose an unequal power relation that Celadon innovates, transforming objectification into a quest for mutuality. If he solicits an "offre" that would "rendre votre juge affectionné" (I, 116), and if Astrée expresses her reluctance to "séduire mon juge par mes paroles," it soon becomes apparent that he seeks neither a bribe, nor a supplicating speech, but a promise of reciprocity.

The ultimate proof of Celadon's submission to the external order, however, is that he abandons his voyeuristic and objectifying subject position. The moment he reveals his true identity, he reestablishes himself as a co-player with Astrée in a drama that he does not control, but rather of which he is but a part. Rather than require Astrée's capitulation as a passive object to his possessive, self-seeking desire, he seeks only her affective ratification of the *a priori* structure that embraces them both. "Scachez que ce que vous m'avez promis, c'est de m'aimer plus que personne du monde, et me recevoir pour votre fidèle serviteur, qui suis Celadon, et non pas Orithie, comme vous pensez" (I, 116).

Far from destroying the intersubjective order by supplanting it with a merely subjective and private meaning, these innovations permit the subject to appear as subject within the confines of an otherwise deadening structure. Both his erotic voyeurism and his deceitful extraction of a vow are variations on the ritual, displacing it in the direction of subjective desire without destroying it, or refusing to play within it.[6] It is precisely because he conforms so nearly to the pre-established pattern that he must supplement each performance with an unmistakably gratuitous, transgressive gesture, for only then will he prevent the effects of inward volition from being entirely attributed to the machinery of an impersonal order. Even the deceit he perpet-rates against Astrée serves only to bring into the open a sentimental truth that Astrée had permitted to remain invisible beneath the perfunctory gestures of ritual action, since, by her own later admission, she really does love him.

Finally, it must be noted that ritual speech no less than ritual gesture facilitates the identification of the subject with a supra-personal order. For the subject who finds his inward truth writ large in the concrete writing of things, and declared yet again in the social and religious institutions of his culture, the function of language is not to represent an inward private truth, nor to refer objectively to the empirical features of external objects, but to clarify, by rendering more explicit, a network of signifying relations in which all phenomena, inward and outward, are mutually involved. Throughout the Festival of Venus Celadon employs speech to interpret phenomena with reference to an order in which they already function as signs. Speech possesses a status in relation to things which, according to Foucault, dominated medieval and Renaissance theory:

> Knowledge therefore consisted in relating one form of language to another form of language; in restoring the great, unbroken plain of words and things; in making everything speak. That is, in bringing into being at a level above that of all marks, the secondary discourse of commentary. The function proper to knowledge is not seeing or demonstrating; it is interpreting.[7]

As an instrument of self-disclosure, Celadon's speech functions as a commentary on the external, visible symbols through which he apprehends his identity, and not, in the manner of objective reference, as a transparent glass through which the mistress peers into the secret recesses of his inner being. The kiss, the garland and the golden apple each possess and harmonize a double signified, one of which lies within the subject, and the other in the social symbolic order. At one and the same time they deliver the lover's identity from its place of concealment and impose upon it an intersubjective meaning provided by the cultural code they activate. They are both subjective epiphanies and articulations of law. Celadon's commentary on the wreath of flowers renders explicit the sentimental meaning: "Voici qui reconfirme ce que je vous ai dit" (I, 114), while the visible gesture already functions within the chivalric code. His commentary on the golden apple is more complete, emphasizing by turns each of the three levels of meaning: publicly he presents the apple "en témoignage" that Astrée possesses "le prix de la beauté" (I, 117). Like Celadon's victory wreath, the apple is a visible sign of the recipient's inherent nature. Astrée already possesses the "prix," the worth or value, that determines her place in relation to her peers, which the apple merely discloses. Celadon's whispered commentary to Astrée, by contrast, indicates both the sentimental and metaphysical levels of meaning, uniting his declaration of love with an invocation of universal order: "Recevez cette pomme pour gage de mon affection, qui est toute infinie comme elle est toute ronde"

(I, 117). Interpretive commentary accompanies Celadon's actions as well: his violation of the law prohibiting men from the Temple, for example, is a "témoignage de mon affection" (I, 116).

Celadon's subversion of the traditional semiotic paradigm appears not in an arrogation of subjective autonomy to himself, but in a tendency to sacrifice his own subjectivity to that of the beloved. This, in fact, is an equally profound departure from the complementarity of souls provided for within the traditional ontological and symbolic structure. While the ultimate orientation of the chivalric lover's words and deeds had been a metaphysical reality of which the mistress herself was but a sign, Celadon elevates Astrée's ego itself to the status of an absolute. She becomes the determining origin of his identity, and the supreme good toward which his actions tend. But because relationships of identity (as opposed to alterity and exchange) are either metaphysical or narcissistic—they can, I think, be explained in no other way—chivalric self-effacement becomes an expression of absolute self-love at the very moment when the lover ceases to recognize the transcendental orientation of his quest. Or, to say the same thing in a slightly different way: By insisting upon a relation of identity after having denied the authority of the ontological order upon which that relation depends, the chivalric lover merely appropriates the mistress as a mirror image of himself, and by doing so renders every act of heroic sacrifice self-regarding. Such deeds, as one wise character explains, express not our love for the other, but rather, "l'amour que nous nous portons" (IV, 246–47).

The discovery of 'narcissistic cathexis' is, I would suggest, one of the most 'modern' of the underlying themes in d'Urfé's critique of the chivalric code. It explains, moreover, why the affirmation of subjective autonomy in *L'Astrée* manifests itself not only in terms of egocentric self-assertion as one would logically expect (e.g. in characters like Hylas, Polemas, and Astrée all of whom, in spite of their differences, are fundamentally self-affirming), but in terms of an imperative of self-annihilation (e.g. in characters like Celadon, Tircis and Ligdamon).

Clearly, for Celadon, erotic desire engenders not a possessiveness that subordinates the other to the self, but the collapse of the self into the identity of the other. Throughout the festival, he fulfills his promise to reveal through signal actions "quel je suis," hazarding first his heart (the lovers' combat), then his reputation (the public competition), and finally his life (his illegal penetration of the temple). His deeds not only place the lovers outside the boundaries of suprapersonal authority—men are prohibited from entering the Temple de la Beauté—but by doing so produce a situation in which he depends on Astrée for his very life. Were she to reveal his transgression he would be summarily stoned to death. The conversations that follow the temple episode confirm the tendency toward individuation that transforms the ontological "conformité des êtres" into a narcissistic appropriation of the other as an idealized self: "Il n'y a ni rigueur de votre cruauté, ni inimitié de nos pères, ni empêchement de l'univers ensemble, qui me puisse divertir de ce dessein" (I, 119). And again, when Astrée reminds him of the obedience he owes Alcippe (his father), Celadon absolves himself of filial duty on the ground that hers is the supreme authority: "Je choisirai plutôt de faillir envers lui, qui n'est qu'un homme, qu'envers votre beauté qui est divine" (I, 120).

From the outset Astrée assumes an entirely different relation to the extrinsic structures embodied in social performance, myth and language. If Celadon affirms the subjective validity of ritualized gesture and speech and finds in them a means of self-disclosure, Astrée experiences them as an alien order, entirely dissociated from her 'true' identity, and employs them as a means of self-concealment. As in the case of the courtiers faced with the arbitrary determinations of Clidaman's lottery, the accidental agreement between her prescribed roles in the dance, the games and the Paris myth serves to mask rather than reveal subjective desire by permitting her expressions of favor to appear as perfunctory gestures imposed by an impersonal structural machinery. She dances with Celadon as protocol requires while "faisant semblant de ne le connaître pas" (I, 113), she accepts his homage at the athletic games "si froidement, que chacun jugea bien, que ce n'avait été que par l'ordonnance de ma tante" (I, 114), and as Venus she kisses him only "parce que c'estait la coutume, que celle qui recevait la pomme, baisait le juge pour remerciement" (I, 117). As we have seen, however, she declines to expose Celadon's transgression, placing herself with him in violation of the law. She presents an appearance of slavish conformity only in order to consolidate her autonomy and control from behind the scenes.

These characteristics of Astrée's relation to the established symbolic order appear in the exchange that takes place between the lovers in the "lieu sauvage" where Celadon, immediately after the Festival of Venus, retreats to lament her cruel indifference to his advances. Removed from the public sphere and the direct supervision of social authority in all of its symbolic manifesta-tions, she permits Celadon for the first time to glimpse her inward feelings, completing the early phase of courtship, and establishing a momentary equilibrium between the characters.

Having refused to acknowledge the subjective validity of the various social performances in which she participates at the Festival of Venus, she graduates to an active production of her identity by means of a parodic inversion of the cultural myths—most particularly that of feminine passivity. Overtly submissive to the authority of the fathers and to the priority of mas-culine desire, she retains interior reserves of autonomy which become the center of her identity, and give all of her actions and words their true, though hidden, meaning. Externally, filial duty outweighs not only her ability to act upon, but even to experience an inward feeling: "Ressouviens toi, berger, de l'inimitié de nos pères, et croi que celle que je te porterai ne leur cédera en rien" (I, 118). She carefully avoids appearing in an active or initiating role, and grants Celadon the responsibility of establishing the "ends" of their relation-ship within the boundaries set by the fathers: "Mais quoi, berger, quelle fin aura votre dessein, puis que ceux qui vous peuvent rendre tel qu'il leur plait, le desapprouvent?" (I, 119)

At the same time, however, she courts Celadon in spite of her father's prohibition, she seizes control of the drama in which she and Celadon now take their places, skillfully managing its pace and turning points so that Celadon's agency is but an illusion he enjoys at her pleasure. A series of dramatic reversals unfolds at her discretion—she rebukes him, he despairs, she seeks him out, he approaches her, she rebukes him, he pleads his case, she relents.

Her power is absolute. Her feigned anger produces a transformation in Celadon so radical that "en peu de jours il devint presque méconnaissable" (I, 118). Knowing full well that she alone can restore him to his former self, she allows him to languish until his absence becomes inconvenient. Upon finding him in his retreat, she lingers over the image of his helplessness: "Je le vis couché en terre de son long, et les yeux tous moites de larmes, si tendus contre le ciel, qu'ils semblaient immobiles" (I, 118). His immobility, and the visibility of his love in his very posture, provides a fitting contrast to the mobility with which she assumes alternative disguises in order to protect, even now when it would seem unnecessary, her inward self from view, thereby securing her position as voyeur and master of the unfolding drama.

> Ne voulant point lui faire paraître que je le voulusse rechercher, je me retirai assez loin de là, où, faisant semblant de ne prendre garde à lui, je me mis a chanter si haut, que ma voix parvint jusques à ses aureilles. Aussitôt qu'il m'ouit, je vis qu'il se releva en sursaut. (I, 119)

When Astrée prefaces the end of her account of these events by announcing her capitulation—"enfin étant vaincue" etc.—we know that suspense has been an illusion, and the outcome fixed in advance, at once for Diane and Phillis entranced by the tale, for d'Urfé's readers, and for Celadon.

It might be argued that Astrée, in so far as she allows Celadon the illusion of agency, is herself submitting to a cultural narrative that fixes active masculinity in structural opposition to feminine passivity, and dooms the female partner to lie inertly, awaiting the animating kiss of a man whose gaze confers identity upon her and becomes the horizon of her existence. If the story of Sleeping Beauty is based on a cultural myth that constructs gender along such lines, it is also possible to see the degree to which Astrée enacts an ironic parody of that myth, demonstrating its irrelevance to her inner truth. In effect, Astrée, as the "sleeping beauty," summons the prince by design, feigns sleep, and when kissed, merely pretends to be awakened:

> A fin de lui donner commodité de m'approcher, je fis semblant de dormir, et toutesfois je tenais les yeux entr'ouverts pour voir ce qu'il deviendrait, et certes il ne manqua point de faire ce que j'avais pensé. Lors que je faisais semblant d'être le plus assoupie, pour lui donner plus de hardiesse, je sentis qu'après plusieurs soupirs, il se baissa doucement contre ma bouche, et me baisa. Alors me semblant qu'il avait bien assez pris de courage, j'ouvris les yeux, comme m'étant éveillée quand il m'avait touchée. (I, 119)

Unlike Celadon who at the last moment utterly relinquishes his privileged subject position by resituating himself within an order that grasps lover and beloved alike, Astrée sustains her self-concealment, and her control of discourse, unwaveringly. Instead of suddenly revealing that, pained by his absence, she had actively sought him in his place of retreat, elicited his approach and even invited his kiss, she remains in character to the end, permitting herself to be persuaded at length only to modulate her categorical rejection into a reluctant acceptance of his devotion: "Nos discours en fin continuerent si avant, qu'il fallut que je lui permisse d'estre mon serviteur" (I, 120).

Astrée is an original pioneer of subjectivity and of the problems that accompany it for intersubjective meaning. The moment she becomes conscious of an inward autonomy she also discovers the inauthenticity of all those forms of cultural life we are accustomed to calling the symbolic order. Only when the totality of signs comes to be regarded as an inessential crust over the truth of the self, as the material of an institutionalized masquerade, can they serve as instruments for private ends, rather than as reflections of the structure of being. She does not reside within and find her inner truth adequately represented by a pre-determined dramatic structure, but governs it from without. Observing without being observed, controlling without being controlled, Astrée construes Celadon as an object, and herself as the self-enclosed subject, the origin and center of her own identity and meaning.

But she will ultimately discover the tenuousness of her control of discourse when Semire bests her at her own game. He promotes, in the form of a cleverly constructed narrative, an interpretation of her relationship with Celadon which supplants her own perceptions, and becomes, as it were, a new subjective truth. It can only be an indication of the distance that separated those living in the early seventeenth century from a naive faith in the metaphysical foundations of the order of temporal signs that Astrée's own victimization, rather than lead her to renounce the arts of deception, merely elicits regret over having lost control. Even though feigning ultimately results in the lovers' estrangement, she remembers her moment of histrionic triumph with pleasure. She invites us to admire the skill with which every action is suspended between an apparent meaning (indifference) and a true (love). Relishing the memory of "ces agréables discours" (I, 119), Astrée associates them with the very pinnacle of her happiness, at the furthest remove from the "maison desastrée" in which she now resides—a "maison" in which she has (by a sequence of events I will examine shortly) become an inscription in another's narrative.

III. Patience, Prudence and the "Travaux d'Amour"

Astrée devotes the remainder of her narrative to a series of four "travaux d'amour." At the most superficial level, the trials are the consequence of obstacles placed in the lovers' paths by feuding parents and jealous rivals. Alcippe (Celadon's father) hopes to put an end to the affair by sending Celadon to Italy. When the lovers are blissfully reunited after an absence of three years, their difficulties only seem to increase. Internally, they contend with jealousy when each imagines the other to have been unfaithful. External obstacles multiply as well. Alcippe sends Celadon to a neighboring village to be wooed by a prospective spouse, Malthée, while Phocion (Astrée's uncle) plans an arranged marriage between Astrée and Corebe. The deception perpetrated by a cunning rival, Semire, is but the last and most devastating in a series of woes.

D'Urfé's "travaux d'amour" distinctly reflect the crisis of meaning that occurs at a certain moment in the early modern shift from the "preuve" to the "confession" as the dominant means of self-representation. Thus, the trials exemplify the epistemological ambiguity that characterizes the work as a whole, in spite of their surface conventionality. Under the object-centered paradigm, the lover reveals his essential identity and his ontologically real relation to the beloved by submitting to "proofs" of character;[8] under the emergent, subject-centered paradigm, lovers strive for reciprocal self-disclosure in confessional speech. In *L'Astrée*, we are betwixt and between the two paradigms. Words and deeds have been detached from their metaphysical horizon of reference without yet being rendered accountable to an authentic, self-present inward truth. As a result, the lovers inhabit an illusionistic, text-ualized universe in which both the "preuve" and the "confession" are under-mined by the autonomy and opacity of signs.

Astrée herself takes responsibility in her confession for having brought about this state of affairs by deciding, upon Celadon's return from Italy, to abandon his ethic of passive suffering, or "patience," in favor of an ethic of self-interested action, or "prudence."[9] Celadon, she recalls, had endured and even welcomed prolonged separations, the threat of arranged marriages, and other persecutions as a means of self-disclosure: "Au lieu que quelqu'autre eut pris ces contrariétés pour peine, il les recevait pour preuves de soi-même, et les nommait les pierres de touche de sa fidélité" (I, 120). In a letter announcing his return from Italy he names his own characteristic virtue: "Belle Astrée, mon exil a été vaincu de ma patience. [...] Permettez-moi donc que je vous voie, à fin que je puisse raconter ma fortune à celle qui est ma seule fortune" (I, 121). Astrée by contrast regards all of the obstacles to desire, of which absence is but the most severe, as effects of youthful naïveté—"nous n'avions pas encore beaucoup d'artifice pour couvrir nos desseins" (I, 120)—and insists that they take measures to forestall further interference in their private affairs: "Nous commençames de nous conduire avec plus de prudence" (I, 122).

By elevating self-interest to the status of an ethical principle, she leaves the metaphysical and symbolic order of chivalric idealism behind forever, and enters the baroque world of disjunction and paradox where subjective privacy and the symbolic order are irreconcilably opposed. From thence forward, the lovers simultaneously inhabit two discursive domains: the public, where they submit to the established structure of social relationships "par apparence," and the private, where they emulate an ideal of confessional transparency. Forming a conspiratorial alliance with Lycidas (Celadon's brother) and Phillis, they publicly "play the field" in order to forestall suspicion—"pour celer nostre amitié, je le priay, ou plustost je le contraignis de faire cas de toutes les bergères" (I, 122)—while expressing their true feelings in private trysts and letters secretly exchanged—"nous inventasmes plusieurs moyens, fut de nous parler, fut de nous écrire secrettement" (I, 128). The ensuing "travaux" arise, without exception, from the impossibility of maintaining the separation of public discourse from private authenticity. Interior privacy destabilizes the conventional sign, while the sign imposes its own reality on the inner self.

The invalidation of the metaphysical horizon of reference engenders a promiscuous circulation of discourses whose meaning cannot be stabilized in relation to either objective being, or subjective experience, but which instead take on a reality and a solidity of their own by virtue of their currency in the public domain of "apparence" and "opinion." First, there is a constant escape of confessional discourse with the result that every act of self-representation, however guarded, implicates them in an external, public discursive structure. "Il est vrai que pour être trop près du chemin," Astrée says of their trysting place in a cavity in a large rock, "pour peu que notre voix haussat, nous pouvions être ouis de ceux qui allaient et venaient" (I, 129). Conversations uttered in private are frequently, and in spite of every precaution, overheard and circulated, as when Celadon's farewell to Astrée becomes a popular ballad (I, 134). Their letters, which they leave for one another in a hollow oak, or pass to and fro in Celadon's hat, are easily intercepted first by Alcippe (I, 132) and then by Semire (I, 147). At the same time, it proves equally impossible to prevent the invasion of subjective privacy by false reports and rumors which, whether disseminated by the lovers themselves as in the first two "travaux," or concocted by their enemies as in the final two, enmesh the lovers in an illusionistic play of empty signifiers which transform their perceptions of each other, and even coalesce into new subjective truths.

Each trial unfolds as a quest for truth in signs which replicates the epistemological structure of the work as a whole. Ontological "rectification"— an attempt to restore the transparency of signs to a metaphysical order—and subjective "verification"—an attempt to verify the truth with reference to a subjectively present object—are tried and abandoned in favor of collective "adequation."[10] The shared perceptions of the community of lovers emerges as the only reliable horizon of symbolic reference. In almost every instance, moreover, the traditionalist response is associated with the masculine characters, Celadon and Lycidas, and the progressive one with the feminine characters, Astrée and Phillis (the few exceptions seem merely to confirm the rule), with the result that only the third term of the dialectic unites the sexes within a single epistemological perspective.

The first response, characteristic of the faithful shepherds, reflects the influence of the traditional "ontological" problematic for which knowledge is a matter of discerning in the changing surfaces of temporal and spatial experience the imprint of an objective metaphysical order, and of restoring the lost correspondence between the sensible and the intelligible, contingent and subsistent levels of reality. When the mistresses appear to be "volage" or unfaithful, they introduce a paradox into the very structure of being itself which the shepherds attempt to resolve or "rectify" by virtue of their heroic and unilateral fidelity. It is almost as though, by approximating in their own single-mindedness the permanence of absolute being, the shepherds hope to recall the mistresses to the transparency and passivity from which they (the mistresses), by their infidelity, have departed. In every case, however, the shepherds are thwarted because the appearances to which they address their efforts conceal not an ontological presence conjoined, by an inherent resemblance, to themselves, but a private and self-enclosed individual. It is as though their "sympathie" journeys forth in vain not because, as in Adamas' explanation, they have mistaken the identity of the object, but because the world itself is no longer infused with that immanent love upon which the entire system of sympathies had been based.

Once the path to transcendence has been foreclosed by the affirmation of the ego—and this, of course has been the effect of the ethic of "prudence" with which they have complied—the attempt to affirm an ontologically real identity between the lover and the beloved (a "conformité des êtres") can only result in a narcissistic cathexis which transforms the mistress, at least in the imaginary world of fantasy, into a mirror image of the lover's self. The failure of the chivalric quest in this debased and "psychologized" form, rendered inevitable by the irreducible otherness (i.e. the subjective self-enclosure) of the beloved, is one of the most frequently reiterated themes of the lover's lament: "Pensons-nous en l'aimant," Lycidas bewails, "Que nostre amour fidelle puisse jetter en elle quelque seur fondement? Helas! c'est vainement" (I, 126). Celadon is similarly aggrieved and perplexed when confronted with rumors of Astrée's infidelity: "Est il possible que [...] une si entière affection que la mienne, n'ait peu arrester l'inconstance de vostre ame?" (I, 131) It also renders psychologically necessary the pattern of paralysis and retreat with which the faithful shepherds meet every rebuff from their mistresses. Only in the solitude of the "lieux écartés," after all, can the narcissistic identification be sustained without threat of contradiction.

The second response to the "travaux d'amour" is predicated on a "representational" theory of signs, and is generally associated with the female characters. Here, we leave the ceaselessly moving world of the *Essais*, and enter the hallucinatory one of the Cartesian "evil genius." Misrepresentation (or deceit) replaces the otherness of being as the principal source of error, and objective verification replaces ontological rectification as the path to knowledge. The numerous instances in which d'Urfé's shepherds and shepherdesses spy on one another while being spied upon in turn, is an expression of the necessity of penetrating the subjective privacy of the other as a means of verifying the truth of his or her discourse. The emergent, subject-centered paradigm fails, however because d'Urfé does not envision the possibility of a "Cartesian" transcendental *cogito*. The consciousness of the knowing subject is continually decentered from without by arbitrary discursive constructions and from within by intra-psychic passions. On the one hand, the suspicion that even scenes which appear to be spontaneous exteriorizations of the "secret hiding places of the soul" are in fact play-acted leads to an infinitely regressive quest for objectivity which plunges the mistresses into ineradicable doubt. On the other, jealousy causes the mistresses to project a self-generated construction upon events even when they are objectively represented.

In each trial, both traditional "ontological" and modern "representational" conceptions of knowledge are explored and abandoned in favor of a third, historicist paradigm. In the absence of either an over-arching *logos*, or a transcendental ego, meaning can only be a function of collectively established norms of interpretation, and error a derogation from orthodox belief. For this reason, error is frequently attributed to strangers and interlopers. Squilindre, the forgerer, inhabits an outer region both geographically and spiritually: "Demeurant sur les lisières de Forests," Astrée says, he is an "homme fin, et sans foi" (I, 142). His forged letter is even delivered by "un jeune berger inconnu" (I, 143). Semire, likewise, had never been seen in the hamlet before his arrival as part of Corebe's entourage.[11] Truth, on the other hand, is reestablished when a trusted member of the community regains control of discourse.

The following paragraphs examine in greater detail the epistemological structure of each of the four trials in turn. It will be demonstrated that the first three contain all of the semiotic alternatives described above, and are therefore resolved within the context of Astrée's confession. The fourth trial, which results in the estrangement of the principal lovers, exhibits only the two failed responses, and awaits the implementation of the third as the precondition of the reconciliation toward which the entire narrative tends.

The lovers first succumb to doubt when the deceptions they perpetrate to conceal their private affairs succeed so well with their enemies that each begins to suspect the others of genuine infidelity: "Il advint que par succession de temps Celadon même eut opinion que j'aimais Lycidas, et moi je creus qu'il aimait Phillis" (I, 129). The idealist and realist responses to doubt are straightforwardly determined by gender. The love-smitten shepherd is obliged by the courtly code to regard every rebuff as a test of his selfless devotion. The shepherdess, on the other hand, seeks to penetrate deception in order to verify the true inward intentions of her suitor.

Neither the "proofs" provided by suffering silently endured, however, nor confessional discourse between autonomous and self-affirming individuals, restores assurance of reciprocal love. The shepherds, afflicted by self-interest in spite of themselves, find "patience" a futile exercise. The more time passes, Celadon declares, the greater his "mal" becomes: "Plus il va vieillissant, plus aussi va-t-il augmentant" (I, 130). At the same time, transparent self-disclosure reaches an impasse when the lovers and their mistresses become as opaque to one another in private discourse as they have made themselves to their enemies in public display: "Nous ne nous voyons plus dans le rocher" (I, 130), Astrée recalls, and the letters they exchange, far from disclosing a stable, inward truth, "étaient si différentes de celles que nous avions accoustumé, qu'il semblait que ce fussent différentes personnes" (I, 130). When Celadon initiates the mutual disclosure that ultimately results in reconciliation this double failure continues to be apparent. The injured shepherds rebuke Astrée and Phillis for being "volages," and invoke their own services, and the vows the shepherdesses have sworn, as binding constraints upon the "changes" to which individuals are susceptible. The shepherdesses, for their part, accuse the lovers of paying lip service to the ideal of perfect love with its vast metaphysical superstructure as a cover for undisclosed personal motives: "Tous ces mots de fidélité et d'amitié sont plus en votre bouche, qu'en votre coeur" (I, 131).

The way beyond incessant change on the one hand, and ineradicable mistrust on the other, lies neither in the recognition of a metaphysical truth that fixes identity from without, nor in transparent self-representation that discloses the self-present inward truth of the individual, but in a collective disclosure that permits each person to become subject and object of the voyeuristic gaze by turns: "Je ne crois pas," Astrée says, "que la vie nous eust longuement duré, si quelque bon demon ne nous eust fait resoudre de nous en éclaircir en présence les uns des autres" (I, 130). Because discourse always carries an intention to produce an effect on its intended audience, words addressed directly to oneself cannot be trusted. It is only when Celadon's momentary silence permits Astrée "d'ouir ce que Phillis repondait à Lycidas" (I, 131) that her doubt begins to dissipate. Glimpsing the inner self of her suspected rival in words addressed to another, she acquires an objective confirmation of Celadon's innocence.

But simple voyeurism alone is insufficient. Collective disclosure frees the lovers from doubt not only because each becomes voyeur to the others, peering behind their masks, but because each knows that he or she is observed in the act of observing. Celadon's declaration that Phillis "n'alluma jamais la moindre étincelle d'amour dans mon ame" (I, 132) gains credence in Astrée's mind not because she sees directly into Celadon's heart, nor even because Phillis's conversation with Lycidas seems objectively to confirm his confession, but because she knows that Phillis has overheard the remarks that Celadon has addressed to herself: "Quant à moi, je vous asseure bien que rien n'eust peu me faire entendre raison, si Celadon ne m'eust parlé de cette sorte *devant Phillis même*" (I, 132). [Emphasis mine.] What I see and hear is real, she seems to be saying, because you have witnessed me seeing and hearing it, and thereby legitimize my experience as true. The reality thus apprehended is not objective, but conventional, a possession of the collectivity rather than of the isolated self. A statement becomes true only when others accept it as such, as though the two couples, by establishing each for the other a normative ground of meaning, reinstate the authority of a collectively ratified symbolic order.

The second trial raises the epistemological vertigo to a new intensity by demonstrating the ease with which pretense becomes reality for the deceiver. When Lycidas finds himself pursued by Olimpe he takes the advice of his companions and feigns a reciprocal interest in order to preserve the secrecy of his feelings for Phillis. Seduced by his own ruse, however, "la feinte en fin fut à bon escient" (I, 135), as Olimpe's pregnancy reveals. The trial enters a second phase which centers on the resulting crisis of estrangement, and concludes, like the trial of jealousy, with a mediated resolution. It is Astrée who breaks the news to Phillis of Lycidas' fault, arguing that guilt is collective rather than individual: "Je lui dis ce qui en était, et ensemble mis toute la faute dessus nous, qui avions esté si mal advisées de ne prévoir que sa jeunesse ne pouvait faire plus de résistance" (I, 136). It is Astrée who coaches the prodigal in his plea for forgiveness: "Lycidas par mon conseil se vint jetter à ses genoux" (I, 137). And finally, it is Astrée who refuses to let the lovers part until the reconciliation is complete: "Je ne les laissais point séparer que toutes offenses ne fussent entièrement remises" (I, 137).

While the first two misunderstandings occur when the lovers become entangled in the meshes of their own deceit, the final two "travaux" portray them as victims of lies perpetrated by others who wish to interfere in their private affairs. When Phocion sets in motion a plan to arrange a marriage between Astrée and Corebe, rumors spring up which represent the event as a *fait accompli*, and Alcippe hires Squilindre to forge a letter in Astrée's hand informing Celadon of her intention to comply. Completely taken in by the reciprocal confirmation of speech and writing—"ce qui lui persuadait plus aisément ce change, c'était que la lettre ne faisait qu'aprouver le bruit commun du marriage de Corebe, et de moi" (143)—Celadon despairs of Astrée's love, and retreats to the wilderness where he plans to spend his final days in solitude. Although the lovers are reunited when Lycidas discovers Celadon's place of hiding and delivers an authentic letter reassuring him of Astrée's love, they almost immediately fall into a second trial. This time Astrée, rather than Celadon, is the dupe. Semire discovers a lost letter that reveals Astrée's love for Celadon. As a cunning rival, he knows that he will never succeed in winning Astrée for himself unless he first destroys her love for Celadon. To this end he misrepresents Celadon's feigned affection for Aminthe as a genuine infidelity, supplanting Astrée's interpretation of the factual evidence with a plausible, but unverified, interpretation of his own. Filled with jealousy, Astrée banishes Celadon from her sight.

Because these two "travaux" befall Celadon and Astrée respectively and in isolation, rather than the two couples collectively, they throw into sharp relief the epistemological and moral weaknesses of each in turn. Lost in a labyrinth of empty signifiers, Celadon's instinct is not to *verify* discourse with reference to an objective signified—in fact it doesn't even occur to him to consult Astrée—but rather to *rectify* a ruptured ontological order in which everything conspires to speak his love. In the "desacralized" universe of the early seventeenth century, however, complementarity can be restored only by virtue of an imaginary projection upon the world, rather than through the discovery of a hidden quality in the world itself. Just as in the first trial he strives to win Astrée's fidelity by appropriating her feelings as a mirror image of his own—literally to arrest the movement of her soul by means of his single mindedness—he now retreats to a solitary place in which his narcissistic imagination can operate without constraint: "Et là tombant évanoui, il ne revint point plutôt en soi-même que les plaintes en sa bouche" (I, 143). Distancing himself from the world by degrees, he falls ill and cloisters himself in his bed chamber where "il demeura tout le jour sur un lit, sans vouloir parler à personne" (I, 143). Finally, he withdraws "dans les bois les plus reculez" (I, 143).

There, in a "Chanson sur le changement d'Astrée," he suggests that a reconciliation between the eternally unchanging core of his identity—conceptualized as the inward writing of the heart—and the transitory nature of the external world—represented by shifting figures he draws in the sand—can be achieved only by the elimination of one of the two terms. He must either renounce the world by accepting death, or, choosing life, resign himself to ceaseless change: "Ou tu devais soudain mourir, ou bien incontinent guérir" (I, 145). Unable to do either, however, he begins, by means of imagination, to remake the world in his own image. His desire becomes, as it were, the absolute reality with reference to which everything else acquires significance and purpose. In the symbolic universe of the *Astrée*, the fact that his place of retreat is near "une des sources du desastreux Lignon" (I, 143) can hardly be accidental. By establishing his abode at the figural source of discourse, d'Urfé's symbol of symbolization, he posits himself—without acknowledging to himself that he has done so—as the autonomous controller of meaning. The love letters he sets adrift on the Lignon verbally proclaim his fidelity and palpably mark the river with a visible sign of his love, transforming it into an expression of his private, inner world.

If Celadon's attempt to rectify signs as a phenomenological reflection of a metaphysical order concludes in a narcissistic inscription of external objects in an idealized dream of love, Astrée's attempt to verify discourse with reference to subjective experience leads to an equally imaginary inscription of external objects within an intra-psychic fantasy of betrayal. We have already examined the dangers inherent in a discourse of objective reference in the "Histoire de Damon et de Fortune." Both the "fontaine de la vérité de l'amour," and the paintings that adorn the tomb of the tragic couple, present themselves as signs that mediate transparently between the mind of the knower and extra-mental, empirical realities which refer to nothing beyond themselves. Those who rely upon either the fountain or the canvasses for their knowledge of others, however, learn that transparency is an illusion created by specifiable techniques of representation. On the one hand, the manipulators of images—Mandrague in the first instance and the demons in the second—impose a perspectival gaze as an omniscient one by removing themselves, and hence their biases and hidden motives, from the field of vision. On the other, they lull the viewer into a suspension of disbelief by sustaining scrupulous accuracy at the level of empirical detail. The arbitrary sign does not present objects as they are in themselves, but renders them up for subjective appropriations—by the viewer in the case of the fountain, and by the painter in the case of the six tableaux.

Semire's deceit, which marks the culmination of the series of "travaux," differs from that of Mandrague and the demons only to the extent that a verbal medium replaces a visual one. D'Urfé has already given us a brief description of the fraud in his opening pages. In Astrée's detailed reminiscence, we are able to recognize more clearly the manner in which Semire's discourse encourages the subjective appropriation of the objects it appears merely to represent.

Semire constructs a narrative of betrayal whose internal logic of suspense and deferral supplants Astrée's thought processes and invalidates subjectivity as a reliable gage of extra-discursive truth. By reminding his dupe of the habitual treachery of shepherds he projects Celadon's guilt as the deferred resolution toward which his discourse inevitably tends: "Nous eumes longuement parlé," she recalls, "des diverses trahisons, que les bergers faisaient aux bergères qu'ils faignaient d'aimer" (I, 148). He not only dwells on the misfortunes of gullible shepherdesses, but encourages her, by means of hints and insinuations, to recognize in their experience a reflection of her own. "Je m'étonne, dit-il, qu'il y ait si peu de bergères qui prennent garde à ces tromperies," and in particular, that "vous ne reconneussiez celle que l'on vous veut faire" (I, 149). At the same time, his half-disclosures and strategic delays awaken a desire for closure that makes Astrée an accomplice in creating the illusion to which she finally succumbs. On the pretext of sparing her a painful revelation, he falls suddenly silent: "Si voudrais-je ne vous en avoir jamais commencé le propos, pour le déplaisir que je prévoi que la fin vous rapportera" (I, 149). In fact, as Astrée retrospectively perceives, he merely exploited the psychology of delayed gratification: "Il ne voulut m'en dire d'avantage," Astrée says, "afin de m'en donner plus de volonté" (I, 149). Before long her conversation is dominated by pleas that he "dire entièrement ce qu'il avait commencé" (I, 149). When at last he offers Astrée an opportunity to "ouir les passionnés discours qu'il [Celadon] tient à son Aminthe" (I, 150), fact has been reduced to a function of the intrinsic logic of discourse. Celadon's "infidelity" is little more than the inevitable, and even ardently longed for, *dénouement* of a narrative whose end is already implied in its beginning. Even as they approach the sequestered couple, he continues to prepare Astrée with an advance report of what she is about to see, replete with a lurid description of their embraces which Astrée ruefully realizes after the fact to have been provided "pour me piquer davantage" (I, 150). When they arrive, she is prepared only "de reconnaître la perfidie de Celadon" (I, 150), and not his innocence. She sees only what the narrative proposes and nothing more.

Subjective desire, far from providing an authentic expression of identity, can hardly be more alienated or inauthentic than in the moment when Astrée, of her own free will, banishes her beloved. The central obstacle to self-fulfillment may no longer be conceived in terms of constraints imposed by an arbitrary, external order upon the true identity of the individual, but rather in terms of an otherness at the heart of the subject herself implanted there by multiple, conflicting discourses of ambiguous origin. Astrée is dispossessed of her true beloved only after having lost her very self—she is, as d'Urfé continually reminds us, "desastrée." One of the poems Celadon recites to Aminthe in Astrée's presence expresses the fundamentally fractured and self-divided condition of the human subject: "Mes contentements conspirent contre moi," he says. The objects he desires, far from bearing within themselves the mark or inscription of the lover's authentic identity, are "traitres miroirs du coeur, lumières infidelles" (I, 151).

IV. Confession as Public Discourse

In as much as the epistemology of meaning is at issue in Astrée's account of her life, we are led, finally, to question the epistemological foundations of her own narrative. As a transparent representation of subjective experience it would seem to be predicated on an epistemology of objective (self-)reference. In the conversational prologue to the tale, Phillis formulates a confessional ideal that suggests the existence of a transcendental consciousness capable of verifying discourse with reference to an object which, in the case of confession, happens to be the affective experience of the speaker: "Je m'assure [Phillis says to Diane] qu'Astrée parlera toujours devant vous *aussi franchement que devant elle même*, son humeur n'étant pas d'être amie à moitié, et depuis qu'elle s'est jurée telle, il n'y a plus de cachette en son âme" (I, 111). [Emphasis mine.][12] No longer does one look to a suprapersonal order of sympathies and antipathies, to the pure intelligences of angels and planets or even to ideas in the mind of God, for the secrets of one's identity and the criterion of truth in self-representation. Rather, for one who posits herself as both author and object of discourse, the foundational reality to which signs refer is nothing other than the consciousness of the speaker herself. The individual is not only the origin of her own desires, but the "proprietor" of her own truth.[13]

The content of Astrée's narrative, however, exposes the ideal of confessional transparency to be an illusion. The four "travaux" prove nothing if not the impossibility of stabilizing meaning with reference to a substratum of objective empirical or psychological fact which presents itself without mediation to a transcendental knowing consciousness. Subjectivity is an unreliable foundation of truth because it is always shaped by the very discourse whose accuracy one seeks to verify, and distorted by intra-psychic desires and fears. We are therefore left with the necessity of viewing the "Histoire d'Astrée" either as a narrative which, by deconstructing its own claim to truthfulness, demonstrates the radically indeterminate status of self-representation, or—and I believe this is the more reasonable view—as a discourse whose horizon of reference is neither metaphysical nor subjective, but collective and social.

I propose that we should apply to the narrative the epistemological norm that prevails within it. In each of the four "travaux" but the last, truth in self-representation has been established on the basis of the shared awareness of the social group. The lovers escape the crisis of jealousy not because they are able to penetrate the secret hiding places of the souls of their partners and rivals, but because the two couples engage in a four-way disclosure that establishes the collective gaze as the criterion of truth for each individual. Phillis accepts Lycidas' penitence not only because she regards his aggressive insistence as a sign of sincerity, but because Astrée testifies that, since his transgression was the consequence of a stratagem invented by his peers (the shepherdesses advise him to feign love for Olimpe), his innocence no less than his guilt is a function of collective agreement. Celadon accepts Astrée's authentic letter in place of Squilindre's forgery not because he verifies its contents by consulting the author herself, but because it is delivered by Lycidas, a trusted intermediary. Astrée's own narrative is less a transparent reflection of objective self-knowledge than an affirmation of a publicly accepted opinion regarding Celadon's fidelity: "Vrayment celle cy est bien une mécognaissance, qui surpasse toutes les plus grandes ingratitudes," Lycidas had declared upon hearing about her suspicions, "puis que ses actions et ses services n'ont pu vous rendre asseurée d'une chose, *dont personne, que vous, ne doute plus*" (I, 18). [Emphasis mine.]

It is indicative of d'Urfé's "historicist" epistemology that, unlike the classical dramatists beginning with Corneille (who have advanced considerably along the continuum toward modernity), he almost never reveals character to us in soliloquies, but rather through various forms of public discourse: tales recounted not to single individuals but to the community of lovers, "procès d'amour" arbitrated by representatives of the collective voice, and prophetic oracles subject to discussion and interpretation. Soliloquies in *L'Astrée* serve primarily to display the symptoms of spiritual malaise or the effects of self-deception, as in the case of Diane's meditation on universal mutability (IV, 46), or Silvandre's struggle against radical skepticism (IV, 219), and not to provide a privileged grasp of a self-present inner reality.

Truth, by contrast, is the possession not of the individual but of the collectivity.[14] The participation of multiple voices in the articulation of character compensates for the distortions attendant upon any single view. The repeatedly interrupted biography of Hylas, for example, begins with the "Histoire d'Hylas" (I, 294–316) narrated in the first person, continues in the "Histoire de Palinice et de Circene" (II, 110–120) as remembered by Palinice, one of his cast-off mistresses, before dissolving into the fragments of the "Histoire de Cryseide" (III, 350–468) supplied by Hylas, by Cryseide herself as remembered by Hylas, and finally by Florice. His story concludes in the narrative present with the *proviso* scene which not only establishes his love for Stelle in the public eye, but secures assent to the radical liberty by which his identity is principally defined (III, 487–494). Similarly, Adamas collects testimony from Leonide and Silvie before taking action to bring an end to Galathée's infatuation with Celadon. Each narrator—Leonide in the "Histoire de Galathée et Lindamor" (I, 323–368), and Silvie in the "Histoire de Leonide" (I, 371–378)—provides a partial view which, though distorted by self-interest in the first instance (I, 368), and by inexperience in the second (I, 378), contributes to a composite representation that becomes the authorized norm. Each of the "procès d'amour," moreover, consists of the presentation of multiple and irreconcilable versions of a single set of events to a representative of collective authority whose judgment determines a normative version of the "truth."

Throughout the narrative, beginning with her autobiographical discourse, Astrée consistently insists upon the epistemological finality of collective opinion rather than subjective experience. Her early acquisition of this insight justifies her status as the title character, and indicates the grounds upon which her estrangement from Celadon will be overcome, and the resolution of the plot achieved.

Astrée's role in mediating the reconciliation of Diane and Silvandre— a couple whose prominence in the frame narrative is second only to that of Astrée and Celadon themselves, and whose story dominates the love interest of Volume IV—serves to illustrate her gain in self-knowledge. On the basis of factual evidence strategically represented by the deceitful Laonice, Diane concludes that Silvandre has been unfaithful (III, 611), and refuses even to listen to him present arguments in his own defense. She succumbs to a radical skepticism according to which the objective verification of discourse is impossible because every subject-position is always already a function of the discourse whose transparency one seeks to prove: "Ne savez-vous pas," she asks her companions, "que les tromperies ne sont tromperies, sinon en tant qu'elles deçoivent ceux à qui elles se font; et c'est pourquoi il faut qu'elles soient toutes faites en sorte qu'auparavant il n'y ait point d'apparence qu'elles deussent arriver ainsi" (IV, 215). Like Astrée who fails to ask Celadon to explain his tryst with Aminthe, and Phillis who regards even Lycidas' solitary monologues as part of a deceptive ploy, Diane doubts the possibility of achieving an extra-discursive position from which discourse itself may be verified. She suspects that she is always *in* discourse.

Astrée's first response to Diane remains within the subject-centered paradigm. She appears to accept Diane's notion that interpersonal knowledge is a function of objective verification, dependent upon the possibility of penetrating, through stratagems of spying, and eavesdropping, the subjective privacy of the other. Diane's fault, she says, is merely to have overgeneralized the dishonesty of shepherds (IV, 215). When the shepherdesses secretly observe Silvandre lamenting her cruelty (IV, 215–20), however, Diane continues to doubt the testimony of her own eyes and ears. From thence forward, the path to reconciliation takes a new, and epistemologically radical turn. Astrée now argues that Diane herself is incapable of apprehending ocular evidence objectively, not because of the deceptions perpetrated by others—a contextualization of her subjectivity by discourse—but because of her own intra-psychic irrational impulses (IV, 222). The remedy cannot lie in empirical data itself, but in the collective mediation of vision: "Mais, ma soeur, reprit Astrée, encore faut-il aux choses douteuses, et qui ne se peuvent pas bien avérer, s'en rapporter, ce me semble, à la pluralité des voix" (IV, 223). She tellingly subordinates even the most empirical of sense data, the perception of color, to the judgment of the social group.

> Quant à moi, j'ai toujours tenu cette règle pour très-asseurée, que, si je voyais que tous eussent opinion qu'une couleur fut jaune, encore qu'elle semblat être rouge, je croirais infailliblement que mon oeil se tromperait, et tiendrais qu'elle serait de la même couleur, que tous les autres yeux la jugeraient. Vous avez opinion que Silvandre aime Madonte, et nous vous disons toutes qu'il n'y a point d'apparence; et que ne vous conformez-vous à la créance que nous en avons? (IV, 223)

A second episode of spying brings Diane's doubts to an end—she and Phillis overhear Laonice reveal the secret of her treachery to Tircis (IV, 257–62)—but the self-evidence of empirical fact is not sufficient in itself to restore Diane's recognition of Silvandre's love. Astrée insists that had Diane's observations not been validated by a second witness her doubts would not have been resolved:

> Je loue Dieu, dit Astrée, qu'il vous ait conduites tant à propos toutes deux, que vous ayez pu ouir ensemble cette tromperie; car je crois que si vous eussiez été séparées, Diane n'eust pas voulu adjouster foi à ce que vous lui en eussiez dit, et encore qu'elle l'eust elle-même oui, s'il n'y eust point eu de témoin, elle eust demeuré longtemps sans se vanter de le sçavoir. (IV, 268)

Given the consistency with which d'Urfé resolves all difficulties by means of reciprocal spying which establishes subjective experience as a collectively ratified reality, it is impossible not to conclude that the logic of the narrative projects a similar means of reconciliation for Astrée and Celadon. Astrée's doubts will be resolved when she witnesses Celadon lamenting her cruelty and affirming his love under circumstances where "il n'y a apparence de feinte," and her observations must in turn be validated by the gaze of her peers so that the knowledge she acquires attains the status of a collective truth.

A different process will be necessary to assure Celadon's submission to collective judgement, however, because he embarks on his mental journey from a different point of departure. From the beginning, Astrée has been strongly implicated in a subject-centered paradigm of knowledge. Her capitulation to the collective voice has been achieved through a series of experiences that reveal the inadequacy of subjective consciousness as the sole criterion of truth in representation. Celadon, by contrast, has been implicated in an object-centered paradigm of knowledge. His reintegration into social life will require the exposure of the self-love that underlies and motivates chivalric idealism once the path to genuine transcendence has been foreclosed. It is not subjectivity, but the fantasy of an objective order, which must be subordinated to a collective, and historically relative, determination of identity and meaning. Much of d'Urfé's narrative is devoted to describing the trajectory of this gradual transformation.

Notes

1. Johan Huizinga, *The Waning of the Middle Ages* (1949; New York: Doubleday Anchor Books, 1954), p. 39.

2. Huizinga, *Homo Ludens: A Study of the Play Element in Culture* (1950; Boston: Beacon Press, 1955), p. 15.

3. *Homo Ludens*, 46.

4. *Homo Ludens*, 17.

5. That the contests are intended to correspond to the characters of the shepherds who win them becomes even more apparent in a later episode. After the "cérémonie de remerciement" that Adamas performs in the Temple d'Amitié: "on proposa le prix pour la course, pour la lutte, pour le sault et pour jetter la barre. De la première Silvandre emporta le prix; de la lutte, Lycidas; du sauter, Hylas; de la barre, Hermante" (III, 534). Again, the advocate of fidelity wins "la course." The jealous lover is the best wrestler, and the inconstant, the best jumper. When Hylas receives "une couronne faite de plume," Silvandre calls attention to the symbolic appropriateness of both his victory and his prize—all of which would seem trivial enough, except

that it reinforces the conception of personal identity as a function of inherent qualities reflected in an external order of signs.

6. For a contrasting view, see Dalia Judovitz, "The Graphic Text: The Nude in *L'Astrée*," *Papers in French Seventeenth-Century Literature* (1988) No. 29, Volume XV, pp. 529–40. Judovitz interprets Celadon's behavior in the Temple de la Beauté as an expression of subjective autonomy that transgresses against the structure of "allegorical" self-representation—the name she gives to "signification," or "resemblance." His voyeuristic gaze and his demand for a bribe in return for a favorable judgment would seem, in her view, to establish him as an observer outside of the scene rather than as a performer of a predetermined role, and Astrée as an object of pleasure, rather than as a co-performer. By placing Celadon squarely on the side of modernity, this interpretation fails, I think, to do justice to the conservative position he actually represents both here and throughout *L'Astrée*. My disagreement notwithstanding, Judovitz' article is among the very few which attend to the juxtaposition of alternative discursive paradigms in the narrative.

7. *The Order of Things*, 40.

8. The "preuve" as a means of self-disclosure figures prominently in several of *L'Astrée*'s intercalated tales, most particularly in the "Histoire de Ligdamon" where the lover reveals through signal deeds that he is, as his name suggests, "a man tied" to his mistress, Silvie.

9. The meaning of the word "prudence" was possibly undergoing a transition in the early seventeenth century. The *Robert* cites two main definitions. According to the first, prudence is the conduct of one's affairs "selon la droite raison," while according to the second, it is the practical foresight required "pour éviter des erreurs, des fautes, des malheurs possibles." The first definition finds the ultimate meaning and purpose of human action in the metaphysical Reason or Prudence that regulates creation as an expression of the divine mind; the second, in the material and experimentally verifiable relations of cause and effect. During the seventeenth century, the two serve as indices of different epistemological models, until, in the early eighteenth century, the realist definition comes into dominance. In *L'Astrée* the two meanings coexist. The wise old man who counsels Dorinde against dangers of skepticism encourages her to trust "cette souveraine prudence" that ensures the moral order of the cosmos (IV, 432). For Hylas, on the other hand, prudence is the fruit of experience which "apprend à mettre les remèdes nécessaires pour éviter les inconvénients" (III,490).

10. The conception of truth as rectitude and the correction of error as rectification is not only implicit in the medieval ontological tradition throughout, but explicitly developed by Saint Anselm in "De veritate," a work devoted in part to the epistemology of signs. See Marcia L. Colish, *The Mirror of Language: A Study in the Medieval Theory of Knowledge* (New Haven: Yale University Press, 1968), pp. 112–23.

11. The pattern holds in other episodes as well. Laonice, whose lies engender the estrangement of Diane and Silvandre, not only arrives from a distant country but disappears from the narrative with an abruptness that calls attention to her detachment from any social milieu whatever: "Elle se jetta d'un autre côté dans le bois, et sans plus se faire voir à personne de la contrée, s'en voulut aller d'où elle était venue" (IV, 260).

12. The ideal of confessional self-disclosure recurs regularly throughout the work, as when Astrée, in an earlier conversation, points to her own transparency as a standard which Phillis should emulate: "Je lui dis, que ces façons de parler étaient à propos avec Lycidas, mais non pas avec moi [...] qui ne lui avais jamais celé ce que j'avais de plus secret dans l'âme" (I, 127–28). Later, when Diane tells her story to Astrée and Phillis, she too posits her discourse as a transparent mirror of a stratum of experience which is subjective, private and hidden, and promises to hold nothing back: "C'est être coupable d'une trop grande faut, que d'avoir quelque cachette en l'âme, pour la personne que l'on aime" (I, 196).

13. I am indebted to Bernard Charles Flynn for clarifying the distinction between the divine mind and subjective consciousness as alternative horizons of being: "According to Heidegger's reading of Descartes, subjectivity [...] installs [...] a new relation between a being and the horizon, or field, in which it can appear as being. In the Middle Ages, the relationship between beings and Being was a relation of creatures to Creator: to be was to have been created by God and to remain in existence by the continuous act of God's creation. [...] In Descartes' thought, the subject, the I, becomes the transcendental ground of the known and the knowable. What can appear is determined in advance as what can be represented to a subject, a subject whose self-representation is the ground of all that it represents to itself." ["Descartes and the Ontology of Subjectivity," *Man and World*, 16(1983), pp. 3–23.]

14. Maurice Laugaa makes a similar point: For d'Urfé, "toute vérité sur les êtres est fragmentaire," he writes. "Chacun recèle une part de la vérité sur autrui." Like Boccaccio's *Decameron* and Balzac's *Comédie humaine*, however, *L'Astrée* integrates multiple perspectives through the agency of a "conscience globale," embodied sometimes in a particular character, sometimes in the reader. ["Structures ou personnages dans *L'Astrée*," *Etudes françaises* 2 (1966): 3–27.]

5

From the Cavern of Memory to the Theater of the World: Subjectivity and Self-disclosure in Celadon's Quest for Identity

Throughout the preceding discussion of the epistemology of self-representation in *L'Astrée*, I have argued that, at a certain moment in the early seventeenth century, a mode of self-representation predicated on the lover's participation in a providentially established symbolic order had been invalidated before a new mode of self-representation, predicated on the subjectively assured transparency of confessional speech, had taken its place. As a result, the "signs of love" were suspended ambiguously between objective-ontological and subjective-empirical horizons of reference. The crisis of meaning occasioned by the peculiar "liminality"—the betwixt and between status—of the "baroque" sign, elicited both progressive and conservative responses from equally thoughtful minds, and the possibility of this double response gives *L'Astrée* its internal structure at every level, and informs its developmental logic.

In d'Urfé's fictional universe, Astrée exemplifies the epistemological advance guard. Proposing to speak of herself to others "aussi franchement que devant elle mesme" (I, 111), she posits subjective self-presence as the unappealable criterion of truth in self-representation. Prior to the theoretical formulation of the "Cartesian" *cogito*, however, early modern epistemology did not admit the existence of an interior *locus* of self-knowledge. Beleaguered by assaults of private fancy from within (jealousy is a case in point), and invasions of inauthentic discourse from without (e.g. Semire's deceit), Astrée at last capitulates to the collective perceptions of a privileged, but historically situated, social group as the only sure foundation of identity and meaning. Celadon, on the other hand, exemplifies those who try to discern in the crude and mutable appearances of the visible world the imprint of an ontological order within which lover and beloved are united by a providentially ordained resemblance. His efforts, in turn, are frustrated by Astrée's irreducible "otherness" continually thrust upon him by her "impossible commands," and, ultimately, by the individuating experience of his own desire. The trajectory of his development, to which we now turn our attention, carries him inexorably toward an acceptance of the legitimizing gaze of a community of like-minded peers with which Astrée has become identified.

The adventures that begin with Celadon's suicidal leap into the Lignon unfold as a spiritual quest or pilgrimage whose stages are distinguished by his sojourns at a series of five symbolic places: the Palais d'Isoure, a watery cave beside the river Lignon, the Temple d'Amitié, the shepherds' hamlet (primarily Astrée's bedroom) and finally, the capital city, Marcilly.

The Palais d'Isoure represents the ethical and epistemological universe to which Astrée's philosophy leads—a world in which individuals are autonomous authors and proprietors of their own identities, and in which collectively authorized norms are trampled under foot. It is, on the surface of things, a pleasure palace where Galathée escapes from royal responsibilities and indulges her fantasy without constraint. Having discovered Celadon near death on the banks of the Lignon, she holds him captive while trying unsuccessfully to restore his health, and (in flagrant disregard for the social hierarchy) to win his love. All of the visual artifacts of the palace, moreover, reinforce its association with rapacious self-interest. When Celadon first regains consciousness in his new surroundings, his eyes immediately encounter a painting that captures the ethos of the place, and provides an obvious ethical commentary on Galathée's behavior. In it, Saturn devours his own children against a background that depicts the destruction of the collective order, or, to be more precise, the defacement of the providentially intended resemblance between historical institutions and their ideal prototypes: "Autour de luy on ne voyoit que des sceptres en pièces, des couronnes rompues, de grands édifices ruinez, et cela de telle sorte, qu'à peine restoit-il quelque legère ressemblance de ce que ç'avoit esté" (I, 42). Clustered about Saturn in ancillary scenes appear a host of other mythical figures—Jupiter, Venus, Cupid—each of whom exhibits a festering scar representing the wound of love in its egocentric form. The palace grounds contain a labyrinth and gardens which evoke the pleasant side of the subjective spirit—the delightful disarray, the giddy disorientation—as well as the tomb of Damon et Fortune adorned with six tableaux which proclaim the twin dangers of jealousy and deceit (I, 37).

If Hylas is an "autre voix" challenging the chivalric idealism that pre-vails among the shepherds and shepherdesses of the Forez, Celadon's arrival at Isoure produces a similar contrast in the reverse. His is the voice of chivalric idealism in the midst of a microcosm of the modern world, and his task is primarily to resist its influence. There, he is tempted to abandon the principle of fidelity—his transparency to an external ideal—and to embrace instead an ethic of self-interested change. It is by his fidelity to Astrée, expressed in his vociferous rejection of Galathée's advances (I, 439), that he reaffirms his identity as a perfect lover within the metaphysical and symbolic code of courtly love. And it is by his fidelity to his inherent nature as a shepherd, ex-pressed in his refusal to consider an alliance with one superior in rank (I, 380–82), that he fulfills his teleological destiny in the social hierarchy.

Although Celadon's opposition to Galathée's "modernity" is equivalent to his rejection of the subject-centered representational paradigm that engen-dered his estrangement from Astrée, his fidelity does not permit the truth of love to be revealed in the traditional chivalric manner. Rather, his attempt to prove his spiritual unity with the mistress by means of an absolute submission to her will can only be represented, in the "liminal" world of *L'Astrée*, as madness. Liberated from his captivity at Isoure by Adamas and Leonide, Celadon retreats to a cavern on the banks of the Lignon where he is able imaginatively to recreate a symbolic universe in which external reality and inward feeling are mutual confirmations of a single truth. Rather than reconfirm his place in a suprapersonal order of which both lover and beloved are part, however, his solitary meditations merely effect the hallucinatory transformation of the world into an allegory of erotic love. It is a world in which Astrée's alterity may be, if not transcended, at least pathologically denied, and in which nothing exists for him except insofar as it refers to her. Increasingly incapable of engaging with the external conditions of life, he succumbs to starvation and illness. It is in this moribund state of withdrawal, legitimized in his own mind by the necessity of proving his identity as a perfect lover, that his rehabilitation begins.

The narrative's major epistemological options are subsequently ex-plored through a period of sentimental and spiritual instruction which falls into three distinct phases: his contemplative life in the Temple d'Amitié; his return to the village disguised as Adamas' daughter, Alexis; and his participation in the "siege of Marcilly."

The first represents an attempt to resurrect the metaphysical and symbolic order of chivalric love which had been preserved only in a debased, psychologized form in the cavern retreat. Astrée's command of banishment continues to be an absolute ethical imperative, enforcing self-repression as the price Celadon must pay to accede to his identity as her lover. But because he learns to regard her as the most perfect work of the creator rather than as the self-sufficient center of his identity, obedience serves the double purpose of implicating him in the collective history, religion and language of Gaul with which she comes to be identified.

In the second phase, the emergence of repressed desire motivates the formation of a new, individuated and self-determining identity. By circumventing Astrée's command, and establishing himself as her "female" companion and erotic voyeur—one who sees without being seen—Celadon arrogates to himself an autonomous subjectivity that places him outside, or establishes an interior distance within, the providential design upon which self-representation in the temple depends.[1] But since truth in self-representation cannot in the mental universe of *L'Astrée* be predicated on subjective self-presence (that is, after all, the point of Astrée's confession), he finds himself consigned to an irremediable invisibility. To affirm the self is to become unrepresentable.

Finally, if the first two phases of his education leave self-representation and subjective interiority unreconciled, the third prefigures an historicist resolution in which self and symbolic order become reciprocal reflections each of the other. When, at the siege of Marcilly, Celadon takes arms in defense of the capital city into which Astrée has been rescued, d'Urfé foreshadows the possibility that the hero's identity as a lover will be legitimized not by his obedience to the command of banishment, nor by the authenticity of his private desire, but by his participation in the collective order. To defend Astrée is to defend the very seat of legitimate social authority. Love no longer implicates him in a transgression of the law, but draws him into its sphere of influence and reaffirms his identity as a social subject.

Celadon's mental progress illuminates the complex series of adjustments by which the ontological structures of the Middle Ages gradually give up their hold on the human imagination to make way for the ascendancy of subjective consciousness. In what follows, I will examine in greater depth the symbolic and polemical material associated with each of his three developmental phases, beginning with the origins of his estrangement from the modern world.

I. Celadon's Madness and the Pleasures of Memory:
The Mentality of the Cave

D'Urfé's prefatory letter "Au Berger Celadon" announces the incompatibility of chivalric love and courtship with the self-serving eroticism of the modern lover. Because Celadon adheres to the values and customs of the knights of the round table and to the traditions of ancient Gaul, he will not only encounter ridicule, but will be regarded by his contemporaries as the victim of an "étrange humeur"—a madman. Thus, we are informed that his state of mind must be understood not in terms of a merely personal pathology, but in terms of an unresolved conflict between cultural systems.

In a phrase, it is an inevitable consequence of the incompatibility of a theory of knowledge predicated on a subject-object dualism, and one predicated on the ontological unity of the mind with its objects—between, that is, a representational paradigm and a hylomorphic one. In the emergent "Cartesian" epistemology that d'Urfé's contemporaries had already in many ways begun to articulate, mind and world, which medieval thought had conjoined in a relation of metaphysical complementarity, are reconceptualized as two distinct and ontologically incommensurate domains. Reason, which had been regarded as an inscription within each soul of the overarching *logos* is now "its own place," and the extra-mental universe which had been construed as a phenomenological reflection of an ideal order becomes a domain of objects referring to nothing beyond themselves. The chivalric lover is one, by definition, who refuses to recognize the disjunction between subjective consciousness and the external world at the heart of the modern episteme, and who clings instead to the notion that they are parallel manifestations of a single cosmic order, the divine *Logos,* or "right reason." The conflation of knower and known underlies the ethic of eternal fidelity and extreme affection codified in the twelve laws of "parfaite amitié." Two individuals love precisely because their souls are imprinted with a single ideal form, and the lover's servility is intended for no other purpose than to render visible, on the very surfaces of things, this ontologically real and *a priori* relation.

From the point of view of an early modern dualist, the traditional insistence upon the unity of self and other (knower and known, lover and beloved) can be interpreted in two ways: as an effect of superior insight relegated to exalted mental states, or as a form of madness in which the subject attributes a specious reality to his own thoughts, and mistakes the ideal order of wishes and dreams for the real world of external, empirical fact. *L'Astrée* includes both evaluations.

On the one hand, Adamas' discourses on the supreme good and on the sympathies uphold a hierarchical model of cognition in which the soul ascends through two degrees of differentiated knowledge before transcending episte-mological dualism altogether. The quest begins at the level of *a posteriori* reason in which the soul is oriented toward objects of sense perception for purposes of utility and possession. It proceeds to judgments based on an *a priori* rationality manifest externally in the cosmic order and inwardly in the innate structure of human understanding. Finally, it passes beyond both the individuated, possessive ego, and the differentiated structure of reason to achieve a recollective union with ideal forms. Aided by its memory of a former existence, the soul recognizes its own participation in the very ground of being. This theory of knowledge reflects the influence of Renaissance neo-platonism, and is the principal manifestation in *L'Astrée* of a philosophical tradition that grants epistemological priority to the objective order. We have already attempted to show that it provides the organizing principle of d'Urfé's love debates.

On the other hand, however, d'Urfé's faithful lovers are frequently represented as madmen exhibiting symptoms that appear in their most char-acteristic and extreme form in the case of the unrequited shepherd Adraste. After losing his suit for Doris in a trial arbitrated by Leonide, Adraste refuses to leave the place where his sentence was imposed, to acknowledge the existence of anyone other than his mistress, or to speak except to pronounce her name. What makes him exemplary of a pervasive "type" of the madman in early seventeenth century is precisely his refusal to accept the reality of the world as "other," its difference from himself—including, of course, the differ-ence that separates him from Doris, who is all the world to him but who remains inaccessible in her autonomy and self-enclosure. It is as though he alone among his contemporaries does not yet realize that a mode of courtship dedicated to revealing the unitive relation with the beloved has been from the outset predicated on an imagined, rather than a real convergence of identities, and has therefore never been but an exercise in self-contemplation which leads to an ever deepening isolation in solipsistic fantasy. He is, as Foucault has said with reference to Don Quixote, "the man who is alienated in analogy. He is the disordered player of the Same and the Other."[2] At the far extreme from the Hobbesian war of all against all engendered by a discourse predicated on alterity and representation, we witness the reductive collapse of autonomous identities into a hallucinatory, erotic monism.

It is the insistence on the unity of lover and beloved that underlies Celadon's typical response to apparent changes or infidelities on the part of his mistress. Confronted by her alterity and self-enclosure, he retreats to the wilderness where he can rectify, in the vain world of imagination if nowhere else, the lost complementarity by which the other is a mirror image of the self, and the entire world a confirmation of his love. The pattern of passivity and retreat recurs in Astrée's confession twice. When Astrée rebukes him for the deception he perpetrates at the Temple de la Beauté he becomes "si particulier, qu'il ne hantait plus que les lieux plus retirés et sauvages de nos bois" (I, 118); and again, when he receives the forged letter announcing Astrée's plan to marry Corebe, he collapses in fit of fainting, falls ill, and finally withdraws "dans les bois les plus reculés" where he intends to lament his fate in solitude (I, 143). The suicidal leap into the Lignon which marks the beginning of the narrative present is but the final and most extravagant example of an established pattern.

Although Celadon's flight from Isoure signals his rejection of a mental universe brought into being by the rational pursuit of self-interest, he cannot return on that account to the pre-modern world in which the individual, at least in theory, finds the reflection of his or her innate identity in a providentially established symbolic order. Once the intensification of subjective self-awareness associated with the birth of love opens a fissure between the interior and the exterior worlds, the self-enclosed isolation of the ego can only be transcended in the world of fantasy. Celadon's escape from Isoure is accordingly structured, both geographically and spiritually, as a retreat into imagination. The landscape through which he progresses is a concrete analogue of the epistemological coordinates of his mental life:

En fin estant parvenu assez près de Bon-lieu, demeure des chastes Vestales, il fut comme surpris de honte d'avoir tant approché sans y penser celle que sa résolution luy commandait d'esloigner. Et voulant s'en retourner, il s'enfonça dans un bois si espais et marécageux en

> quelques endroits, qu'à peine en peut-il sortir; cela le contraignit de
> s'approcher d'avantage de la rivière, car le gravier menu luy estait
> moins ennuyeux que la boue. (I, 483)

The ideal order uniting the inner and outer worlds is symbolized by the
convent of the vestal virgins from which he is banished; the illusionistic,
textualized universe in which individuals are inscrutably self-enclosed is symbolized by the impenetrable and boggy forest through which he makes his way;
and the inner world of fancy is represented by the river Lignon, and by the
watery cavern, formed by the river and permeated by rain, to which he finally
withdraws.

From the outset, solitude intensifies his self-absorption: "Et d'autant
que la solitude a cela de propre de représenter plus vivement la joye ou la
tristesse, se trouvant seul, il commença à estre traitté de sorte par le temps, sa
fortune et l'amour, qu'il n'y avait cause de tourment en luy qui ne luy fust
mise devent les yeux" (I, 483). Far from seeking company to alleviate his
sorrow, he purposely avoids companionship, because it would disturb the
integrity of his emotional state. "Faisant dessein d'aller si loing que jamais on
n'entendist de ses nouvelles" (I, 483), he speaks to a passer-by only because
he perceives that the other's mood resembles his own. In the cave, his
introspection is heightened by the absence of anything extra-mental "qui le
pust distraire ailleurs (car rien ne se présentait à ses yeux que le cours de la
rivière)" (I, 484), and he achieves complete withdrawal from the objective
universe in his nocturnal meditations: "car l'obscurité a cela de propre qu'elle
rend l'imagination plus forte" (I, 487). If he attends to the external conditions
of life at all, it is only to perpetuate the inner world of imagination:

> Et n'eust été la crainte d'offenser les dieux en se laissant mourir et plus
> encore celle de perdre par sa mort la belle idée qu'il avait d'Astrée en
> son coeur, sans doute il eust été tresaise de finir ainsi le triste cours de
> sa vie. (I, 486)

When d'Urfé returns to the affairs of his hero just past the middle of the
second volume, he attributes his isolation and suffering to a pathological
tyranny of memory—the capacity for conjunctive awareness—over will and
reason, which ground the subject in empirical and rational structures of

identity and difference. Celadon lives "dans sa caverne, sans autre compagnie que celle de ses pensées qui n'avaient autre sujet que son bon-heur passé et son ennui présent" (II, 273). Astrée's portrait and love letters serve as memnonic aides in a contemplative love religion by which he renders ever present to the world of thought the mistress whose real presence he has been denied. The portrait bears an inscription which clarifies its commemorative function: "Privé de mon vrai bien, ce bien faux me soulage" (II, 275). Her letters, likewise, are "heureux témoignages de ta félicité passée" (II, 277).

Memory, as we have seen, occupies a privileged position in the idealist conception of the "vérité d'amour" because it permits the lover to achieve, beyond the differentiated modes of awareness associated with sense perception and discursive reason, a unitive knowledge of his mistress—a knowledge in which all sense of self and other, knower and known gives place to an immediate, and supra-rational intuition of the ideal form by which both he and she are "imprinted," and consequently conjoined as one soul. In a mental universe that consigns unitive knowledge to the domain of fancy, however, memory ceases to be esteemed as the avenue to the highest insight, and comes instead to be regarded as a source of error. Memory prevents the lover from recognizing real, and irreducible, differences—his autonomy from the mistress, and their inscription as social subjects in a differentiated rational order— and causes him to collapse distinct identities into an endless repetition of the Same—a single *idée fixe*.[3]

For Celadon, a figure at the threshold of the modern episteme, to live by memory is not to ascend to highest truth, but to lose touch with reality of the individuated ego. His meditation on Astrée's portrait, his most treasured mnemonic aid, reveals the impossibility of reconciling the "otherness" of the mistress, exemplified by her command of banishment, with the ideal unity of self and other. It is as though he confronts the self-enclosure which renders *anamnesis* ineffective as a path to truth. Whereas a contemplative saint adoring an icon would ordinarily expect to achieve a unitive awareness of the reality beyond the image, Celadon's "triste exercice" produces only an endless string of paradoxes: (1) It is impossible that he should have displeased his mistress because they share a single will, and yet he *has* displeased her. (2) If he had displeased her, it would be impossible for him to survive the knowledge of his transgression because her displeasure is his own, and yet he *has* survived. (3) Separation is equivalent to death because she is the source of his being, and yet a command that imposes banishment rather than death implies that he *must* live without her.

We are made privy, as it were, to the collapse of chivalric idealism and the object-centered paradigm of which it is but a part as Celadon tries without success to assimilate the unassimilable fact of subjective autonomy: "Ce qui est raisonnable au jugement des autres, est sans force de raison en elle" (II, 276). And what is the logic she violates? None other than that of reciprocity, the unity of souls, that lies at the heart of the chivalric philosophy of love: "Il semble à chacun que c'est chose juste d'aymer celuy dont il est aymé, et que l'amitié ne se paye que d'amitié; et au contraire, elle juge raisonnable de hayr ceux qui l'adorent" (II, 276). As a result of her opposition to *a priori* structures, Astrée's commands are deprived of their signifying function. Rather than serve as "touchstones of fidelity," which permit Celadon to prove the conformity of his will with hers, they are at best gratuitous—intended only "pour me faire souffrir davantage"—and at worst incompatible with his innate teleological destiny: "A-t'elle jamais demandé de moy que des preuves impossibles?" In the end, Celadon resolves the conflict between the real alterity and the ideal unity of lovers not by holding Astrée accountable to a higher truth, but by establishing her will as an autonomous, and self-suffi-cient law, a transcendental signified in its own right: "Or sus, disait-il, vivons donc pour sa gloire, puis que nous ne le pouvons faire pour nostre con-tentement" (II, 276).[4]

With the bliss of conjunctive awareness out of reach, memory acquires the hallucinatory quality of subjective fantasy, and it is in a world composed of memories irreconcilable with either empirical or ideal reality that Leonide and Adamas discover Celadon. As spiritual mentors, each offers a corrective point of view designed to reawaken one of the two differentiated modes of knowing that he neglects. In a series of philosophical conversations, Leonide advocates a practical materialism oriented toward self-preservation, while Adamas represents the authority of "right reason"—the objective ontological and ethical structure, the *Logos* of Being, from which each creature receives its essential identity, and teleological purpose.

The conversations, in turn, exhibit the three-fold structure of the idealist dialectic we have already outlined (see chapter 3), but in a parodic or subverted form imposed by Celadon's demented state. Rather than begin, at the lowest level of awareness, with an *a posteriori* rationalization of the chivalric code, Celadon insists upon the irreducible paradox between self-preservation (one of the principal goals of a *posteriori* reason) and perfect love; instead of advancing in the next phase of demonstration to deductive arguments based on *a priori* reason, he declares the incompatibility of the reason of lovers with the reason of men; and finally, in response to the objection that love so conceived is incompatible with happiness, he does not follow Silvandre in resolving the paradox at the level of metaphysical intuition—because the lover and the beloved are one, self-sacrifice is equivalent to self-fulfillment—but rather declares the superiority of the pleasures of imagination, "les biens des pensées." The mode of knowing at the end of the journey is "unitive" in the sense that it is predicated on the collapse of subject-object alterity, but whereas recollective knowledge of the divine ground not only transcends but provides the ultimate metaphysical support for lower modes of awareness, Celadon's ecstatic union renders them null and void. Love is incommensurate with, rather than a dialectical progression from, the lower orders of knowledge. Celadon's logic concludes not in self-transcendence but in self-absorption.

Leonide encounters Celadon in the course of one of her visits to the hamlet, and is astonished to find him starving himself in solitude rather than courting Astrée for whom he had been willing to refuse the affections of the high-born ladies at Isoure. Her concerns from the outset are those that come naturally to an *a posteriori raisonneur.* For her, the preservation and integrity of the individual ego is the *sine qua non* of rationality: "Comment, dit-elle, est-il possible que l'amour d'autruy vous ayt fait mespriser de ceste sorte vostre propre conservation?" (II, 281). Confronted with the spectacle of Celadon's self-sacrifice, she assumes the existence of an explanation which would render his behavior comprehensible in terms of the rational pursuit of self-interest: "Si j'avois à mourir, j'en voudrois demander la raison à celuy qui me condamneroit" (II, 281–2). Retributive justice preserves the rights of the individual by means of equitable exchange. For Celadon, however, love dissolves the distinction between self and other, rendering the notions of exchange and retribution irrelevant. He requires no other reason for his suffering than Astrée's arbitrary will: "Et quelle autre meilleure raison, adjousta Celadon, dois-je désirer d'en sçavoir, sinon que celle qui peut tout sur moy le veut ainsi? Tellement que la raison de mon mal sera que mon bien luy desplait" (II, 282).

Appalled by the apparent illogic of his position, Leonide attempts to bridge the gap between their frames of reference by justifying self-preservation in terms of an ethical imperative imposed by *a priori* reason. In this view, the identity and worth of each creature is a function of its place in an external relational structure, and the care and nourishment of the self is an act, not of self-assertion, but of submission. Celadon is obliged to love and care for himself because, within an overarching design, he is Astrée's beloved: "Si vous l'aymez, continua la nymphe, vous devez donques aymer ce qui est à elle; et si cela est, pourquoy ne vous aymez-vous, puis que vous estes tellement sien, que vous cessez d'estre vous-mesme?" (II, 282) Her attempt, however, reaches an impasse in the command of banishment which, by Celadon's own testimony, cannot be reconciled with the ontologically real relation presumed to exist between the (chivalric) lover and the beloved. The shepherd merely reiterates the paradox of his earlier soliloquy. His identity has been subsumed in that of a mistress who hates him. It therefore follows that he must hate himself: "Puis que j'ayme Astrée, répliqua le berger, je dois hayr tout ce qu'elle hait" (II, 282).

Finally, if Celadon's self-sacrifice can be coherently justified neither in terms of a logic of alterity and exchange, nor in terms of his participation in an all-encompassing *logos*, it must be admitted to be merely irrational. When Leonide reiterates for the third and final time her objection that "chacun est plus obligé à sa propre conservation qu'à la haine ou amitié d'autruy" (II,282), Celadon demonstrates the extent of his departure from the traditional, idealist hierarchy of knowledge by construing love not as a dialectical *advance beyond* but as a *negation of* practical reason: "Ces loix, interrompit incontinent le berger, sont bonnes et recevables parmy les hommes, mais non pas parmy les amants" (II, 282). Insofar as they lack an autonomous will and judgment, he explains, lovers are not men:

> je nie que l'amant soit homme, puis que des l'heure qu'il commence de devenir tel, il se despouille tellement de toute volonté et de tout jugement, qu'il ne veut ny ne juge plus que comme veut et juge celle à qui son affection l'a donné. (II, 283)

As in the conventional love debates, the final phase of the argument addresses the apparent conflict between self-sacrificial love and happiness.

Throughout the conversation, Leonide expostulates on the practical disadvantages of Celadon's position. When he declares his abdication of self-will: "Misérable condition, dit la nymphe en le plaignant, que la tienne, Celadon!" (II, 282) And, again, when he explains that lovers lack not only self-will, but an autonomous faculty of judgment: "O misérable estat que celuy de l'amant!" (II, 283). Just as Silvandre (the idealist dialectician) insists that lovers enjoy their greatest happiness in the absence of sensory pleasure, however, Celadon declares that even the draconian self-repression under which he lives affords superlative bliss: "Je ne sçaurais désirer plus de bien que le mal que je souffre; car en pourrais-je point souhaitter un plus grand que de luy plaire?" (II, 282). Those who cling to the impoverished rationality of alterity and exchange will never know the pleasure that accompanies the sacrifice of judgment: "Misérable celuy qui n'ayme point, puis qu'il ne peut jouyr des biens les plus parfaits qui soient au monde" (II, 283). The "biens" he has in mind, however, are neither the empirical objects of sensory pleasure proposed by Hylas and other egocentric lovers, nor the transcendent ideas with which the soul achieves contemplative union proposed by Silvandre and the other idealists, but rather imaginary objects that afford the soul an hallucinatory gratification: "Y a-t'il rien de si aisé à divertir que les biens qui sont en la pensée?" (II, 283) He proceeds to describe the power of imagination to generate its own satisfactions by conjuring up images not merely of the mistress herself, but of any object which, by virtue of its association with her, has been subjectively invested with erotic value:

> Quand un amant se représente la beauté de celle qu'il ayme, mais encore cela est trop, quand il se remet seullement une de ses actions en mémoire, mais c'est trop encores, quand il se resouvient du lieu ou il l'a veue, voire quand il pense qu'elle se resouviendra de l'avoir veu en quelque autre endroit, pensez-vous qu'il voulust changer son contentement à tous ceux de l'univers? Tant s'en faut, il est si jaloux et si soigneux d'entretenir seul cette pensée, que pour n'en faire part à personne, il se retire ordinairement en lieu solitaire et reculé de la veue des hommes, ne se soucie point de quitter tous les autres biens que les hommes ont accoustumé de chérir et rechercher avec tant de peine, pourvue qu'avec la perte de tous il achette le bien de ses chères pensées. (II 283)

In this account of imaginary erotic gratification, d'Urfé crosses the threshold from a theory of mind which grants epistemological priority to the objective order to one that grants priority to the subject. He explains the lover's unitive knowledge and enjoyment of the beloved not in terms of an ontologically real relation, but in terms of psychological projection. What had once been regarded as a function of an *a priori* order is now regarded as a function of erotic desire itself. Expressing her contempt for such pleasures, Leonide "l'estime misérable de le voir réduit aux imaginations pour avoir quelque contentement" (II, 284). And when Celadon attributes a mystical efficacy to his fidelity on the ground that Love—that is, the divine intentionality which draws all things toward their teleological fulfillment—has banished him and will bring him home, she dismisses the notion as fantastical: "Si vos imaginations, répliqua la nymphe, pouvaient autant sur les autres que sur vous, il y aurait quelque apparence en ce que vous dites" (II, 284). For those who have crossed the cultural divide into the modern era, the route to health and happiness lies primarily through self-directed action: "Mais croyez que les dieux n'aident guière à ceux qui ne s'aident point eux-mesmes" (II, 284).

When Celadon's physical and mental decline continues in spite of her ministrations, Leonide persuades Adamas, the chief druid, to intervene. Upon his arrival in the forest, Adamas completes the analysis of Celadon's error and provides instruction conducive to his health and reintegration into community life. While Leonide emphasizes his neglect of the instinct of self-preservation, Adamas calls attention to his transgression against the suprapersonal rational order:

> Vous estes nay, Celadon, à quelque chose de meilleur, vous, dis-je que le grand Taramis a particulièrement doué de la raison, ne serez-vous condamné par son infaillible jugement si à la nécessité vous ne produisez les effects qu'il attend de vous? (II, 316)

By retreating to the cave, he abdicates his responsibilities in the structure of economic and social relationships in which each individual possesses a providentially established status and role:

Encore qu'il [i.e. the creator, Taramis] nous ait remis sous nostre volonté, si ne sommes-nous pas nostres, et faut que nous attendions un rude chastiment, si nous avons diposé de nous-mesmes autrement que nous n'avons deu. (II, 316)

Since erotic love, precisely because it arises from the individuated and self-seeking ego, places the authority of the objective rational order in abeyance, Celadon's retreat from society might be justified as proof that he cannot sustain the loss of Astrée's favor "sans perdre aussi pour quelque temps l'usage de la raison." The suspension of reason, however, is a suspension of human nature itself and must, he warns, be temporary not only because it violates his teleological destiny, but because it removes him from the ontological category (rational beings) in which Astrée must find her objects of affection. In direct response to Celadon's dictum that "lovers are not men," he declares that lovers must in the last analysis remain men as well, and his final advice is that Celadon return to himself in the sense of submitting to his predestined place in the cosmic scheme:

Mais à ceste heure il est temps que vous reveniez en vous-mesme, et que vous luy fassiez paroistre que vous n'estes pas seulement amoureux, mais homme aussi, et que si le desplaisir vous a jusques icy osté l'usage de la raison, la raison toutesfois vous est demeurée qui, peu après, a repris sa force, afin qu'elle ne se repente pas d'avoir affectionné un amant qui n'estoit pas homme. (II, 317)

If Celadon in the first dispute insists that lovers sacrifice their individuated will and hence the capacity for a rational pursuit of self-interest, he now acknowledges the lover's abdication of *a priori* reason in both its extra- and intra-mental manifestations—that is, the divine *logos* or cosmic order both as imprinted in the rational soul and as displayed visibly in social institutions, and the "book of nature." He has, he declares with psychological precision, neither the will nor the understanding proper to human beings, but only the memory—the faculty responsible for unitive knowledge: "Il ne m'est resté autre chose de l'homme que la mémoire, n'en ayant plus ny l'entendement ny la volonté" (II, 317). As we have seen, in the traditional object-centered paradigm, will and understanding counterbalance the unifying impulse of memory by assuring the recognition of differences as well as similarities. Now, with their role in the cognitive process eliminated, memory appropriates all objects as metaphorical substitutes for the one reality that matters—the beloved— without regard either for their irreducible difference from himself, or for their location in a suprapersonal order.

Celadon elaborates the consequences of the ascendancy of memory over the various modalities of *a priori* reason. On the one hand, his identity ceases to be a function of his place in a differentiated structure of status and role, and comes instead to depend upon his transparency to the beloved. He becomes, as it were, a commemorative monument bearing the imprint of Astrée's character. What we see before us, he explains, is no longer "Celadon, fils d'Alcippe et d'Amarillis [...] mais seulement une vaine idole que le Ciel conserve encore parmy ces bois pour marque que Celadon sceut aymer" (II, 317). At the same time, the differentiated structure of language imprinted in the rational soul succumbs to a powerful unifying impulse that imposes upon all signs a single, endlessly repeated meaning: "Et toutefois, puis que réduit en cette extrémité, l'usage de la parole m'est permis pour répondre au grand Dieu Tharamis, et à tout ce que vous m'opposez, il suffit que je vous dise seulement ce mot, J'AYME" (II, 371).

Rejecting ethical imperatives predicated on either self-interest (which protects the rights of the individuated will) or duty (which protects the authority of a suprapersonal order), Celadon establishes his obedience to Astrée as the governing principle of his identity:

> Et quant à ce qui me touche, celuy-la se peut-il dire amant qui a des yeux pour voir autre chose que ce qu'il aime? Ah! mon père, c'est sans doute que j'ayme, et c'est sans doute aussi que je suis aveugle pour moy, pour mes troupeaux, pour mes parents, et pour tout le reste des hommes. Car je n'ay des yeux que pour celle a qui je suis. (II, 317)

Finally, as in the conventional tripartite debate structure, the apparent conflict between "parfaite amitié" and happiness must be addressed. Adamas objects, as had Leonide, that Astrée's absence prevents the real, physical consummation of his love: "Mais si vous aymez, continua le druide, comment ne vous efforcez-vous de voir celle que vous aymez?" True to the chivalric tradition, Celadon reminds Adamas that the lover sacrifices self-gratification in order to enjoy a higher pleasure: "Si j'ayme, respondit-il, comment voudrois-je desplaire à celle que j'ayme, ou comment luy desobéir? ou plustost comment ne recevray-je un extrême contentement de luy plaire et de luy obéir?" (II, 318) But isn't chivalric obedience intended to render visible a metaphysical reality—the unity of souls—that legitimizes a real social relationship? And doesn't Celadon's hiddenness therefore undermine its true purpose, which is its signifying function? These considerations would seem to resonate in Adamas' reply: "Mais, dit le druide, elle ne sait pas que vous luy obéissez" (II, 318). Instead of arguing as he might have done that his actions are intrinsically worthy as the confirmation of his place in a supra-personal order, Celadon once again reverts to the self-sufficient "biens des pensées." As the solitary witness of his own fidelity, he derives his pleasure from the knowledge of his own perfection: "Pour notre satisfaction, nous sçachons que nous avons fait ce qui a esté de nostre devoir. Il n'y a point de plus fidelle tesmoin, ny de juge plus rigoureux contre nous que nous-mesmes" (II, 318).

II. Spiritual Exercise and the Rectification of Signs: The Mentality of the Temple

In the previous section, we have seen that Celadon, unable to accept the irremediable alterity and self-enclosure of his mistress, retreats into an imaginative universe symbolically represented by the wilderness cavern where he lives on memories of a unitive relation once enjoyed but now forever lost. From his meditation on Astrée's portrait we learn that he regards himself as being conjoined by an intrinsic and indissoluble bond with a mistress whose refusal to return his love transgresses against the objective rational order in which love and aversion, sympathies and antipathies, are signs of ontologically real relationships. Rather than abandon love in favor of reason, however, he sacrifices reason to love. Here we have the origin of his madness, for in the absence of reason, love—the subjective experience of unity—triumphs over his awareness of difference. The distinctions between himself and objects along one axis, and among objects themselves along another, lose their relevance as he succumbs to a debilitating monism. Celadon's dialogues with Leonide and Adamas reveal his refusal to acknowledge either his individuated ego or his place in the suprapersonal structure from which he would normally receive his social status and role. The remainder of his sojourn in the forest is devoted to a heuristic process that draws him away from the mentality of the cave in which a thwarted eroticism projects upon all objects the image of the beloved, and toward the mentality of the Temple in which his love for Astrée reaffirms his place in a differentiated cosmic and social order embodied in the authentic ceremonial life of Gaul.

The process unfolds as a progressive reorientation of thought from the inward concerns of the self, to the external order of nature, and concludes in the contemplation of the attributes of the creator. In the first stage, Adamas encourages Celadon to express his feelings in verse because "les playes d'amour estant de telle condition que plus elles sont cachées et tenue secretes, plus aussi se vont-elles envenimant" (II, 320). In the second, Celadon's self-absorbed lyricism gives place to, or is at least accompanied by, an outwardly directed activity: Adamas "luy conseilla de passer son temps dans le boccage sacré, qui estoit auprès de là, fust à graver sur les escorces des jeunes arbres des chiffres et des devises, fust à faire des tonnes et cabinets, pour l'embellis-sement du lieu" (II, 320). Like our "first parents" of the Biblical myth, the shepherd becomes a care-taker of the garden, transforming and beautifying the wood. If he is fully to recover his identity as a human being, however, he must not only fulfill his pre-determined *telos* (even the beasts do that), but achieve an enlightened awareness of his role. This can only occur when he knowingly submits to the objective rational order within which all things—including the beauty of the mistress and the deeds of the lover—are signs directing the soul toward God.

The centerpiece of Adamas' instruction in the Temple is a discourse on the history of druidic religion, coupled with the construction of the Temple de l'Amitié in honor of "Teutates, Hesus, Belenus, Tharamis nostre Dieu." The discourse is an extended reflection on the epistemology of signs which draws an implicit parallel between Celadon's mistaken interpretation of the signs of love and the misinterpretation of religious symbols in the society at large. Verbal and visual representations of theological truths—the names of God, icons, and sacred architecture—have suffered the same alienation from transcendent guarantees of meaning as the signs by which the lovers seek to represent themselves to each other. Having once possessed a providentially assured resemblance to their referents, they have become impenetrably opaque.

Rather than stabilize meaning with reference to subjective experience, however, Adamas employs etymology (when dealing with words) and allegory (when dealing with visual icons) to rectify a symbolic universe in which creation is a vast web of signs revealing the attributes and intentions of the creator (II, 320–329). The temple discourse, in other words, elaborates precisely the resolution to the problem of symbolic reference toward which Celadon is naturally inclined, but which the individuating experience of erotic desire prevents him from achieving except in the realm of imagination.

In Adamas' account, the decisive event in the history of signs occurs at Babel which marks the dividing line between a mythical transparency forever out of reach, and the deepening opacity that follows. In the Biblical story, the transgression that prompts the foreclosure of meaning is, of course, the construction of a tower by which people intended to climb into the heavens on their own volition—an act of collective self-assertion which signifies a turning away from transcendence toward the natural order, from creator to the domain of creatures.[5] The linguistic "fall" is followed by a brief golden age under the leadership of Dis Samothés who received a revelation of theological and "scientific" truth in the original, perfectly transparent, speech, and whose authority therefore derives from the link he maintains with the pre-lapsarian era:

> Ce grand Dis Samothés, incontinent après la division des hommes, à cause de la confusion des langues, estant bien instruit par son ayeul, fust en religion du vray Dieu, fust aux sciences plus cachées, s'en vint descendre par l'Océan Armorique en cette terre que jusques à ceste heure nous nommons Gaule. (I, 320)

The cultural order that emerges after Babel is characterized by a plurality of discursive communities at odds with each other but internally coherent as each in its own way refers its symbolic universe back to the originary discourse of the mythical ancestors. The fact that Gaul occupies a position of ethical and military preeminence in this pluralistic world makes it pedagogically useful as an exemplary case: Samothés "regna longuement en paix et après luy sa postérité, avec tant d'heur, qu'il n'y a eu endroit de la terre qui n'ait cogneu le nom, et la valeur des Gaulois" (II, 322).

While the collective turning away from the transcendent toward the natural order, signified by the construction of the tower, introduces the first displacement of signs from their providentially intended or "inherent" meanings, an intensification of subjective self-awareness, signified by the assertion of personal ambition, initiates the second displacement by disrupting the adequation between the self and the conventional (historical, cultural) symbolic order:

> Que si ce peuple que nous nommons Romain, s'est usurpé la domination des Gaulois, ce n'a point esté par les armes, mais plustost par chastiment de nos dissensions qui, estant pleines d'animosité entre nous, ont esté cause de nous le faire appeller. (II, 322)

The community reaches the extreme limit of its decline during the Roman occupation when the introduction of linguistic impurities and pagan religious customs further increases the distance between signs and their pre-lapsarian meaning, and makes it impossible to determine which discourses, ceremonies and customs are indigenous and authentic, and which imported and false. It is as though the very souls of the people are re-formed by the introduction of an alien symbolic order:

> Mais d'autant que le vainqueur donne des loix qu'il luy plaist au vaincu, ils en firent de mesme en Gaule, où s'usurpant avec une extrême tyrannie, non seulement nos biens, mais nos âmes aussi, ils voulurent changer nos cérémonies, et nous faire prendre leurs dieux, nous contraignant de leur bastir des temples, de recevoir leurs idoles, et de représenter Teutates, Hesus, Belenus et Tharamis avec des figures de leur Mercure, Mars, Appollon et Juppiter. (II, 325)

Finally, the expulsion of the Romans by the Franks initiates a return to the legitimate political authority (II, 322), and to the authentic religious traditions of the golden age: "Il semble que nostre authorité [that of the druids] et nos sainctes coustumes reviennent en leur splendeur" (II, 325).

A parallel degenerative sequence may be traced in the love plot—a sequence so nearly identical, in fact, that it can scarcely be unintended. In a mythical past, prior to the advent of love's tyranny, an external fabric of speech and symbol concretely embodies a providential design perfectly harmonized with the aspirations of the inner self. The birth of love, like the construction of the Tower of Babel, inaugurates a decisive rupture between the self and the transcendent order, foreclosing access to providentially established meanings. Astrée's confession[6] describes the events that follow. An initial post-lapsarian period of "patience" and tranquility equivalent to the golden age after Babel gives place to a second period dominated by "prudence" which seals individuals off from each other in the impenetrable privacy of self-interest. Jealousy, the first consequence of "prudence," is an intestine evil just as "nos dissensions pleines d'animosité entre nous," and interposes a layer of subjective fantasy between signs and their referents. At the same time, the lovers are subject to an invasion of discourses which originate elsewhere, and which parallels the arrival of the Romans with their inauthentic religious practices. Both difficulties reveal the impossibility of sustaining a privileged representational space in a symbolic universe where discourses proliferate endlessly with neither subjective nor metaphysical guarantees of meaning. We have entered the illusionistic, textualized universe of the baroque.

In the light of Adamas' discourse, it appears that Celadon's striving to apprehend and represent his true relation to Astrée replicates the epic *travail* of mankind to read through the opacity of words and things the traces of an *a priori* order. Although that order, the very structure of being, had been plainly manifest in language in its original, pre-lapsarian state, at present, it may be seen only dimly and with great effort. The healing of the lover, and the return religious purity, both require a rectification of signs. Adamas restores the purity of language by means of etymology, reverses the error of paganism by instructing Celadon in the art of allegorical interpretation, and returns Astrée to her proper place as an icon in the larger, ontological and symbolic structure of the Temple de l'Amitié.

For Adamas, etymology is a science not merely of words, but of the things to which words refer. His attitude, so foreign to later seventeenth-century linguistics for which verbal signs are arbitrary representations, reflects the "cratylist" view that words originally possessed an intrinsic, and providentially established, resemblance to their referents. By clearing away morphological distortions and refuting mistaken derivations, Adamas restores the immediacy of the original likeness, and permits language once more to function as a true reflection not of created objects as such, but of the metaphysical order of which the objects themselves are signs. Etymology is a form of rational proof. What is true of the word, the name, is true of the thing. In his disquisition on the word "druid," Adamas rejects two false derivations before stating the true. The first is the name of a prominent religious teacher, Druys, while the second is the Greek word for oak (drys), an object of religious veneration. What these derivations share, and what distinguishes them from the third, is that they terminate the quest for meaning in the phenomenal world (the man, the tree), rather than pointing beyond the world of appearances to an ideal order. Adamas by contrast recalls the word's original form as it had been in a perfectly transparent language of inherent signs, and by doing so restores its power to reveal the inner *telos* of the priesthood:

> Le nom du druide [...] au langage de l'ayeul de Samothés [the language prior to Babel], signifie *contemplateur*, du mot Drissim, parce que, comme vous sçavez, mon enfant, notre principale vocation consiste en la contemplation des oeuvres de Dieu. (II, 322)

Adamas applies a similar method in response to Celadon's query regarding the four names of God in the druidic theology: "Comment, mon père, respondit Celadon, vous en nommez quatre, et vous ne dites que nostre Dieu? Il faudrait dire nos Dieux" (II, 321).[7] Just as the name "druide" traced to its source in the "langage de l'ayeul de Samothés" teaches us the purpose of the priestly vocation, the names of God in the original language teach us, directly and without interpretation, the divine attributes. The historical distortion of names, however, conceals the reality to which they inherently refer. Adamas retraces the degenerative path from the unity of God to the multiplicity of his attributes, to the plurality of gods, and at last to the veneration of men as gods, in order to expose the illusion created by darkened signs. The first mutation is carried out within the original language itself:

> Et parce que l'ignorance du peuple grossier estait telle qu'il ne pouvait comprendre cette suprême bonté et toute puissance, qu'ils nommaient THAU, c'est à dire Dieu, sans en apprendre quelques effects, ils [Dis Samothés and Druys] lui donnerent trois noms: IEHUS qui signifie fort, Belenos, c'est à dire Dieu homme et Taharamis qui signifie repurgeant, nous voulant enseigner par ces trois noms, que Dieu est tout puissant, Créateur et conservateur des hommes. (II, 323)

The ignorance that prefers the multiplicity of the effects to the unity of the cause produces only a slight displacement. The path back from effects to cause remains visible in the language itself in the fact that the names of God are adjectival rather than substantive. Before long, however, a purely arbitrary, conventional element in language sullies over the original morphology of the names, and renders the return more difficult. Since sign and signified are joined by an inherent resemblance, every deviation in form obscures the meaning itself:

> Mais depuis, par les changements que le temps et l'ignorance du peuple apporte en toutes choses, mais principalement aux noms, au lieu de THAU ils dirent THAUTA, et en fin THAUTATES et THEUTATES. Au lieu de IEHUS BELENOS et THAHARAMIS, desquels l'aspiration sur le milieu estait un peu mal-aisée, ils dirent HESUS, BELENOS et THARAMIS. (II, 323)

The deepening opacity of signs leads at last to the practice of venerating the attributes of God as separate deities—a mistake made first by the inhabitants of Gaul who invoke different names for different needs, then by the Roman invaders who assume that their new subjects are invoking several gods analogous to the pagan pantheon, and finally by Celadon whose theological ignorance both parallels and helps to explain his own deification of Astrée: "Et quoi? mon père, respondit le berger, Teutates, Hesus, Tharamis et Belenus, ne sont-ce pas les dieux que l'on nous dit, à sçavoir Mercure, Mars, Jupiter et Apollon, mais un Dieu seulement?" (II, 323) If idolatry results from the separation of names from the things they inherently signify, the defeat of idolatry lies in the recognition that beyond the diversity of cultural forms lies the transcendent One. Names which seem to designate multiple deities, Adamas explains, "ne sont proprement que surnoms de ce grand Teutates" (324).

Historical accretions similarly obscure the meanings concealed in visual symbols. If the transparent language of the age before Babel gives place to darkened speech of men, natural signs in the book of creation are displaced by artificial symbolic structures. The ancient Gaulois had worshiped in open air with no other sacred spaces than the fields and groves because they recognized the impossibility of representing the ineffable (II, 324). Under the influence of their Roman masters, however, they adopted the practice of praying in temples adorned with images not only of gods but of men.

If etymology permits the seeker to find his way back to a transparent word, allegory permits him to find his way among divergent religious practices to the hidden truth within. In keeping with the "natural theology" propounded by many Renaissance neo-Platonists, d'Urfé suggests that all symbolic forms whatever their immediate historical derivation—natural objects, man-made structures and images, the heroes of Roman history, and figures from pagan mythology—reveal the attributes and intentions of the creator when properly understood. In pagan temples, Adamas tells Celadon, "il faut que vous y alliez fort retenu, et que sur tout vous ne preniez pas cela pour des dieux séparés, mais pour les vertus, puissances et effects d'un seul Dieu [...]. Par ce moyen les adorant comme je dis, vous refererez tout à nostre grand Teutates" (II, 326).

The rectification of signs prepares Celadon to recognize first Astrée's place, and then his own, in the suprapersonal order represented in authentic religious doctrines and ceremonial practices. The notion that heroes may be venerated as patterns of virtue, in particular, sets the stage for the construction of the Temple de l'Amitié where he will adore Astrée as the embodiment of a divine idea rather than as an object of egocentric desire. If at the beginning of his sojourn in the forest, Celadon posits Astrée's will as the center of his identity and as the reality to which all signs refer, he learns through Adamas' instruction to recognize the epistemological priority of a suprapersonal order within which his mistress *is* a sign, and from which his actions must therefore derive their final cause and purposiveness. Adamas authorizes him to dedicate part of the temple to Astrée "non pas comme à une première divinité, mais comme à un très-parfait ouvrage de cette divinité" (II, 321).

Celadon's life in the Temple, however, fails to resolve the conflict between authorized representations of identity on the one hand, and personal authenticity on the other. If his obedience to Astrée's command acquires a suprapersonal meaning by virtue of her position in the metaphysical and symbolic order of the Temple, it nevertheless continues to entail the sacrifice of the individual ego. Beneath the orderly structures we hear the whisper of another, inconsolable and unrepresented self which must inevitably break forth to express its truth as well.

From the outset, Adamas recognizes the impossibility of eradicating the ego, and has accepted the more modest goal of redirecting its desires toward metaphysical objects, effecting, as it were, a kind of transference of affective value from the mistress to an ideal order with which she has come to be identified: "Mais tout ce qu'il faisoit, c'estoit par le dessein du druide qui aussi, comme un bon médecin s'accommodant avec son malade, luy assaisonnoit tous ses conseils par quelque dessein d'amour" (II, 320). If Celadon adores Astrée as one of the most perfect works of the creator, and "refers" her as a sign to a transcendent ideal to which he gives up his ego, his motives are clearly sexual: "Mais d'autant que le druide avait opinion que, s'il ne flattoit un peu le mal de Celadon, il perdroit peu à peu la dévotion et la volonté d'y travailler, il nomma le temple du nom de la déesse Astrée" (II, 327). The ambiguity of Astrée's "double inscription" as the embodiment of an ideal reality and as an ontologically self-sufficient object appears in the double status of the portrait in the temple that bears her name. The painting is both an icon and a quasi-pornographic image, inspiring both metaphysical and sexual longings:

> Le druide, l'ayant quelque temps considérée: Vrayment, dit-il, mon enfant, ta folie est belle, et faut advouer que je ne crois pas qu'il y ait visage plus beau, ny auquel il se lise une plus grande modestie d'amour, ny une plus douce sévérité. Heureux le père qui a un tel enfant! Heureuse la mère qui l'a eslevée! Heureux les yeux qui la voyent, *mais plus heureux celuy qui aymé d'elle la possedera*! (II, 328) [Emphasis mine.]

Astrée's sudden appearance in the temple (she arrives with a group of shepherds led by Silvandre) represents the brutal intrusion of concrete reality into the ideal world of thought, and initiates the next phase of Celadon's mental development: "Et parce qu'il s'en alloit tout en ses pensées, sans prendre garde a ce qui luy estoit autour, jamais homme ne fut plus estonné que luy, quand tout à coup il apperceut Astrée" (II, 330). The sight of her half-dressed figure reclining in the grass reawakens sexual desire, and exposes the poverty of substitute gratifications. She ceases to signify, and becomes a self-present object under her shepherd's decidedly unspiritual gaze. Her petticoat "peu retroussé par mesgarde" displays a portion of her leg. Through a thin gauze handkerchief "la blancheur de sa gorge paroissoit merveilleusement," and her sleeves, turned back to the elbow, reveal "un bras blanc et potelé" (II, 330).

The episode concludes with the construction of a "vain tombeau"—an empty tomb in Celadon's memory—intended to give his soul a final resting place. Insofar as the edifice combines both verbal and visual symbolism, and occasions an elaborate ceremony of consecration, it would seem to represent the conventional symbolic order itself—a sort of symbol of symbols. But insofar as it is without content—the tomb is "vain" in the sense of being empty—it would also seem to bear the weight of d'Urfé's ironic commentary on a paradigm of self-representation predicated on suppression of the subject. The tomb does not contain the individual whose identity it purports to represent. It is an empty structure, a text without (subjective) meaning.

III. Erotic Voyeurism and the Emergence of Subjectivity: The Cross-dressing Episodes

If the temple exercises entail the sacrifice of subjective interiority to a suprapersonal order, the cross-dressing episodes reverse the process. Celadon's encounter with Astrée sets in motion the dynamics of the paradigm shift that informs, on a much larger scale, the narrative as a whole and leads to the emergence of subjectivity as an alternative center of personal identity. Self-representation in the temple is predicated on his transparency to an external order—a sacrifice of all that is merely subjective by virtue of which he accepts his "inscription" within the official discourses and ceremonial practices of chivalric love. His erotic reawakening opens a gap between private experience and conventional signs, compelling him to reveal himself to Astrée directly rather than through the elaborate display of icons and quasi-sacred texts. To do so, however, would not only call into question his status as perfect lover by placing him in violation of the command of banishment which, for him, represents the ethical imperative of the code. It would also, by affirming the epistemological value of subjective experience, invalidate the structure of signifying relations upon which self-representation in the temple depends. Hence his dilemma: he can obey Astrée's command at the expense of an emergent, inward truth, or he can affirm his inward truth at the expense of the entire object-centered structure of identity and meaning. Faced with this intolerable set of alternatives, he takes a peculiarly baroque middle course. He assumes a disguise.

One of the most startling and frequently analyzed features of *L'Astrée* is the fact that beginning a little less than halfway through the narrative, and continuing for some one thousand pages thereafter, Celadon successfully impersonates a woman. Dressed as Adamas' daughter, Alexis, a druidess in the convent of Carnutes, he enjoys the companionship of Astrée and her friends without detection. However implausible the disguise to modern readers, it aptly illuminates the split between the inner self and the external order of signs which prevents the reconciliation of the lovers. The ruse is Celadon's paradoxical and doomed attempt to satisfy both the inward impulse, which forecloses the path to interpersonal knowledge, and the imperative of obedience upon which his representation as a lover depends.

But the strategy hardly resolves the problem of self-representation. Instead, the dual personality "Alexis-Celadon" entails an internalization of the very paradox between the ossified symbolic forms and an autonomous inner self from which he would like to escape. Just as Montaigne pays lip service to orthodox ideas while giving free reign to his unbridled mind in the "privacy" of his essays, the false but publicly represented self permits the hero to preserve an outward appearance of obedience to the code (encapsulated, we must always remember, in the command of banishment), while the inner, private self emerges only in nocturnal soliloquies. Insofar as the disguise is a concession to Astrée's command, "Alexis" represents, in the economy of the hero's personality, a lingering attachment to the old order. Insofar as the authentic or true self is increasingly identified with interior privacy, "Celadon" represents his leaning forward toward the new.[8]

The inauguration of this split is clearly apparent in the casuistic arguments with which Adamas persuades Celadon to adopt the Alexis disguise. Obedience to Astrée's command, which Celadon had envisioned as an expression of his intrinsic being, is reduced to the status of mere play acting, and his true identity is reformulated as a function of the inward, private self whom he continues to *be* regardless of the external appearance he assumes: "Pensez-vous, adjousta le druide, qu'elle vous voye, si elle ne vous cognoit? et comment vous cognoistra-t-elle ainsi revestu?" At first, Celadon insists upon a conjunctive relation between being and appearance, self and sign. He would in fact "be" Celadon however he were dressed, with the result that his appearance in Astrée's presence would belie his identity as perfect lover whether she knew it or not: "Mais répliqua Celadon, en quelque sorte que je sois revestu, si seray-je en effect Celadon, de sorte que véritablement je luy desobéiray" (II, 398). But Adamas will not relent. Astrée has not forbidden Celadon to "be" himself, but only to "appear" as himself: "Que vous soyez Celadon, il n'y

a point de doute, respondit Adamas, mais ce n'est pas en cela que vous contre-
viendrez à son ordonnance, car elle ne vous a pas deffendu d'estre Celadon,
mais seullement de luy faire voir ce Celadon" (II, 398). The argument cuts to
the core of the intrinsic relation between appearance and being. The true self
is inward and inscrutably hidden: "Or *elle ne vous verra pas en vous voyant,*
mais Alexis. Et par conclusion, si elle ne vous cognoit point, vous ne
l'offencerez point" (II, 398). [Emphasis mine.]

   With Celadon's identity divided between an external play-acted self and
the interior "true" self, he leaves the mental universe of chivalric idealism
behind and enters the proto-modern world of baroque illusion. The ideal love
relation will no longer be conceived in terms of an innate conformity of beings,
but in terms of alterity and exchange, and the obstacle to interpersonal knowledge will no longer be attributed to the ontological disparity between material
forms and transcendent ideas, but to subjective self-enclosure and misrepresentation. D'Urfé insists on precisely the psychological interiority that forecloses access to "la vérité d'amour" when summarizing the plot situation at
the opening of Volume III and projecting the direction for later development.
As Astrée and Alexis-Celadon anticipate a gathering at Adamas' house where
they will meet for the first time, they burn with mutual desire, but an entrenched habit of concealment on the one side, and the garb of a druidess on
the other, render their feelings invisible and prevent reconciliation:

> Et combien Amour est mauvais maistre, et combien il paye mal la peine
> de ceux qui le servent: il donne à ces amants tout ce qu'ils sçauraient
> désirer, car il faict qu'ils meurent d'amour l'un pour l'autre, et il n'y a
> point de désire en leur âme plus ardent que celuy de cette réciproque
> volonté; mais comme s'il estait jaloux que les humains jouyssent de ces
> contentemens qui sont le plus grands que les immortels puissent avoir,
> il veut qu'ils ignorent le bien qu'il leur faict, et que dans cette igno-
> rance, ils n'en jouyssent point! (III, 12)

   Although the hero continues to be torn between the external, obedient
"Alexis" and the internal, self-seeking "Celadon" he develops inexorably toward an affirmation of the latter. An initial period of passivity associated with
his lingering nostalgia for a metaphysical conception of identity gives place to
an increasingly intense experience of subjective privacy which leads, in the
final stage, to his emergence as a self-determining individual.[9] The first phase

begins with his arrival at Adamas' house and ends with his return in the company of Astrée and her companions to the Temple d'Amitié. Throughout this interval, he persists in the strategy of deceit only out of respect for Adamas. Privately, he adheres to an ideal of obedience as the true expression of his identity, and regards his concealed passions as inauthentic and potentially subversive. A collective visit to the temple marks a turning away from the chivalric ideal toward possessive individualism.

When Celadon takes up residence in the hamlet as Astrée's female companion, the pressures impelling him toward a decisive break with the chivalric past gather additional force. The intolerable conflict between the symbolic order of courtly love (which his obedience preserves) and subjective interiority (the authentic self which his disguise conceals) reaches its highest pitch of intensity in two episodes of erotic voyeurism and interrupted sexual foreplay. His identity hangs in the balance between two incompatible systems of self-representation. On the one hand, erotic desire introduces an experience of inward privacy that cannot be reconciled with the conjunctive logic of chivalric idealism. On the other, it has not yet become possible for Celadon to imagine subjective consciousness as an alternative criterion of truth in self-presentation. As a result, he finds himself compelled to preserve the illusion of conjunction by imaginary means—means in which the modern reader inevitably recognizes the characteristics of a "substitute gratification."

The third and final phase begins when Adamas and Leonide leave Celadon alone in the hamlet at the end of Volume III. Under the individuating pressure of erotic desire he decisively abandons the chivalric ideal. His identity as Astrée's lover ceases to depend on his obedience to her command, and comes instead to depend on the authenticity of his inner life. But the ideal of confessional transparency has already been tried, and proven unattainable. Astrée and Celadon can never enter fully into that new symbolic order in which appearances—all of the institutionalized roles and modes of speech—will be reestablished as transparent representations of autonomous individuals. In the final episodes of the narrative, Celadon must progress beyond the privacy of the bedroom, *locus* of erotic desire and confessional speech, to enter the domain of public action. At the Siege of Marcilly he at last establishes his identity as a social subject, united with Astrée neither by an innate ontological conformity, nor by a subjective emotional affinity, but by the authority of the collective gaze.

During the two days the lovers spend together at Adamas' house, the individuating, interiorizing impulse that helped to motivate Celadon's strategy of disguise makes little headway against his lingering adherence to the imperative of obedience in terms of which he continues to conceptualize his "true" identity. As he anticipates Astrée's arrival he is torn between a desire to see her and the knowledge that were his ruse exposed, his status as "perfect lover" would be in jeopardy (III, 12). At one moment he is overwhelmed with joy: "La voila, dit-elle, la plus belle, et la plus aimable bergère de l'univers, imitant presque en ce transport Adraste en sa folie." At another he suffers the agony of guilt: "Mais, ô Dieu, dit-elle, comment m'oseray-je présenter devant ses yeux, puis qu'elle m'a commandé le contraire?" (III, 61) Prohibited, banished, repressed, the erotic subtext in the lovers' conversations remains almost entirely submerged. In the course of two consecutive interviews, elaborate exchanges of conventional compliments are followed by equally conventional professions of reciprocal friendship (III, 72–75; 221–26).

Although Adamas suggests that true identity is inward and private, and that Celadon should assert his autonomy by actively pursuing Astrée regardless of her command, the shepherd continues to conceptualize identity as a function of his passive submission to external structures. He only brings himself to disobey Astrée by deferring to the priestly status of Adamas, merely substituting one command for another.[10] Unable to project himself as maker and molder of his destiny, he succumbs to resigned fatalism: "Souviens-toi du bonheur où tu t'es veu, et si jamais il y a eu berger qui ait eut plus de sujet de se dire bien heureux que toi! Et incontinent tourne les yeux sur l'estat où ceste fortune t'a réduit, et considère si tu pouvois tomber en un précipice plus profond" (III, 243). His disguise—his concession to the code—is a continuous reminder of his lack of entrepreneurial will: "Tu desrobes sous le nom d'autruy ce que non seulement on refuserait au tien, mais que tu ne serais pas mesme si effronté que de recevoir ny d'oser entreprendre" (III, 243). Locked in his role as a victim of external determining forces represented variously by Astrée, by Adamas, and at last by the goddess "Fortune," he yearns for a life of solitude and imaginary gratifications: "Peu s'en fallut qu'il ne retournast à ses premiers desseins de vivre esloigné de tout le monde puis qu'il ne pouvait espérer quelque changement en ses misères" (III, 244).[11]

The journey to the Temple d'Amitié tips the scales in the direction of the emergent voice of subjective interiority. The temple is a transitional place through which the hero passes not only on his journey toward the suprapersonal, but in his progress toward subjectivity. It is a point of intersection between the authorized and the covert discourses of the self, and its principal symbols—the sacred architecture, and the icons and laws of chivalric love—are suffused in equal measure with the metaphysical and the erotic. If the former had been the focus of Celadon's initial experience of the temple, the latter comes to the foreground on the occasion of his return. Everywhere, there are traces of an unspoken empirical and subjective truth just beneath the patina of the external forms. The idealist mimesis characteristic of religious iconography shades into realism in the portrait of a goddess who not only bears an astonishing resemblance to the historical Astrée, but who, at variance with tradition, appears in the garb of a shepherdess. The hymns to the goddess strewn about the grass are love poems written in a hand that closely resembles that of Celadon. It is, moreover, the subjective presence and not the ceremonial superstructure, that captures the imaginations of the pilgrims. While Adamas instructs Alcidon and Daphnide in the history of Forezian religious practices (III, 476–77), the shepherds examine the temple not for distant reflections of divine ideas, but for evidence that would reveal the identities of the real lovers represented in the icon and texts. The portrait occasions yet another exchange of amorous compliments between Astrée and Alexis (III, 9, 478), and the love poetry elicits an obsessive curiosity from Phillis and Diane: "Malaysément ces belles bergères eussent peu laisser un seul de ces rouleaux qui estaient sur les autels, sans les desployér et les lire" (III, 481).

The processes contributing to the emergence of subjectivity as the authenticating ground of self-representation continues when Celadon returns to the hamlet for the first time since his leap into the Lignon, and lives on intimate terms with Astrée. From thence forward, he engages her in intimate conversation during the days, and sleeps in her bed chamber at night where he enjoys the privileges of an intimate female companion. A sexual imperative replaces chivalric obedience as his dominant motivation, and awakens a subjective self-awareness that must ultimately find expression in reciprocal enjoyment and confessional self-disclosure. At present, however, his adherence to a chivalric conception of personal identity enforces the repression of desire. It is impossible to enjoy sexual fulfillment without disobeying the command of invisibility, and it is impossible to disobey Astrée's command without sacrificing his identity as her perfect lover. Nowhere is his dilemma more clearly represented than in two nocturnal vigils when his rigorous obedience results in a reversion to imaginary gratifications. Unable to achieve a consummation of love in an act that is at once sexual and symbolic—an expression of desire and a representation of identity within an external symbolic order—he manufactures it as an imaginative projection upon the world. This first occurs in his commemorative promenade through the "sacred" topography of love, and again, in his famous exchange of clothing with Astrée.

On the first night, physical intimacies as they help each other undress carry the lovers far beyond the range of behavior consistent with feminine friendship, and into that of sexual foreplay: "si quelquefois sa main passoit près de la bouche d'Astrée, elle la luy baisoit, et Alexis, feignant de ne vouloir qu'elle luy fist ceste faveur, rebaisoit incontinent le lieu où sa bouche avait touché" (III, 548). The details of presentation, however implausible—"une grande partie du reste de la nuict se passa de cette sorte" (III, 548)—serve still to emphasize d'Urfé's central point regarding his hero's inward progress: his slavish submission to, and self-definition in terms of, the chivalric code has begun to give way before the gathering force of a repressed eroticism. Not only have the lovers come to the verge of making love, but Celadon's "true" identity, the self which he must actualize and reveal in order to be who he most authentically is, comes less and less to be associated with the ideal image of the "parfait amant," and more and more with the altogether realistic image of the aroused shepherd. "Combien de fois faillit-elle, cette feinte druide, de laisser le personnage de fille pour reprendre celuy de berger et combien de fois se reprit-elle de ceste outrecuidance!" (III, 549)

Unable to sleep, and encouraged by his success, Celadon considers waking Astrée and revealing his true identity. His disobedience, however, would not only open the way toward sexual fulfillment, but invalidate his identity as "parfait amant" by establishing his autonomy from the beloved. He hesitates at the precipice, and at the last moment retreats: "Non, non, disait-il alors, mourons, mourons plustost, et portons avec nous dans le tombeau nostre amour innocente, pure et sans reproche" (III, 552). Confronted by an intransigent "otherness" which nevertheless cannot be acknowledged, he consoles himself by reverting to the "cavern of memory" where the offending—the *inassimilable*—difference can still be denied. "Elle sortit de la chambre pour aller revoir les lieux où autrefois elle avait été si contente" (III, 552). Like a pilgrim reviewing the sacred relics of a shrine, Celadon conceptualizes the world as a Temple d'Astrée in which present objects derive their meaning neither from their inherent beauty, nor from their utility in his pursuit of self-determined ends, but from their commemorative associations with an idealized past in which he enjoyed a unitive relation to the beloved. By means of memory, the external is made to signify the internal. Each stop along the way elicits an explanatory gloss. On a fountain in the garden of Phocion's house:

> C'est bien, disait-elle, icy le lieu où si souvant Astrée m'a juré que son amitié serait éternelle! (III, 553)

on a grove of almond trees:

> Ce lieu fut bien celui qui lui remit en la mémoire les plus doux ressouvenirs de son bon-heur passé (III, 554)

on the Lignon:

> qui avait esté presque présente à tous ses bonheurs passé, et qui aussi avait vu naître le commencement de son extrême malheur (III, 555)

on the hollow willow where they exchanged letters:

> O saule! disait-elle en soi-même, que sont devenues les lettres que j'ai confiées si souvent sous ta foi! (III, 557)

on a tree where he had carved a complaint in verse against the necessity of feigning to love Aminthe:

> O combien cette vue lui donna de mortels ressouvenirs! (III, 558)

When d'Urfé next turns his attention to his two principal characters, he picks up the thread of their adventures on the second night of Celadon's sojourn in the hamlet. Events parallel those of the previous night, beginning with a nocturnal vigil that intensifies erotic desire, and titillates us with the prospect of sexual indiscretion and scandal. Beneath the superficial suspense, however, Celadon faces yet again the intolerable choice between obedience and disobedience to Astrée's command. The determining center of his identity once more hangs in the balance. Again, the tension builds until Celadon is on the very point of committing an act that would expose his ruse and transform his world forever: "Quelquefois transportée de trop d'affection, elle s'approchoit pour en desrober un amoureux baiser, mais soudain le respect l'en retiroit" (III, 594). Again, he is deflected from his impulse at the last moment, this time, significantly, by the circumstantial fact of Leonide's awakening rather than by the renewal of his dedication to the laws of love. His resolve appears to be weakening. Finally, just as before, repressed desire finds an alternative outlet in "les biens des pensées"—pleasures that the idealists of a former age had considered to be more real, and more worthy, than the "troubles mouvements des sens," but which the materialists of the early seventeenth century can only regard as imaginary gratifications—poor substitutes for possessive enjoyment.

This time, the route to gratification takes the form of an exchange of garments which evokes the neoplatonic ideal of a "conformité des estres" and calls attention to Celadon's refusal to participate in a representational paradigm of self-enclosure and objective reference. The exchange of clothes reproduces the sequence of events represented by Eros and Antéros in the second tableau of the "Histoire de Damon," and in the icon of the two cupids in the Temple d'Amitié. In each case, the lover demonstrates his submission to the mistress' will in order that she may recognize in his "caractère"—the very imprint of his identity—a perfect image of her own. Only then does she reciprocate by accepting his services as signs of love in its metaphysical sense as a "conformité des estres." On the first day of the clothing exchange, Alexis dresses as Astrée, while Astrée remains in her own costume. On the second day Astrée completes symbolic convergence of their identities by dressing as Alexis (IV, 37). (D'Urfé's readers waited five years, from 1619 to 1624, and endured the appearance of several unauthorized sequels, before the event was properly finished!)

Because the modern mentality has re-evaluated the chivalric ideal as a cultural fiction, the clothing exchange is parodic. It cannot be taken seriously as an external corollary of an ontologically real relation. Instead, it merely illustrates Celadon's unwillingness to acknowledge difference, and his resulting entrapment in a world of imagination. The clothes are not signs of an essential conformity of beings but of an egocentric, sexual desire. Denied access to real objects, the lovers appropriate the clothing metonymically, just as a dreamer invests otherwise indifferent objects with an erotic value which has been displaced by a prohibition or cultural taboo. Alexis-Celadon lavishes the garments with an affection he would have preferred to have given Astrée her-self—clutching them to his breast, kissing them repeatedly. By the same token, Astrée not only longs to dress as a druidess, but to take religious orders in order to secure erotic access to Alexis. Precisely because the clothing exchange is substitutive, it serves not to disclose the truth of the self, but to conceal a hidden interiority. An unacknowledged awareness of the sexual motivation makes both lovers furtive, guilty:

> Alexis mourait d'envie de posseder tout le jour cet habit, lui semblant que le bon-heur de toucher cette robbe qui souloit estre sur le corps de sa belle maistresse, ne se pouvoit égaler. Astrée qui aymait passionne-ment cette feinte druide, et qui désirait de laisser tout à fait l'habit de bergère pour prendre celuy de druide, afin de pouvoir demeurer le reste de sa vie auprès d'elle, avait un désir extrême de porter les habits d'Alexis, et toutesfois ny l'une ny l'autre n'osait en faire semblant, pour ne donner quelque cognoissance de ce qu'elles vouloient cacher.
> (III, 596)

All of this, of course, is so fundamental to our "Freudian" understanding of the erotic that it scarcely needs explaining. I would simply stress that, as indicators of Celadon's mental progress, the appropriation of the external world as an allegory of sexual love and the exchange of clothes have precisely the same value, which is at one and the same time psycho-sexual and cultural historical. Triggered by the repression of sexual desire, they are indeed instan-ces of erotic displacement, but they also represent, and find their ultimate justification in, attempts on Celadon's part to reach back behind the cultural divide to a time before the emergence of the subject-object dualism which posits the difference and self-enclosure, the ontological isolation, of the lover from the world and from his mistress. To the extent that alterity is denied, and ideas are considered to be more real than things, the world indeed bespeaks the inner truth of the self like a book of signs, and the mistress herself is a sign of the lover's true identity. It is only retrospectively, from the alien perspective of a mental universe predicated on alterity and exchange, that the denial of difference has been re-interpreted as an imaginative projection on objects that are essentially "other," with roots in a narcissistic passion: "l'amour que nous nous portons."

As Volume III comes to a close, a soliloquy in which Celadon weighs the possibility of setting aside his disguise reveals the distance he has moved toward an acceptance of subjective self-enclosure and the representational paradigm that it inevitably entails. The composite personality, "Alexis-Celadon," has from the beginning been the mark of the hero's double inscription in two entirely different and incompatible psychological models. As a concession to Astrée's command it represents his continued adherence to the chivalric ideal of love as a unity of souls; as a strategy for securing erotic access, it affirms his interior privacy and ontological difference from the beloved. With the intensification of sexual desire, however, the self-enclosed, desiring self begins to crystalize as the determining center of his identity—the "true" self—and incrementally supplants the "parfait amant" of the chivalric ideal.

When the unity of souls gives place to reciprocal possession as the model of the love relation, the transparency of the lover's will to an external order (i.e. obedience) gives place to the transparency of speech to subjective consciousness as the criterion of truth in self-representation. On a superficial level, Celadon has to give up his role as a druidess in order to achieve sexual satisfaction. But the deeper source of his discontent with a life of concealment is not that it imposes sexual restraints, but that it deprives the sexual favors he receives of their representational value.

> Que si j'estais véritablement Alexis, et non pas Celadon, que je serais heureuse de recevoir ces faveurs d'Astrée, mais combien le serais-je encore plus si, estant Celadon, elles ne m'estaient pas faites comme estant Alexis! Fut-il jamais amant plus heureux et plus malheureux que moi? heureux pour estre chéry et caressé de la plus belle et de la plus aimée bergère du monde, et malherueux pour sçavoir asseurément que ces faveurs qui me sont faites seraient changées en chastiments et en supplices, si je n'estais couvert du personnage d'Alexis. (III, 604–05)

"Celadon" remains unhappy in spite of the caresses that "Alexis" receives not because they (the favors) don't go far enough, but because they do not, when granted to *another*, affirm his identity as Astrée's lover. Insofar as he has become an autonomous, self-determining subject, self-representation no longer depends upon his obedience to Astrée's will, but upon his visibility as the one who possesses her love. Only when he receives her favors *as Celadon* will his identity appear once more in the field of representation.

At the end of the soliloquy Celadon brutally silences the voice of interior privacy. The suppression is tenuous, however, and the tone wistful. Obedience to the command now serves less to prove his status as the true lover than as a means for securing erotic access which he would lose were he to disclose his hidden identity:

> Tay-toy, tay-toy, Celadon, disoit-il, contente-toy d'estre mort une fois, sans vouloir par ta présomption remourir encore avant que d'avoir revescu. N'envie point le bon-heur d'Alexis, et puis que tu n'en peux jouyr, ne sois point marry qu'elle le possède, car si tu dois espérer quelque meilleure fortune que celle que tu as, c'est sans plus par l'entremise de ceste druide.

And although he finally takes solace in the knowledge of an ethical perfection which, under the traditional paradigm affords the lover a contemplative bliss, he no longer embraces the "biens des pensées" as the highest good, but accepts them reluctantly as an inadequate substitute for possessive enjoyment:

> Et puis, s'il y a quelque chose en toy qui te puisse contenter, n'est-ce pas pour sçavoir en ton âme que jamais tu n'as manqué aux loix d'une parfaite affection? [...] Ayme donc, o Celadon! et obéis, et te tais si tu veux vivre et aimer sans reproche. (III, 605–06)

The stage is set for the final volume in which Celadon emerges as self-enclosed and self-determining individual in the modern sense by positing reciprocal exchange and confessional transparency as a consciously acknowledged ideal.

At the opening of Volume IV, Adamas and Leonide have departed from the hamlet, thereby forcing Celadon to determine an independent course of action, and to sustain his ruse without external supports. Though filled with self-doubt, he abandons the passive obedience of the chivalric lover, posits himself as maker and molder of his identity through self-interested action, and formulates a plan of courtship which projects confessional self-disclosure as his explicit goal:

Il luy sembla qu'il estait très à propos d'engager toujours davantage
cette bergère en l'amitié qu'il cognoissoit qu'elle avait pour luy, jugeant
avec beaucoup de raison que, venant après à le recognoistre pour tel
qu'il estait, malaisément pourrait-elle consentir à un second es-
loignement. (IV, 35–36)

Now, as an advocate of modernity, Celadon temporarily assumes a position in the narrative's epistemological drama previously occupied by Astrée
herself, effecting a peculiar reversal of roles. And if the ideal of reciprocal
exchange and confessional transparency had been, in Astrée's narrative,
associated with a community of four lovers who separated themselves from the
world in order to pursue a course of private intimacy,[12] it is now associated
with the religious community of the Carnutes, the convent where druidesses,
including the real Alexis, receive their spiritual instruction. In the symbolic
totality of the narrative, Carnutes stands at the farthest extreme from the
"école des Massiliens" where Silvandre, the neoplatonic *raisonneur*, is said to
have received his education. It becomes for the lovers the symbol of an ideal
society where institutions reflect the inner truth of the individual, and where
language is transparent, not to an objective order of Ideas, but to the human
heart. As such, it serves as the imaginary and perpetually deferred destination
of the proto-modern subject, the homeland that d'Urfé's fictional lovers long
to discover, and the ideal which they, provisionally even in the midst of the
secular society of the hamlet, begin to emulate.

As the "myth" of the convent of Carnutes develops in the imaginations
of Celadon and Astrée, it takes on with increasing clarity the characteristics we
have come to associate with a subject-centered paradigm of identity and
meaning. For Astrée, who has already asked Leonide to help her gain admission to the order (III, 619), the prospect of renouncing the world represents not
self-loss, but the triumph of self-will—the freedom to express an authentic
inwardness. The religious vocation will permit her to escape the authority of
anyone "qui puisse tyranniser ma volonté" (IV, 40).

The requirements of membership described by Alexis-Celadon are
reciprocal desire and, although it cannot yet be explicitly stated, confessional
disclosure: "Il faut seulement que vous fassiez deux choses, l'une, que vous
m'aymiez autant que je vous ayme, et je vous diray l'autre quand je cognois-
tray que vous aurez mis en effect cette première proposition" (IV, 41). Life in

the "antres des Carnutes," in other words, will be nothing other than the fulfillment of the dream of a lovers' paradise: a retreat from the world in which they
live in "honnête liberté" (IV, 43), and in which their speech is a transparent
window to their souls. Since Astrée and Celadon already satisfy the first requirement, all that prevents the resolution of the plot in terms of a subject-
centered ideology is the accomplishment of the second: "Elles s'embrasserent
avec un tesmoignage de si bonne volonté qu'il ne fallait, pour le contentement
de toutes deux, sinon qu'Alexis osast dire: Je suis Celadon" (IV, 42).

The trajectory of Celadon's development is henceforth oriented toward
the implementation of confessional transparency as a new discursive norm. In
the midst of the secular society of the hamlet, it can be practiced only in secret,
while in public they must conform to inauthentic roles. Echoing language we
encountered in Astrée's confession, Celadon advises that "nous vivions quand
nous serons en particulier, avec la mesme franchise que nous ayons fait
jusques icy," but that "devant le reste des bergers et des bergères, il est à
propos d'estre un peu plus retenues" (IV, 44). At the same time, he offers the
convent as a model society in which the discrepancy between private and
public discourse, so fatal to the lover's happiness in the past, will be overcome. In a community where subjective consciousness is the collectively acknowledged criterion of truth, the names by which lovers are publicly represented, and inscribed as social subjects, correspond to private, affectional
relations:

> La coustume des filles druides qui sont aux Carnutes, est de ne s'ap-
> peller jamais par leurs propres noms, mais par d'autres que l'amitié
> qu'elles se portent leur fait inventer, et qui tesmoignent la bonne
> volonté qu'elles ont les unes pour les autres; et ces nouveaux noms
> parmi elles sont appellez des alliances, comme si l'on voulait dire que
> par la on se lie de plus fort devoirs et de plus forte affection. (IV, 45)

The events that initiated the estrangement of the lovers in the narrative's
pre-history have already, of course, exposed subjective self-presence as an illusion, and transparent self-disclosure as an unattainable ideal. A private and
authentic interiority cannot be sustained in the midst of the discursive anarchy
that characterizes the textualized universe of d'Urfé's "baroque" imagination.
Discourses, detached from either metaphysical or subjective horizons of refer-

ence proliferate in all directions, enmeshing and imposing alien structures upon the lovers' identities. The ideal associated with the religious order is as unattainable now as it ever was. Its status as a myth, a wish fulfillment fantasy, is reinforced by the fact that neither Astrée nor Celadon have the slightest historical knowledge or first hand experience of the community they seek. Its unattainability is built into the plot itself, since it is merely an aspect of Celadon's disguise, his false identity. Were he to practice transparent self-disclosure, he would forthwith expose the prospect of an idyllic life in the convent as a fiction. In yet another poignant soliloquy, Celadon contemplates the impasse to which his stratagem has led, and which seems to preclude the possibility of resolution. He again laments that the favors he receives fail to satisfy desire because they leave his identity shrouded in doubt. As Alexis he is loved only on the condition that he vanish from the field of representation, and as Celadon he appears in the field of representation only on the condition that he sacrifice the consummation of love. The goal of his quest remains the simultaneous enjoyment of both:

> Je suis sans doute un meslange, et d'Alexis et de Celadon; et aussi, comme Celadon, je desire recouvrer le bonheur qui m'a esté tant injustement ravy, et, comme Alexis, je crains de perdre celuy que je possède. Je suis donc et Alexis et Celadon meslez ensemble; mais maintenant que je sçay qui je suis, que ne recherchons-nous un moyen de contenter Celadon, et d'assurer Alexis?
>
> Ah! disait-elle alors, c'est la l'oeuvre et la peine! (IV, 252)

IV. Converging Journeys: The Lovers at Marcilly

It is time for us to return once more to the question with which this essay began and upon whose answer depends our assessment of the narrative's place in the evolution of early modern culture—that of its resolvability. In Chapter 1, I intimated the existence in *L'Astrée* scholarship of two entrenched positions. On the one hand there are those who stabilize the meaning of the text at the expense of its internal ambiguities. For our purposes it matters little whether they do so in terms of an objective, metaphysical conception of order, or in terms of a subjective, representational one, whether, in other words, they attempt to assert the medieval or the modern features of the work as normative for the whole. On the other hand, there are those who regard *L'Astrée* as a "transitional" work suspended between incompatible systems of thought, but who affirm its "undecidability" at the expense of an intrinsic coherence that has rarely failed to impress attentive readers from the seventeenth century to the present. D'Urfé's original audience universally proclaimed his masterpiece a marvel of logic and order, while an eminent modern critic like Henri Coulet still discovers in its rambling and unwieldy bulk an impressive "unité de signification." My position, by contrast, has been not only to acknowledge the text's liminality—its place at the threshold of two cultural epochs—but to suggest that it escapes the condition of irreducible *aporia* by projecting a characteristically "baroque" resolution. The lovers will be reunited, and their union legitimized, neither by an intrinsic metaphysical bond, nor by the personal authenticity of their reciprocal desire, but by the authority of the collective gaze. Consensus becomes in *L'Astrée* the unappealable criterion of truth in self-representation, and the foundation of "la vérité de l'amour."

We have already seen that Astrée's confession not only describes the double failure of the object-centered and the subject-centered epistemological paradigms, but establishes the collective voice as an alternative to both, and that it reinforces this position in three different ways. Internally, the tale describes a series of "travaux d'amour" in which two couples (Astrée and Celadon, and Phillis and Lycidas) collectively verify the love professed by each individual. The confession, moreover, derives its legitimacy as a discourse of truth from the collective perceptions of the community rather than from the subjective self-presence of the speaker. It signals Astrée's capitulation to the testimony of Lycidas who argues that Celadon's fidelity is no longer doubted by anyone except herself, and coincides with her reentry into social life after a period of solitude and mourning. Finally, public confession becomes the verbal medium in which a new society emerges and gradually expands throughout the remainder of the narrative. By submitting their life stories for collective arbitration in a series of "procès d'amour," an interminable procession of exiles and pilgrims of love permit themselves to be inducted as social subjects into a community that forms around Astrée, Phillis and Diane—three shepherdess who are themselves united by a pact of mutual self-disclosure.

A similar mechanism is at work in Celadon's development. The two periods in his mental journey thus far—the religious instruction in the Temple d'Amitié and the cross-dressing episodes in the hamlet—represent the nostalgic, and the proto-Cartesian solutions respectively, which must both give way to the third, collectivist one. The final pages of the narrative as d'Urfé wrote them[13] effect a global shift in thematic and diagetic emphasis away from the ontological hierarchies of the temple, and the private intimacies of the hamlet, toward the public, political sphere. All of the principal characters—knights and ladies, princes and princesses, shepherds and their mistresses—converge through divergent routes upon the capital city, Marcilly, to play their parts in the *dénouement* of a deepening political crisis that has been brewing over several thousand pages. In consequence we are led to expect that the epistemological dilemmas of the narrative will be resolved, if at all, as a matter of *public policy* and not through an unexpected breakthrough in the perceptions of individuals.

Still dressed each in the other's clothes, Astrée and Celadon are violently removed from the privacy of their erotic dalliances and forced, in spite of themselves, to take positions on the grand stage of the world. Mistaken for Alexis, Astrée is kidnapped by the henchmen of Polemas, an illegitimate pretender to the throne of Amasis, the rightful queen. Celadon, dressed as Astrée, follows her into captivity at Surieu, the enemy camp. The following day, both are tied and used as human shields by soldiers who intend to set fire to the city with torches. The plan is foiled when Semire emerges from the ranks of Polemas' army to liberate the lovers he wronged. In the final scenes, Astrée is hoisted into the city, while Celadon takes arms in its defense.

From the kidnapping forward, episodes in the lives of the lovers seem calculated to reiterate the impasse to which the quest for "la vérité de l'amour" has arrived. Although Astrée and Celadon demonstrate the reciprocity of a desire which has become the determining center of their identities, they nevertheless remain impenetrably hidden, unable to represent their inner truth except through the ossified structures bequeathed to them, and to the early seventeenth century as a whole, by the chivalric tradition. At Surieu, each attempts to convince Polemas that s/he is the true Alexis in order to save the life of the other (IV, 747–52). Later, they spend the night before their anticipated martyrdom developing extravagant and irrefutable arguments, in which no possible variation on the "unity of souls" theme is spared, why s/he should be allowed to make the ultimate sacrifice (IV, 793–96). Neither, however, will relent. Each values the other's life more than his or her own. Neither is willing to survive the other's death. The thematics of unity reaches its zenith when, approaching the gates of the city, each strives to precede the other in death: "Exemple remarquable d'une entière et parfaite affection" (IV, 798).

But the exchange of clothing, the formal vows, the will to self-sacrifice—in short, all of the external trappings of an idealized and egoless love—merely defer the simple and necessary acknowledgement on Astrée's part that she loves Alexis for "her" resemblance to Celadon, and Celadon's that he is indeed the shepherd for whom she longs, and not the druidess he appears to be. It is as though desire must still be constrained within the confines of an inauthentic structure, and represented indirectly through the mediation of a "marque étrangère." Subjective self-presence cannot yet serve as a reliable criterion of truth in self-representation because the unbridled mind continues to be regarded by d'Urfé and his contemporaries as the *locus* of chimeras and grotesque monsters. Descartes has not yet proclaimed the *cogito.*

The induction of the couple into public life, however, seems to foreshadow precisely the kind of collectivist resolution to the problem of self-representation that prevails in all of the "travaux d'amour" recited in Astrée's confession. Celadon's defense of the city into which his mistress has been rescued effects a convergence of public and private registers of personal identity. Erotic love, which had introduced a gap between subjective consciousness and the external symbolic order, now becomes a motive for public action. To protect his mistress is to preserve the very seat of legitimate political and religious authority. He is neither the ideal lover represented in the sacred architecture of the temple, nor the possessive individualist condemned to invisibility (literally, banished to the domain of the unrepresentable) in the cross-dressing episodes, but a social subject, a "subject of discourse," inscribed within an historically situated social order. And because he has become a man of action, a hero whose identity is a function of the public gaze, Astrée will be forced to acknowledge his fidelity. She who has claimed that she would deny the testimony of her own senses in order to conform to collective opinion on the color of a flower, will be unable to gainsay his love not only because he has risked his life in her behalf, but because he has done so in the presence of spectators that include the highest authorities in the land. What Astrée sees may be believed not merely because she sees it, but because the community bears witness to her seeing, and thereby legitimizes her knowledge as an intersubjective truth.

Notes

1. In contrast to my contention that the ethic of the temple represents a provisional moment in Celadon's development to which the cross-dressing episodes provide a corrective measure, Paul Koch regards the first as normative for the entire work, and the second as a test. At the end of his instruction in the temple, Celadon's love "sera suffisamment contrôlé par la raison pour permettre au berger de vivre dangereusement avec Astrée, sous les habits d'Alexis." ["L'Ascèse du repos ou l'intention idéologique de *L'Astrée*," *Revue d'histoire littéraire de la France*, nos. 3–4 (1977), p. 396.]

2. *The Order of Things*, 49.

3. Twentieth-century readers of Freud will find it impossible not to recognize the potential for an interpretation of Celadon's "madness" in terms of regression which is at one and the same time psycho-sexual and cultural. The approach would seem to be all the more valid in the light of an analogy suggested by Freud himself in *Totem and Taboo* between the evolutionary patterns of psychic and cultural life. Both begin, he says, with a conflation of thought and reality and progress toward the delineation of difference. On the one hand, a "primary" narcissism in which infants perceive external objects only as extensions of themselves precedes the differentiation of the ego and the emergence of "object-love." On the other, an animistic system of thought which conflates the external world of natural phenomena with the ideational world of wishes and dreams historically precedes the recognition of the subject-object dichotomy as an epistemological principle. If the chivalric lover tries to recapture a lost complementarity of inner and outer registers of being, it is because he recoils before the harsh but "mature" perception of difference. Insofar as we consider him as an individual, he resembles the neurotic who regresses to an infantile stage of psychic development. Insofar as we view him as an historical type, he represents an atavistic element in early modern culture.

4. We have already witnessed this precise line of reasoning in one of the letters Astrée discovers after Celadon's disappearance.

5. Foucault explains the significance early modern philologists attached to the Biblical story of Babel as follows: "In its original form, when it was given to men by God himself, language was an absolutely certain and transparent sign for things, because it resembled them. The names of things were lodged in the things they designated, just as strength is written in the body of the lion [...]. This transparency was destroyed at Babel as a punishment for men. Languages became separated and incompatible with one another only insofar as they had previously lost this original resemblance to the things that had been the prime reason for the existence of language. All languages known to us are now spoken only against the background of this lost similitude, and in the space that it left vacant" (*The Order of Things*, 36).

6. For a detailed discussion of the semiotic crisis described in the confession, see Chapter 4.

7. D'Urfé here follows Plotinus rather than Augustine in his view of the trinity. The three "persons" are hypostatizations of a transcendent and ineffable One rather than coincident with subsistent Being itself. When, near the end of the temple discourse, d'Urfé has Adamas introduce the Augustinian tradition as a "higher mystery," we detect a nervous concession to orthodoxy on the part of a *ligueur* who recognized the heretical element in neo-Platonism. For a discussion of the difference between neo-Platonic and Christian views of Godhead, see the chapters devoted to Plotinus and Augustine in Knowles, *The Evolution of Medieval Thought*.

8. Mitchell Greenberg argues that cross-dressing epitomizes the repression rather than the reassertion (as I am suggesting) of subjective interiority and difference: "The *Astrée*, as 'androgynous' text, would therefore be a text that refuses the differentiating gesture, that establishes itself as existing before scission, before the division of the world into subject and object, into fixed, sexed, gendering." When Celadon, already disguised as Alexis, takes the further step of dressing as Astrée, he completes the eradication of individuated selfhood that the erasure of sexual difference had begun: "What the cross-dressing permits, of course, is the elimination not only of the sexual and social barriers but of all difference, so that in the end Alexis and Astrée become one—the Androgyn." I believe that this formulation gives short shrift to the fact that disguise as such is always in *L'Astrée* an affirmation of subjective autonomy and self-enclosure, and that the voyeurism it facilitates establishes interpersonal knowledge on the foundation of a subject-object dichotomy. ["*L'Astrée* and Androgyny" in *Subjectivity and Subjugation in Seventeenth-Century Drama and Prose: The Family Romance of French Classicism* (Cambridge University Press: 1992), pp. 40–43.]

9. Once again, Celadon's progress unfolds in three phases. It seems impossible to envision any developmental sequence in *L'Astrée* except in terms of threes—an effect, possibly, of d'Urfé's neoplatonism. We have already established the importance of a tripartite dialectic in the love debates. Jacques Bonnet finds a triadic motif in the narrative's visual symbols: "Lorsque dans *L'Astrée*, l'autel du Temple d'Astrée construit par Celadon sur les indications d'Adamas est situé dans un triangle contenant le chêne porteur du 'guy sacré,' on peut y voir la marque du roman lui-même." [*La Symbolique de "L'Astrée"*(St-Etienne: Le Hénaff, 1982), p. 71.]

10. When, at the end of the first day at the druid's house, he declares that he would prefer death to being discovered in a transgression against the code of perfect love—"Si Astrée me venait reconnaitre, je jure et je proteste qu'il n'y a rien qui me peut jamais retenir en vie" (III, 241)—Adamas rebukes him for clinging to error, and reasserts, by way of a countermeasure, his authority as spiritual director:

> Eh bien!, répliqua Adamas, je voy bien que vostre mal n'est pas encore en estat de recevoir les remèdes que je luy voulois donner. Il faut attendre que le temps l'ait meury davantage, et cependant resolvez-vous de ne me point desobeyr en ce que je vous ordonneray. (III, 241)

11. I am omitting any discussion here of the "doctrine of sympathies," the elaboration of which occupies a large part of the sojourn at Adamas' house. Because of its importance as one of the narrative's clearest statements of an idealist theory of interpersonal knowledge, I have discussed the doctrine at length in an earlier section. In the present context, suffice it to say the doctrine serves an immediate heuristic purpose for Celadon by teaching him to distinguish between the arbitrary fatality of which he complains, and the "souveraine prudence" governing a rational cosmos and drawing all creatures toward a unitive consummation in love. Although both are external determining structures, the first destroys the lover's integrity and leaves him no alternative but to retreat helplessly from the world, while the second compels each person to bring to fruition a providentially intended potential, an intrinsic *telos*.

12. See the "Histoire d'Astrée et Phillis" (I, 111–152), and my analysis in Chapter 4.

13. A fifth and final volume of *L'Astrée* was written by Baro, d'Urfé's personal secretary, with the aid of a few notes the author left at his death. At its conclusion, all of the principal couples are able at last to verify the truth of the love they profess to each other by peering at the enchanted surface of the "fontaine de la vérité de l'amour." Having done so, Celadon and Astrée marry.

Although our exposition of epistemological paradigms would permit us to assess the sequel's compatibility with the inner logic of the whole, such an analysis does not fall within the scope of the present study which is addressed only to those portions of the narrative composed by d'Urfé. I would only like to suggest that throughout the text, the fountain exemplifies the status of the "baroque" sign. The double epistemological failure that engenders the lovers' estrangement—the foreclosure at one and the same time of both objective-ontological and subjective-empirical foundations of discourse—is symbolized by the destruction, in the narrative's pre-history, of the fountain's ability to speak to the inhabitants of d'Urfé's fictional world. Thenceforth, the fountain represents a promise of interpersonal knowledge that cannot be realized. Its restoration would logically coincide with the resolution of the narrative's central problem, the crisis of self-representation. By the same token, the conditions under which it imparts its truths would reflect the epistemological status of discourse in general.

Brief remarks on Baro's role in the posthumous publication of Volume IV and his decision to write the fifth and final volume outright may be found in Reure, pp. 209–14. A more recent publication history appears in Paul Koch, "Encore du nouveau sur *L'Astrée*," *Revue d'histoire littéraire de la France*, mai-juin 1972. Again, however, it includes only passing references to Volume V.

Epilogue

As a text embedded in the liminal space between alternative epistemological models, *L'Astrée* addresses itself to human minds in the throes of negotiating the distance between them. It reflects the delicate shifts and adjustments by which early seventeenth-century intellectual culture gradually and with difficulty came to accommodate subjective privacy as a meaningful fact in human self-understanding rather than, as was initially the case, a mere anomaly to be dismissed or laughed away. Hence, I have argued, the narrative's universal popularity in cultivated circles not only in France, but everywhere on the continent and in England, at least until about 1660.[1]

L'Astrée's magic was not to last. Already, by 1660, the frenzy that had accompanied the appearance of each new volume (readers had waited anxiously outside the print shop to make away with individual pages as they came off the presses) was but a distant memory. Although the work continued to enjoy a select readership well into the eighteenth century, it had already, as the Sun King began his climb toward immortality, begun a slow but inexorable descent into a sea of forgetfulness. There, it was destined to remain for approximately 200 years like a great, lost civilization—a magnificent, sprawling Atlantis, dimly remembered but no longer accessible without the peculiar equipment of specialists in deep sea exploration. It would seem that, just as the narrative's initial popularity reflects its cultural function in the early modern crisis of meaning, its decline was an inevitable consequence of the resolution of that crisis in the mode of Cartesian subjectivity—a child whose birth d'Urfé helped to foster, but whose existence he could never entirely embrace.

Curiously enough, however, beginning in the late nineteenth century, and with gathering intensity during subsequent decades up to the present moment, d'Urfé's masterpiece of premodernity has captured the serious attention if not of a popular audience, at least of an impressive group of students and critics of literature. This, I would like to suggest, is because, as Foucault has so famously announced, "the ground is once more stirring under our feet."[2] After having been treated for at least two centuries with condescension and even ridicule, *L'Astrée* once again impresses us with its wisdom and relevance as we, in the late twentieth century, confront our own crisis of meaning and recognize with renewed poignancy the unsettling liminality of signs.

In a remarkable way, critical responses to *L'Astrée*, from the late nineteenth century onward, bear witness to the final moments of ascendancy and to the hastening decline of the subject-centered semiotic model whose troubled emergence helped to produce the upheaval of early modernity. Challenged at once by a psychology of the unconscious and by ethnology, subjective self-presence in our own time, much like transcendent Being in an earlier age, has come to be regarded as non-existent or inaccessible, and, in either case, unreliable as a foundation of knowledge and authenticating well-spring of discourse. Each of the two interpretive strategies which (as I have argued) dominate the last century of critical commentary on *L'Astrée*—the search for unity and the analysis of difference, or heterogeneity—occupies a distinctive position in the evolutionary process that has brought us full circle back to an overdue admiration of *L'Astrée*, and, perhaps, to an historicist theory of meaning that bears comparison with d'Urfé's own.

Critics who emphasize the intrinsic unity of the text at the expense of its contradictions invariably seek to stabilize literary meaning with reference to one of the two sides of the subject-object relation engendered by the the-oretical formulation of the transcendental ego as the guarantor of inter-subjectjectivity. Either the referential relation of literature to an objective historical context, or the internal coherence of a self-enclosed authorial consciousness, undergirds the unity of signification sought by the critic, while the transcendence and self-enclosure of the critic's own subjectivity *vis à vis* the evidence he examines renders that meaning objectively retrievable across the centuries. Such criticism, in other words, functions as a discourse of objective reference by aiming to represent to the reader a substratum of textual meaning that refers to nothing beyond itself.

Those responsible for reviving interest in d'Urfé during the first three decades of the present century—Gustave Reynier, O.-C. Reure, André Le Breton, Henri Bochet and Maurice Magendie—generally emphasized the referentiality of the text to its historical *milieu*. André Le Breton takes this view to an almost absurd extreme when he says that the authors of prose fiction in the seventeenth century "ont été les historiographes de leur temps."[3] Some were more subtle in defining the inter-relation between literature and life, attributing to *L'Astrée* a limited role in shaping history in addition to merely reflecting it.[4] All, however, admired the narrative primarily as an accurate portrayal of the aristocratic society of the period, and as a precursor to that seventeenth-century variety of literary realism, *vraisemblance,* which though hardly realistic in the Balzacian sense, nevertheless seeks to induce a suspension of disbelief by emulating a discourse of objective reference.[5]

Other critics, by contrast, have sought to establish the organic coherence of *L'Astrée* in terms of authorial intention, thereby shifting the ground of literary meaning from the objective to the subjective side of the Cartesian equation. Thus, Bernard Yon argues that if modern readers knew "ce que l'auteur a voulu faire," the undecipherable complexity and apparent anomalies of the narrative would fall into place, and we would see that "la composition de l'oeuvre" produces an "effet d'ensemble."[6] In a similar vein, several critics— Christian Wentzlaff-Eggebert, Clifton Cherpack, and Georges Molinié, for example—have insisted that d'Urfé consciously employs rhetorical figures, generic conventions and other compositional devices, current in the seventeenth century but unfamiliar to ourselves, to organize the diverse and unruly material of his work. A renewed historical awareness of these procedures would enable us to appreciate previously unrecognized patterns of order, and hence the integrity of the author's unifying vision.[7]

Phenomenology, which produced at least one influential piece of commentary on *L'Astrée*, might be said to traverse the gulf between the objective and the subjective sides of Cartesian dualism. In so far as human thought is concerned, these critics tell us, there can be no object without a subject, and no subject without an object. "Thought," the famous slogan goes, "is always of something," and the inter-dependence of subject and object in the production of mental phenomena means that literature can never be the representation of reality as such, but must always be "the embodiment of a state of mind."[8] In this vein, Jacques Ehrmann's *Un Paradis désespéré,* which in 1963 was the first book-length study of *L'Astrée* to appear in over three decades,[9] argues that d'Urfé's preoccupation with the "phenomenon" of illusion enables us to recognize many otherwise disparate and conflicting elements of *L'Astrée* as expressions of a single "effort créateur." Nevertheless, phenomenology remains within the Cartesian paradigm insofar as the self-presence and logical priority of authorial consciousness is a necessary corollary of the intrinsic unity of the phenomenological life-world itself. The moment we imagine an "effort créateur" besieged by conflicting psychic energies or informed by cultural mentalities that pre-exist the individual, we are constrained to relinquish the ideal of unity, and to accept the inevitable dispersion of creative consciousness.[10]

Beginning in the 1960s numerous critics, recognizing the limitations of the autonomous, knowing subject as a *locus* of self-present truth in much the same way as d'Urfé and his contemporaries did, have insisted upon just such a dispersion. They have come to regard the internal divisions and contradictions in literary texts as precisely those phenomena in which the human condition appears most clearly. Features which had once been treated as anomalies to be either digested (i.e. reconciled with an idea of coherence by means of complex argument) or expelled (i.e. identified as aesthetic flaws) suddenly become objects of analysis in their own right.[11]

If the critics of unity may be grouped according to which side of the Cartesian paradigm they emphasize in the stabilization of literary meaning, the critics of heterogeneity may be grouped, in a manner that cuts across other methodological differences, according to the sources of subversion to which they attribute its ambivalence—although this distinction can never be more than a matter of emphasis. A psychoanalytic current in poststructuralism emphasizes the anarchic eroticism which destabilizes authorial and critical consciousness from within, and finds its way into the text as an insurmountable semantic ambivalence, and into critical discourse as interpretive free-play—a celebration of the "jouissance" of the text. Alternatively, an ethnographic current avers that the cultural symbolic order decenters authorial and critical consciousness from without by the fact that thought itself takes place only in the dimension of external, and pre-existing, discourses which are historically variable and culturally relative. On this view, literary and interpretive texts become battlegrounds where various discursive voices, irremediably estranged because enclosed in incompatible modes of symbolization, compete for cultural dominance without any prospect of discovering common ground. Gérard Genette[12] and Nicole Chabert[13] have written illuminating studies of *L'Astrée* in the first, psychological, mode. Maurice Laugaa,[14] Yvonne Jehenson,[15] Herbert De Ley[16] and Mitchell Greenberg[17] exemplify the second, cultural, mode.

It is as though, at the end of the era of which *L'Astrée* marks the beginning, we are once again confronted with the intolerable alternatives faced by Astrée and Celadon themselves. The fissure between interior privacy and the symbolic order that resulted from the foreclosure of Being has reopened with the dispersion of the *cogito*. With the demise of the theoretical fiction which, for over three centuries, has knit them together, self and sign once again confront each other across an unbridgeable void. Although no two historical moments enact identical semiotic dramas, it cannot but be noticed that metamorphosis and ostentation—the two elements of the baroque aesthetic as defined by Rousset—seem to have reappeared as the free-play of the signifier and the tyranny of "discursive practices." Indeed, it might almost be said that the critics of heterogeneity represent the "Montaignian" phase in our own, late twentieth-century epistemic transformation. Like Montaigne, they oscillate between the anarchy of the unbridled mind and a resigned fideism, offering their readers a choice between the total relativization of meaning, or the imposition of an artificial construction on the objects, in this case a literary text, we wish to comprehend.

While a criticism of difference escapes the anachronistic project of attributing aesthetic unity to *L'Astrée* on epistemological grounds—the self-presence of the transcendental subject *vis à vis* extra-discursive objects of perception—which d'Urfé himself rejected, it nevertheless proceeds at a level of analysis which dissects the narrative without putting it back together again. It leaves us in an unresolved state of *aporia* characteristic of the earliest phase of an epistemological shift, but ultimately, as I have argued, uncharacteristic of *L'Astrée*. For a theoretical perspective that both illuminates the formal and thematic integrity the work, and demonstrates the uncanny symmetry between pre- and postmodernity, we must turn to a more recent current in contemporary literary theory—a current which recognizes at once the relativity of culturally established systems of signification *and* their legitimate, stabilizing function.

In the mid-1980s, a number of avant-garde theorists began to express weariness with a deconstructive criticism which fails to envision a reconstructive project. A disillusionment with epistemological giddiness for its own sake was perhaps one of the primary impulses behind the "neo-historicist" movement which devoted much of its energy to elucidating the process of identity formation within divergent cultural paradigms.[18] Such concerns also emerge forcefully in lectures delivered between 1982 and 1985 at the University of California, Irvine for a series of colloquia entitled "The Aims of Representation: Subject/Text/History,"[19] and were most eloquently summarized by David Carroll: "Perhaps the most serious consequence of this relativization of all discourse and the 'crisis' of legitimation associated with it is the destruction of traditional notions of society and the social subject" (86). Turning to Bakhtin and Lyotard in search of an emergent foundation for intersubjective meaning, he elucidates "critical strategies that indicate indirectly an Idea (or 'fiction') of heterogeneous humanity as the foundation of the social, an Idea that must be pursued in the name of justice, in the name of an obligation to others and alterity in general" (103). This idea is "unpresentable as such" (103), but it is nevertheless, he concludes, "imaginable" (103).

It is precisely this kind of creative imagining that d'Urfé undertakes in *L'Astrée*. He is not content merely to play the role of an iconoclast, rejecting the objective ontological order as a specious, culturally generated fiction, and the self-presence of subjective consciousness as an impossibility. His recognition of the inadequacy of two conceptual paradigms leads to the discovery of a third. In the course of their development, Astrée and Celadon learn that individuals are neither determined by their location in an ontological hierarchy, nor autonomous and self-determining, but shaped by the customs of a particular time and place. The normative subject is the subject of history. And for that reason, interpersonal knowledge is a function neither of the individual's identification within a structure of providentially given signs, nor of the objective representation of an autonomous interiority, but rather, of his or her participation in a social symbolic order which is both subjectively compelling, and open to historical transformation.

I would like to suggest, then, that postmodern culture shares with baroque premodernity not only an epistemological crisis characterized by the double peril of semantic free-play and the imposition of inauthentic discourses of power, but a tendency to resolve the crisis through a positive and hopeful affirmation of the historical origins of meaning. D'Urfé's search for a criterion of truth in symbolic reference leads him directly to conclusions that closely resemble views put forward in our own period by poststructuralists such as Foucault, Althusser, Geertz and Lacan, all of whom, in their various idioms— history of philosophy, political economy, anthropology and psychology—insist upon the priority of discourse to truth. Like d'Urfé, they envision the foundations of intersubjectivity in terms neither of a transcendental objective order, nor of a transcendental subject, but rather, in terms of an historical *a priori* to which the individual has been made "subject" through institutionalized processes of "interpellation," or "subjugation." And, although many theorists emphasize the deterministic implications of this line of thought, it may also be that the historicity of meaning enables a perpetual, change-producing interaction between collectively ratified, stabilizing structures and the myriad potentialities of the self. It is as though by being premodern, d'Urfé was most clairvoyantly postmodern, and, in the most representative work of early modernity, assumed an epistemological stance that was later rejected but to which we have recently, after several centuries, returned.

If this is true, students of seventeenth-century French literature have good reason to return to *L'Astrée* in anticipation that they will find something more than an aesthetic curiosity of marginal relevance. It will no longer suffice to dismiss the work as a specimen of an eccentric historical moment which prefigured but failed to attain the glories of neoclassical "vraisemblance," or to reduce it to a collection of hopeless paradoxes that arise from the conflict between two cultural periods. Rather, *L'Astrée* should be studied as a poly-semic "fontaine de la vérité" which illuminates the origins of our own crisis of meaning, and models a process by which cultural transitions may be negotiated, and new forms of consensus reached.

Notes

1. For a history of *L'Astrée*'s reception, see Reure p. 303, according to whom the work enjoyed its greatest popularity in the decades from 1607–1660. See also my discussion and relevant notes in Chapter 2.

2. *The Order of Things*, xxiv.

3. Le Breton supports this view with statements that presuppose the representational transparency of literary language. He writes, for example, that we find in the pages of the old romances "la physionomie d'un monde qui n'est plus" (viii), and that "La société de Mme de Rambouillet vivait, aimait, comme aiment et vivent les per-sonnages de *L'Astrée*" (25). [André Le Breton, *Le Roman au dix-septième siècle* (Paris: Hachette, 1912).]

4. In keeping with a traditional conception of literature as an instrument of moral instruction, Reynier affirms that sentimental novels not only "made manifest" the

social ideal of the aristocracy under Henri IV, but also provided a medium in which that society "s'est en quelque sorte définie" (176). For Reure as well, *L'Astrée* exerted a salutary influence "en présentant aux classes éclairées un idéal supérieur" which directed "des aspirations confuses vers une conception plus raffinée de la vie" (276). Magendie perhaps offers the most complete and complex formulation of the reciprocal relation between text and context: "D'une part, *L'Astrée* procède des tendances, plus ou moins conscientes, des personnes distinguées, vers un idéal plus noble, plus élevé. D'autre part, elle a éclairé et fortifié ces tendances, et précisé cet idéal. Il y a ici un échange d'influences, d'ailleurs inégales. Les moeurs, déjà épurées, ont, en partie, déterminé le livre, et le livre, à son tour, a amélioré les moeurs" (253). It should be noted, however, that even Magendie takes for granted the extra-discursive status of the ethical ideal which literature illuminates and offers for emulation. He therefore differs radically from the postmodern, textualist view of discourse as the origin of "the real," and of the values it imposes.

5. The criteria upon which these critics base both praise and blame reveal their overwhelming admiration for classical verisimilitude. They approvingly note that d'Urfé's characters strike us as credible individuals complete with complex personalities and particularized social origins rather than as lifeless types or mouthpieces for philosophical arguments (Reynier, 347; Reure, 232–233; Magendie, 337–359); that d'Urfé subordinates plot to character, producing an impression that events flow from the inner motivations of characters acting freely rather than being imposed upon them arbitrarily (Reynier, 348); he achieves logical order by subordinating subplots to the main action, and by other techniques which prevent confusion (Reynier, 350; Reure, 233; Magendie, 314); our empathy with characters and our desire to see their difficulties resolved creates suspense which d'Urfé skillfully intensifies by means of strategic interruptions and delays (Magendie, 315); d'Urfé's style conveys an impression of reality unclouded by the fantastical decoration or cabalistic allusiveness of his predecessors, and in that respect he prefigures Guez de Balzac and Corneille (Reynier, 248; Reure, 266; Magendie, 373–378).

Dispraise as well as admiration rests on an uncritical acceptance of classical norms. Reure complains of *L'Astrée*'s excessive length (233), fragmented narratives (233), *invraisemblance* (234) and anachronism (241). Magendie reiterates Reure's censures with a few additions: tediously long conversations whose import ought to have been conveyed in an economical summary, a taste for irrelevant detail and displays of erudition (315–318), the repeated use of a few narratological techniques borrowed from the chivalric romance (318–326), redundancy and digression which give the reader an unpleasant sensation of walking in place (322), an inability to convey the gradual transformation of a character's inner life (361). In general, anything that derogates from a scheme of logical subordination, interferes with the mechanism of suspense, or disturbs the inner coherence of character constitutes a fault. Only Reure seems to intimate the inadequacy of classical aesthetic standards when he writes that *L'Astrée* is "d'une certaine manière trop riche" (234).

6. Armed with this premise, Yon sets out to demonstrate the logical necessity that determines the placement and thematic content of the intercalated tales, and concludes that the narrative unites formal patterns and ideological purpose in an intentional confirmation of cosmic order: "Les soucis esthétiques d'ordre, de variété, d'enchainement, de logique, sont alliés à un sens de la complexité de la vie et à une sôrte de leçon sur l'ordre du monde" (25). [Bernard Yon, "Composition dans *L'Astrée*, composition de *L'Astrée*," *Papers in French Seventeenth-Century Literature* 10, 2 (1978), p. 10.]

7. Wentzlaff-Eggebert argues that d'Urfé borrowed a variety of narratological techniques from sixteenth-century predecessors, and subordinated them all to the harmonizing structure of a dominant trope, the parentheses, much in vogue in his own era. A key episode at the center of each volume provides the point of reference in relation to which fragments of the main plot as well as intercalated tales are symmetrically distributed according to principles of parallelism and contrast. [Christian Wentzlaff-Eggebert, "Structures Narratives de la Pastorale dans L'Astrée," in *Cahiers de l'Association Internationale des Etudes Françaises* No. 39 (May 1987): 63–78.] Cherpack and Molinié both argue that d'Urfé emulates principles of composition typical of the Greek Romance. For Cherpack, a slavish technical borrowing explains the proliferation in *L'Astrée* of "serious inconsistencies which involve not only what the characters do and say but also the very form of the work itself" (323). [Clifton Cherpack, "Form and Ideas in *L'Astrée*," *Studies in Philology* 69 (July 1972).] Molinié provides many examples from *L'Astrée* in support of his thesis that the Greek and the Baroque novel adhere to a single, trans-historical, set of generic conventions. [Georges Molinié, *Du roman grec au roman baroque: un art majeur du genre narratif en France sous Louis XIII*, Travaux de l'Université de Toulouse-le-Mirail, Serie A, Tome XIX (Toulouse: U.T.M., 1982).]

8. J. Hillis Miller, "The Geneva School: The Criticism of Marcel Raymond, Albert Béguin, Georges Poulet, Jean Rousset, Jean-Pierre Richard, and Jean Starobinski," *Critical Quarterly*, VIII (1966), p. 306. See also Ian W. Alexander, "The Phenomenological Philosophy in France," in *French Literature and the Philosophy of Consciousness: Phenomenological Essays*, Ed. Busst (Cardiff: University of Wales Press, 1984), p. 93. Alexander writes: "literary creation is a sense-giving and sense-revealing activity whereby the writer constitutes his self and a world for himself."

9. Jacques Ehrmann, *Un Paradis désespéré: l'amour et l'illusion dans "L'Astrée"* (New Haven: Yale University Press, 1963).

10. For the definitive contemporary critique of subjective self-presence as it appears in phenomenology, see Jacques Derrida, *Speech and Phenomena and Other Essays on Husserl's Theory of Signs*, trans. Allison and Garver (Evanston, Illinois: Northwestern University Press, 1973).

11. Though predominantly a development of the last three decades, at least one early proponent of this view may be found. Bernard Germa shares the contemporary fascination with the suppressed ideological conflicts that troubled the peace of the early seventeenth century and with *L'Astrée*'s resistance to totalizing or reductive interpretation. In contrast to Reynier and Magendie who dwell upon the progress of manners and the flowering of genteel culture under Henri IV, he argues that a harmonious society devoted to pleasant conversation and the pursuit of *parfaite amitié* was, in the France of Henri IV and Louis XIII, an unrealized aspiration: "Si *L'Astrée* est 'un enfant de la paix,' c'est d'une paix idéale [...] c'est d'une paix souhaitée" (217) rather than real. The text, like the society in which it appeared, is traversed by unresolved tensions: "D'Urfé ne se pique pas d'unité, et après tout il n'a pas tort; ce n'est pas un philosophe, qui à grand renfort d'arguments édifie une doctrine qui lui est chère; c'est un romancier, qui, dans une oeuvre touffue, subissant tour à tour des influences diverses, reproduit la complexité de la vie et accommode ses théories, soit aux personnages, soit aux événements qu'il représente" (76). [Bernard Germa, *"L'Astrée" d'Honoré d'Urfé, sa composition et son influence* (Paris: Alphonse Picard, 1904).]

12. Gérard Genette's influential "Le Serpent dans la bergerie," strikes a new note in *L'Astrée* criticism by identifying a psycho-sexual imperative operating beneath the threshold of authorial consciousness. Celadon and Astrée, Genette says, make use of the chivalric ethic of self-denial only to enhance sexual pleasure by means of indirection and delay. The officially sanctioned code serves "comme un instrument non de perfec-tion spirituelle, mais de raffinement érotique" (121). This destabilizing paradox, more-over, reflects the ambiguity of the historical moment: *L'Astrée* is "l'étroit goulet par où tout l'ancien se déverse, se renverse dans tout le moderne" (110). While the code reflects the lingering influence of an antiquated ethical idealism, the latent eroticism heralds the emergence of a modern, psychological realism. His thesis takes issue persuasively with Ehrmann's *Un paradis désespéré* which had, only the previous year, presented the work as an internally consistent expression of neo-platonic idealism. [Gérard Genette, "Le Serpent dans la bergerie," in *Figures* (Paris: Sueil, 1966),

pp. 109–22. Originally published in *L'Astrée* (Paris: Union generale d'éditions, Collection 10/18, 1964).]

13. Chabert proceeds in the psychologizing vein established by Genette, but frames her argument in terms of semantic free-play, or, as she says, the commutability of the sign, rather than in terms of a larger thematic ambivalence. [Nicole Chabert, "L'Amour du discours dans *L'Astrée*," in *Dix-septième Siècle* 33 (Oct.-Dec. 1981), pp. 393–407.]

14. Laugaa describes the ambiguous interpenetration of two literary genres in a way that enriches his essentially formalist approach with historical relevance. Lyric, associated with the ideal, timeless world of myth and dream, and narrative, associated with the materiality and temporal sequences of real life, compete inconclusively for dominance, leaving us suspended between incompatible points of view: "Nous sommes sans cesse renvoyés de l'agitation au repos, du temps à l'age d'or, du récit au lyrisme" (24). *L'Astrée*, he concludes, is "une synthèse inachevée" (26). [Maurice Laugaa, "Structures ou personnages dans *L'Astrée*, in *Etudes françaises* 2 (1966), pp. 3–27.]

15. For Jehenson, d'Urfé paradoxically affirms both the idealism of conventional pastoral, and the epistemological realism which had begun, in the early seventeenth century, to engender new ethical and aesthetic norms. As a result, he produces a work disturbingly incoherent at its core: "[D'Urfé] pits a harsh reality against his fiction, and a discrepancy thereby results between the author's formulation of his literary intentions and their actual realization" (114). [Myriam Yvonne Jehenson, *The Golden World of Pastoral: A Comparative Study of Sidney's "New Arcadia" and d'Urfé's "L'Astrée"* (Ravenna, Italy: A. Longo, 1981).]

16. De Ley was perhaps the first to employ Foucaultian ideas in an analysis of "*L'Astrée*'s hetergeneous epistemological assumptions." He identifies two distinct "modes of thought" in the narrative but does not attempt to demonstrate their relevance to either the formal organization or ideological aims of the whole. [Herbert De Ley, *The Movement of Thought in Seventeenth-Century France* (Urbana: University of Illinois Press, 1985), pp. 39–53.] An earlier version of the essay appeared in the mid-seventies.

17. Greenberg has framed the debate in terms of the discursive construction of gender. Demonstrating the thwarted emergence in *L'Astrée* of the modern "gendered" subject, he attributes the narrative's ambivalence to its position between two hegemonic cultural epochs, each with its own conceptualization of sexual identity. As an

"androgynous" text, *L'Astrée* is once more implicated in an unresolvable paradox. [Mitchell Greenberg, "*L'Astrée* and Androgyny," in *Cahiers du Dix-Septième: An Interdisciplinary Journal* (Spring 1987), pp. 169–78.]

18. The now classic introductions to neo-historical theory are Jean E. Howard, "The New Historicism in Renaissance Studies," *English Literary Renaissance*, 16(1) (winter 1986), pp. 13–43; and Louis Montrose, "Renaissance Literary Studies and the Subject of History," *English Literary Renaissance*, 16(1) (winter 1986), pp. 5–11. Montrose is particularly clear in his acceptance of the provisional, yet relatively stable, determination of meaning within cultural contexts subject to change: "Recent theories of textuality have argued persuasively that the referent of a linguistic sign cannot be fixed; that the meaning of a text cannot be stabilized. At the same time, writing and reading are always historically and socially determinate events [. . .] We may simultaneously acknowledge the theoretical indeterminacy of the signifying process and the historical specificity of discursive practices" (23). Frank Lentricchia had made a similar argument several years earlier in *After the New Criticism* (Chicago: University of Chicago Press, 1980), when calling for a middle way between the philosophic idealism of the old New Critics for whom the aesthetic word "plumbs the nature of things" (119), and the vertiginous skepticism of the new New Critics who celebrate semantic free play. Both groups, he says, "fail to credit the coercive power of the historical determination and cultural enclosure of semantic potential" (121).

19. David Carroll, "Narrative, Heterogeneity, and the Question of the Political: Bakhtin and Lyotard," in *The Aims of Representation: Subject/Text/History,* ed. Murray Krieger (New York: Columbia University Press, 1987).

Bibliography

I. Primary Texts

Aristotle. "Metaphysics." *The Basic Works of Aristotle*. Ed. Richard McKeon. New York: Random House, 1941.

Bacon, Francis. *Novum Organum*. Reprinted in *Seventeenth-Century Prose and Poetry*. Ed. Witherspoon and Warnke. New York: Harcourt Brace, 1963.

Descartes, René. *The Philosophical Works of Descartes*, Vol. I. Trans. Haldane and Ross. Cambridge: Cambridge University Press, 1975.

La Bruyère, Jean de. *Les caractères*. Paris: Garnier-Flammarion, 1965.

La Rochefoucauld, François IV de. *Maximes et réflexions diverses*. Paris: Librairie Larousse, 1975.

Montaigne, Michel de. *Essais*. Ed. Alexandre Micha. Paris: Garnier-Flammarion, 1969.

Pascal, Blaise. *Pensées*. Ed. Lafuma. Paris: Editions du Seuil, 1962.

Urfé, Honoré de. *L'Astrée*. 1607–1627. Ed. Hugues Vaganay. Lyon: Pierre Masson, 1925.

II. *L'Astrée* Criticism

Adam, Antoine. *L'époque d'Henri IV et de Louis XIII*. Paris: Domat, 1948. Vol. I of *Histoire de la littérature française au XVIIe siècle*. 5 Vol. 1948–1956.

Bonnet, Jacques. *La Symbolique de "L'Astrée."* Saint-Etienne: Le Hénaff, 1981.

Chabert, Nicole. "L'Amour du discours dans *L'Astrée*." *Dix-septième Siècle* 33 (Oct.-Dec. 1981): 393–407.

Cherpack, Clifton. "Form and Ideas in *L'Astrée*." *Studies in Philology* 69 (July 1972): 320–33.

Coulet, Henri. *Le Roman jusqu'à la révolution*. New York: McGraw-Hill, 1967.

De Ley, Herbert. "Two Modes of Thought in *L'Astrée*." *The Movement of Thought: An Essay on Intellect in Seventeenth-Century France*. Urbana: University of Illinois Press, 1985.

Ehrmann, Jacques. *Un Paradis désespéré: l'amour et l'illusion dans "L'Astrée."* New Haven: Yale University Press, 1963.

Gaume, Maxime. *Les Inspirations et les sources de l'oeuvre d'Honoré d'Urfé*. Saint-Etienne: Centre d'Etudes foreziennes, 1977.

Genette, Gérard. "Le serpent dans la bergerie." 1964. *Figures*. Paris: Seuil, 1966. 109–22.

Germa, Bernard. *"L'Astrée" d'Honoré d'Urfé, sa composition et son influence.* Paris: Alphonse Picard, 1904.

Greenberg, Mitchell. *"L'Astrée* and Androgyny." *Cahiers du dix-septième* 1 (Spring 1987): 169–178.

———*L'Astrée*, Classicism, and the Illusion of Modernity." *Continuum* II (1990): 3–25.

———*"L'Astrée* and Androgyny." *Subjectivity and Subjugation in Seventeenth-Century Drama and Prose: The Family Romance of French Classicism.* Cambridge: Cambridge University Press, 1992.

Gregorio, Laurence A. "Implications of the Love Debate in *L'Astrée.*" *The French Review: Journal of the American Association of Teachers of French* 56.1 (October 1982): 31–39.

———*The Pastoral Masquerade: Disguise and Identity in "L'Astrée.*" Saratoga, CA: ANMA Libri, 1992.

Harth, Erica. *Ideology and Culture in Seventeenth Century France.* Ithaca: Cornell University Press, 1983.

Hinker, Monique. "La Préciosité." *Manuel d'histoire littéraire de la France.* Vol. II. Paris: Editions Sociales, 1975.

Jehenson, Myriam Yvonne. *The Golden World of Pastoral: A Comparative Study of Sidney's "New Arcadia" and d'Urfé's "L'Astrée.*" Ravenna: A. Longo, 1981.

Jourlait, Daniel. "La Mythologie dans *L'Astrée,*" *L'Esprit Créateur* XVI.2 (1976): 125–37.

Judovitz, Dalia. "The Graphic Text: The Nude in *L'Astrée.*" *Papers in French Seventeenth-Century Literature* XV.29 (1988): 529–541.

Koch, P. "Encore du nouveau sur *L'Astrée.*" *Revue d'histoire littéraire de la France* No. 3 (mai-juin 1972): 29–45.

———*"L'Ascèse du repos, ou l'intention idéologique de *L'Astrée.*" *Revue d'histoire littéraire de la France* Nos. 3–4 (1977): 386–98.

Lafond, Jean. Chronologie. *"L'Astrée": textes choisis.* Paris: Gallimard, 1984.

Laugaa, Maurice. "Structures ou personnages dans *L'Astrée.*" *Etudes françaises* 2 (1966): 3–27.

Le Breton, André. *Le Roman au dix-septième siècle.* Paris: Hachette, 1912.

Magendie, Maurice. *Du Nouveau sur "L'Astrée.*" Paris: Champion, 1927.

Molinié, Georges. *Du roman grec au roman baroque: un art majeur du genre narratif en France sous Louis XIII.* Travaux de l'Université de Toulouse-le-Mirail, Série A, Tome XIX. Toulouse: U.T.M., 1982.

Morel, Jacques. "Honoré d'Urfé." *La Renaissance, 1570–1624.* Paris: Arthaud, 1973. Vol. 3 of *Littérature française.* 229–57.

Reure, O.-C. *La Vie et les oeuvres de Honoré d'Urfé.* Paris: Plon, 1910.

Reynier, Gustave. *Le Roman sentimental avant "L'Astrée.*" Paris: Armand Colin, 1908.

Rousset, Jean. *La Littérature de l'âge baroque en France.* Paris: Corti, 1954.

Wentzlaff-Eggebert, Christian. "Structures Narratives de la Pastorale dans *L'Astrée.*" *Cahiers de l'Association Internationale des Etudes Françaises* No. 39 (May 1987): 63–78.

Yon, B. "Une autre fin de *L'Astrée*, la quatrième partie de 1624, les cinquième et sixième parties de 1625 et 1626." Thèse de troisième cycle, Lyon, 1972.

_____."Composition dans *L'Astrée*, composition de *L'Astrée.*" *Papers in French Seventeenth-Century Literature* 10.2 (1978): 9–27.

III. History and Theory

Abel, Lionel. *Metatheater: A New Vision of Dramatic Form.* Clinton, Mass.: Colonial Press, 1963.

Alexander, Ian, W. "The Phenomenological Philosophy in France." *French Literature and the Philosophy of Consciousness: Phenomenological Essays.* Ed. Busst. Cardiff: University of Wales Press, 1984.

Althusser, Louis. "Ideology and Ideological State Apparatuses." *Lenin and Philosophy and Other Essays.* Trans. Ben Brewster. New York: Monthly Review Press, 1971.

Burckhardt, Jacob. *The Civilization of the Renaissance in Italy.* Trans. S.G.C. Middlemore. 2 Vols. London: Phaidon Press, 1960.

Carroll, David. "Narrative, Heterogeneity, and the Question of the Political: Bakhtin and Lyotard." *The Aims of Representation: Subject/Text/History.* Ed. Murray Krieger. New York: Columbia University Press, 1987.

Cassirer, Ernst. *The Individual and the Cosmos in Renaissance Philosophy.* Originally published in German, 1927. Trans. Mario Domandi. New York: Harper & Row, 1963.

Caton, Hiram. *The Origin of Subjectivity.* New Haven: Yale University Press, 1973.

Church, William. *Richelieu and Reason of State.* Princeton: Princeton University Press, 1973.

Colish, Marcia. *The Mirror of Language: A Study in Medieval Theory of Knowledge.* New Haven: Yale University Press, 1968.

Curtius, Ernst Robert. *European Literature and the Latin Middle Ages.* Trans. Willard Trask. Bollingen Series, 36. New York: Pantheon Books, 1953.

Derrida, Jacques. *Speech and Phenomena and Other Essays on Husserl's Theory of Signs.* Trans. Allison and Garver. Evanston: Northwestern University Press, 1973.

Dollimore, Jonathan. *Radical Tragedy: Religion, Ideology and Power in the Drama of Shakespeare and his Contemporaries.* Brighton: The Harvester Press Limited, 1984.

Fish, Stanley. "Literature in the Reader: Affective Stylistics." *Reader-Response Criticism: From Formalism to Post-Structuralism.* Ed. Jane P. Tompkins. Baltimore: Johns Hopkins University Press, 1980. 70–100.

Flynn, Bernard. "Descartes and the Ontology of Subjectivity." *Man and World* 16 (1983): 3–23.

Foucault, Michel. *The Order of Things: An Archeology of the Human Sciences.* New York: Random House Vintage Books, 1973. Trans. of *Les Mots et les choses.* Gallimard, 1966.

Freud, Sigmund. *Totem and Taboo.* 1913. Trans. Brill. New York: Random House Vintage Books, 1961.

Geertz, Clifford. *The Interpretation of Cultures.* New York: Basic Books, 1973.

Howard, Jean E. "The New Historicism in Renaissance Studies." *English Literary Renaissance* 16.1 (winter 1986): 13–43.

Huizinga, John. *The Waning of the Middle Ages.* 1919. Trans. F. Hopman. New York: Doubleday Anchor Books, 1954.

———*Homo Ludens: A Study of the Play Element in Culture.* 1938. Boston: Beacon Press, 1955.

Judovitz, Dalia. *Subjectivity and Representation in Descartes: The Origins of Modernity.* Cambridge: Cambridge University Press, 1988.

Kenny, Anthony. *The Anatomy of the Soul: Historical Essays in the Philosophy of Mind.* Bristol: Basil Blackwell, 1973.

Knowles, David. *The Evolution of Medieval Thought.* Baltimore: Helicon Press, 1962.

Kuhn, Thomas S. *The Structure of Scientific Revolutions.* Second Edition Enlarged. Chicago: University of Chicago Press, 1970.

Lentricchia, Frank. *After the New Criticism.* Chicago: University of Chicago Press, 1980.

Lewis, C. S. *The Allegory of Love.* New York: Oxford University Press, 1958.

MacPherson, C. B. *The Political Theory of Possessive Individualism: Hobbes to Locke.* London: Oxford University Press, 1962.

Matar, N. I. "Peter Sterry and the 'Lovely Society' of West Sheen." *Notes and Queries* 227 (February 29, 1982): 45–46.

Miller, J. Hillis. "The Geneva School: The Criticism of Marcel Raymond, Albert Beguin, Georges Poulet, Jean Rousset, Jean-Pierre Richard, and Jean Starobinski." *Critical Quarterly* VIII (1966): 305–21.

Montrose, Louis. "Renaissance Literary Studies and the Subject of History." *English Literary Renaissance* 16.1 (winter 1986): 5–11.

Pinto, Vivian de Sola. *Peter Sterry: Platonist and Puritan, 1613–1672.* Cambridge: Cambridge University Press, 1934.

Reiss, Timothy. *The Discourse of Modernism.* Ithaca: Cornell University Press, 1982.

Rorty, Richard. *Philosophy and the Mirror of Nature.* Princeton: Princeton University Press, 1979.

Turner, Victor W. *Dramas Fields and Metaphors: Symbolic Action in Human Society.* Ithaca: Cornell University Press, 1974.

Van Gennep, Arnold. *The Rites of Passage.* 1909. Trans. Monika B. Vizedom and Gabrielle L. Caffee. Chicago: University of Chicago Press, 1960.

Warnke, Frank, J. *Versions of Baroque: European Literature in the Seventeenth Century.* New Haven: Yale University Press, 1972.

White, Hayden. "Interpretation in History." *Tropics of Discourse: Essays in Cultural Criticism.* Baltimore: Johns Hopkins University Press, 1978. 51–80.

Willey, Basil. *The Seventeenth Century Background: The Thought of the Age in Relation to Religion and Poetry.* 1934. New York: Doubleday Anchor Books, 1953.

Yates, Frances A. *Astraea, the Imperial Theme in the Sixteenth Century.* London and Boston: Routledge & Kegan Paul, 1975.

Index

Abel, Lionel: 40n

Adamas: as Celadon's mentor, 29, 33, 172, 176–193; in the Grotte de Damon et Fortune, 59–63; house of, 190, 192; as institutional authority, 63; theory of cognition and, 81–83, 168

Adraste: madness of, 33, 168; trial of, 85

Alcé: 129

Alcidon: 193

Alcippe: 129, 130, 145, 147, 152

Alexander, Ian: 219n

Alexis: 30

Allegory: 180–181, 183, 185–186

Althusser, Louis: 29, 41n, 216

Amarillis: 129

Amasis, Queen: 34

Aminthe: 84, 152, 195

Androgyne: 221–222n

Anselm. *See* Signs; epistemology of, Anselm and

Aquinas: 37n

Aristotle: 37n, 120n

Artemis: 136

Artist: in Pico's *Oration,* 74n

Astraea, in myth and literature: 28, 41–42n

Astrée: autobiographical narrative of, 27–28; command of banishment and, 1, 27, 28, 30, 85; declaration of love by, 141–144; as metaphysical and sexual object, 187; epistemology and, 158–159; gender and, 142–143; hamlet of, 191; at Marcilly, 204–206; mental journey of, 84–90;

modernity of, 144, 163; portrait of, as mnemonic aid, 171; prudence of, 145–146; ritual performance and, 141; self-representation and, 25, 26–28, 123, 143–144, 205; social ideal, embodied by, 31–32, 71–72; in the Temple d'Amitié, 187; *travaux d'amour* and, 149–155;

Astrology, the birth of love and: 126–127

Augustine: theories of cognition and, 119n; interiority and, 23; d'Urfé influenced by, 207n

Bacon, Sir Francis, epistemology of language and, 108, 121n

Bakhtin: 216

Balzac, Honoré de: 162n

Baro: and *L'Astrée,* Volume V, 208n, 209n

Baroque: epistemology and, 1–4, 107; metamorphosis and, 215; narrative form and, 1, 3; ostentation and, 215; periodization of, 3–4

Belenus. *See* Gaul, religious history of

Boccaccio: 162n

Bochet, Henri: 212

Bonnet, Jacques: 208n

Burckhardt, Jacob: 36n

Calidon: 33;

Carrefour de Mercure: 71

Carnutes, religious community of: Ecole des Massiliens and, 200; self-representation and, 200–202

Carroll, David: 215, 222n